Microsoft Dynamics AX 2012 Reporting Cookbook

Over 50 recipes to help you build Dynamics AX reports faster by simplifying your understanding of the report model

Kamalakannan Elangovan

BIRMINGHAM - MUMBAI

Microsoft Dynamics AX 2012 Reporting Cookbook

First published: September 2013

Production Reference: 1170913

Published by Packt Publishing Ltd.
Livery Place
35 Livery Street
Birmingham B3 2PB, UK.

ISBN 978-1-84968-772-0

www.packtpub.com

Cover Image by Prashant Timappa Shetty (sparkling.spectrum.123@gmail.com)

Credits

Author
Kamalakannan Elangovan

Reviewers
Deepak Agarwal

Emad Mokhtar Habib

Umesh Pandit

Nasheet Ahmed Siddiqui

Saptha Wanniarachchi

Acquisition Editor
James Jones

Lead Technical Editor
Amey Varangaonkar

Technical Editors
Iram Malik

Manal Pednekar

Larissa Pinto

Project Coordinator
Apeksha Chitnis

Proofreader
Chris Smith

Indexer
Tejal R. Soni

Graphics
Ronak Dhruv

Production Coordinator
Manu Joseph

Cover Work
Manu Joseph

About the Author

Kamalakannan Elangovan has over eight years of development experience in Dynamics AX. He shares a passion for product development and has pioneered multiple ISV solutions on Dynamics AX. In the past he worked with Innovites to create the first multidimensional ISV solution for cable industries called "Innovites for cable". Building the solution from scratch, he has gained great insights into building, selling, and promoting the product among customers and partners in the Microsoft Ecosystem. You can learn more about him at `http://about.me/casperkamal`.

He is enthusiastic about sharing his learning with the community which led him to create one of the first few blogs for AX in 2006. It is currently available at `http://kamalblogs.wordpress.com`. He is active through twitter and the community, popularly by his pseudonym Casperkamal.

First of all, I would like to thank my wife Sangeetha and my little daughter Anu for their considerable support during the long hours I have put behind this book. I also want to apologize for the time I have stolen from them to invest in this book.

Thanks to Dhangar Naveen who has spent considerable hours working along with me in making the examples involved in each recipe.

Special thanks to the wonderful team at Packt who have patiently guided and supported me in making this book a reality.

Also, a big thanks to the readers of my blog, my fellow bloggers, and the Dynamics AX community who have directly and indirectly inspired me in this work.

This book is dedicated to Dick De Jong, who selflessly mentored and trained me in the art of software development.

About the Reviewers

Deepak Agarwal [B.Tech, MBA] is a Technical Consultant and has been working professionally on Dynamics AX since 2011. He is a team member of the very first AX project in the Manufacturing Domain. Though his strengths are rooted in X++ development, he is a highly regarded developer and has solid knowledge of technical aspects of Dynamics AX and X++ reporting.

Deepak blogs on Dynamics AX on his blog `http://theaxapta.blogspot.in/`.

A big thanks to my dear sister Khushbu Agarwal for her support and understanding of my long hours spent on this work.

Emad Mokhtar Habib is a passionate and an enthusiastic software developer, loves to learn new technologies, and is always seeking for the better to be the best. He has worked with many Microsoft partners. He is builds software to improve and help businesses. He runs a professional and technical blog, `EmadMokhtar.com`, and shares his thoughts and readings on Twitter and LinkedIn. He is working for Arabesque Group now and as a freelance Web Developer.

I want to thank my lovely wife who helped me in reviewing this book and always took care of me and my environment. I also want to thank my family and friends for motivating me and always pushing me to do my best.

Umesh Pandit is a Techno Functional Consultant with KPIT Cummins Infosystems Ltd. He has done Masters of Computer Applications with first division, having specialization in ERP from Ideal Institute of Technology, Ghaziabad.

He has worked with the top IT giants, such as Google India and Cap Gemini India. He has a deep understanding of ERP systems, such as Microsoft Dynamics AX. He has worked with different versions of Axapta, such as AX 3.0, AX 4.0, AX 5.0 (AX 2009), and AX 6.0 (AX 2012). He has a vast knowledge of Microsoft Technologies, such as SQL, CRM, TFS, Office, Windows Server 2008, Windows Server 2003, Office 365, Microsoft Dynamics NAV, SSRS, SSAS, VSS, and VCS.

I would like to thank my friend Pramila, who encouraged me in this passion.

Nasheet Ahmed Siddiqui has studied Computer Science at the University of Karachi, Pakistan. He has over seven years of consulting experience, playing a variety of roles, including Software Engineer, Senior Software Engineer, Team lead, and Technical Consultant in Dynamics AX and Microsoft technologies.

He started working in 2006 for e-Creatorz, where he was developing and managing web applications. He started his Dynamics AX career with MazikGlobal (a subsidiary of Tyler Technology Ltd, U.S.A and Microsoft Corporation). He was the core developer in the development of the Dynamics AX 2012 and AX 2012 R2 features for Microsoft. He was directly involved with the Microsoft team to build the features for the AX 2012 and AX 2012 R2. Since 2012, he has been working for Othaim Markets, where he is responsible for the customizations, development, and implementation of new verticals (Property Management System and Maintenance Management System).

He has a solid knowledge of and skills in technical aspects of Dynamics AX 2009 and 2012. He is also working as a freelance Dynamics AX Technical Consultant. He has provided development services to many organizations in Pakistan, Saudi Arabia, and Canada. He is also a Microsoft Certified Professional (MCP) for Dynamics AX Development and MorphX Solution Development.

He lives in Riyadh, KSA with his family. He is always happy to share useful AX development tricks on his blog (`nasheet.wordpress.com`). He can be contacted via LinkedIn at `http://sa.linkedin.com/in/nasheet`.

Saptha Wanniarachchi is a certified and experienced IT professional from Sri Lanka with quite extensive professional experience, in particular with Microsoft Dynamics-based Business Solutions. She is currently employed with SML, Sri Lanka, an international global branding and packaging company. She takes particular pride in her ability in infrastructure design and implementations for Microsoft Dynamics AX/NAV ERP Systems, system automation, and CRM solutions.

She has worked on the book:

- *Microsoft Dynamics AX 2012 Security How-To*

www.PacktPub.com

Support files, eBooks, discount offers and more

You might want to visit www.PacktPub.com for support files and downloads related to your book.

Did you know that Packt offers eBook versions of every book published, with PDF and ePub files available? You can upgrade to the eBook version at www.PacktPub.com and as a print book customer, you are entitled to a discount on the eBook copy. Get in touch with us at service@packtpub.com for more details.

At www.PacktPub.com, you can also read a collection of free technical articles, sign up for a range of free newsletters and receive exclusive discounts and offers on Packt books and eBooks.

http://PacktLib.PacktPub.com

Do you need instant solutions to your IT questions? PacktLib is Packt's online digital book library. Here, you can access, read and search across Packt's entire library of books.

Why Subscribe?

- ▶ Fully searchable across every book published by Packt
- ▶ Copy and paste, print and bookmark content
- ▶ On demand and accessible via web browser

Free Access for Packt account holders

If you have an account with Packt at www.PacktPub.com, you can use this to access PacktLib today and view nine entirely free books. Simply use your login credentials for immediate access.

Instant Updates on New Packt Books

Get notified! Find out when new books are published by following @PacktEnterprise on Twitter, or the *Packt Enterprise* Facebook page.

Table of Contents

Preface

Reporting capabilities are the turn-key decision makers for choosing an ERP system. They cater from the low-level shop floor users to the board room members giving them the right insight into their business. That is one of the many reasons why report customizations dominate at customer implementations. Strengthening your reporting capabilities as a Developer not just makes you but also the users of your report confident than ever.

Microsoft Dynamics AX 2012 is a phenomenal release that took AX to a different breadth and depth. The SSRS has brought in huge thrust to the leap forward. This book has been written to help you understand and acquire the skills necessary to be good at Reporting based on SSRS.

What this book covers

Chapter 1, *Understanding and Creating Simple SSRS Reports*, walks you through creating a basic report that introduces you to several basic features of Dynamics AX reports.

Chapter 2, *Enhancing Your Report – Visualization and Interaction*, focuses on further controlling and improving your report through parameters, data regions, expressions, new report and style templates.

Chapter 3, *A Report Programming Model*, helps you in understanding the programmatic model of the reporting framework inside AX and introduces you to programmatically modifying report UI and validations.

Chapter 4, *Report Programming Model – RDP*, delves into creating advanced reports using the new report data contract framework. It also details how to design reports through Precision Design.

Chapter 5, *Integrating External Datasources*, showcases how reports can be extended beyond AX to include other data sources, such as Cubes, XML Cloud Service, or through the integrations framework.

Chapter 6, Beyond Tabular Reports, dives in to using the other types of report formats, such as chart and matrix reports. It further details the use of other interesting controls, such as gauges, lists, and rectangles with clearly drafted examples.

Chapter 7, Upgrading and Analyzing Reports, shows you the approach to adopt when moving reports from MorphX-based reports to SSRS and discusses several repeated customization patterns in reports.

Chapter 8, Troubleshooting and Other Advanced Recipes, is a collection of assorted topics that can be applied to your SSRS reports, such as deploying through your code, using Enum provider and localization of reports. This chapter also introduces you to the log viewer through which you can analyze and identify report usage, report logs, and more.

Appendix, Introduction to SSRS, will help you run through the basic architecture of AX SSRS, followed by a brief introduction to different reporting components and the comparative advantage over the legacy reporting system from the previous releases of Dynamics AX.

What you need for this book

To practice the content in this book, you need the following software:

- ▸ Microsoft Dynamics AX 2012
- ▸ SQL Server Reporting Services
- ▸ SQL Server Analysis Services
- ▸ Microsoft Visual Studio 2010

Alternatively, you can use the Virtual Image available for Microsoft Dynamics AX 2012/AX 2012 R2 through Microsoft Learning Download Center.

Who this book is for

This book aims at IT administrators looking to get their hands on to develop their own reports for their internal demands and for X++ developers who want to deepen their understanding of SSRS reports.

This book requires some basic knowledge of Microsoft Dynamics AX 2012, X++, and MorphX. Some examples are based on C# and .NET. However, they are not must to read this book.

Conventions

In this book, you will find a number of styles of text that distinguish between different kinds of information. Here are some examples of these styles, and an explanation of their meaning.

Code words in text, database table names, folder names, filenames, file extensions, pathnames, dummy URLs, user input, and Twitter handles are shown as follows: "Set the name as `PKTReleasedProducts`."

A block of code is set as follows:

```
public static void main(Args args)
{
    PktRdlCustTransController srs;

    srs = new PktRdlCustTransController ();
    srs.parmReportName(ssrsReportStr(PktRdlCustTransList,
        CustTransList));
    srs.parmArgs(args);
    srs.startOperation();
}
```

Any command-line input or output is written as follows:

```
# cp /usr/src/asterisk-addons/configs/cdr_mysql.conf.sample
    /etc/asterisk/cdr_mysql.conf
```

New terms and **important words** are shown in bold. Words that you see on the screen, in menus or dialog boxes for example, appear in the text like this: "Click on **Next** and from the available fields drag-and-drop the required fields".

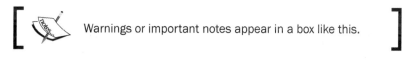

Warnings or important notes appear in a box like this.

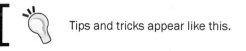

Tips and tricks appear like this.

Reader feedback

Feedback from our readers is always welcome. Let us know what you think about this book—what you liked or may have disliked. Reader feedback is important for us to develop titles that you really get the most out of.

To send us general feedback, simply send an e-mail to `feedback@packtpub.com`, and mention the book title via the subject of your message.

If there is a topic that you have expertise in and you are interested in either writing or contributing to a book, see our author guide on `www.packtpub.com/authors`.

Customer support

Now that you are the proud owner of a Packt book, we have a number of things to help you to get the most from your purchase.

Downloading the example code

You can download the example code files for all Packt books you have purchased from your account at `http://www.packtpub.com`. If you purchased this book elsewhere, you can visit `http://www.packtpub.com/support` and register to have the files e-mailed directly to you.

Errata

Although we have taken every care to ensure the accuracy of our content, mistakes do happen. If you find a mistake in one of our books—maybe a mistake in the text or the code—we would be grateful if you would report this to us. By doing so, you can save other readers from frustration and help us improve subsequent versions of this book. If you find any errata, please report them by visiting `http://www.packtpub.com/submit-errata`, selecting your book, clicking on the **errata submission form** link, and entering the details of your errata. Once your errata are verified, your submission will be accepted and the errata will be uploaded on our website, or added to any list of existing errata, under the Errata section of that title. Any existing errata can be viewed by selecting your title from `http://www.packtpub.com/support`.

Piracy

Piracy of copyright material on the Internet is an ongoing problem across all media. At Packt, we take the protection of our copyright and licenses very seriously. If you come across any illegal copies of our works, in any form, on the Internet, please provide us with the location address or website name immediately so that we can pursue a remedy.

Please contact us at `copyright@packtpub.com` with a link to the suspected pirated material.

We appreciate your help in protecting our authors, and our ability to bring you valuable content.

Questions

You can contact us at `questions@packtpub.com` if you are having a problem with any aspect of the book, and we will do our best to address it.

1
Understanding and Creating Simple SSRS Reports

This chapter will cover the following topics:

- ▶ Using a query as a datasource in a report
- ▶ Creating an auto design from a dataset
- ▶ Grouping in reports
- ▶ Adding ranges to the report
- ▶ Deploying the report
- ▶ Creating a menu item for the report

Introduction

Reports are the key to any business process. A successful ERP implementation is gauged by the efficient reports that can be generated through the data present in the system. Reports are introspective tools that help top-level business users to asses the condition of their business and help them make critical decisions.

This chapter will help you understand the development artifacts related to reports development, by designing a simple report which is broken down into smaller recipes. We will design a report that is applied with simple formatting capabilities and then deployed to the server to make it available for the end users, after which it is made accessible inside the rich client.

Reporting overview

Dynamics AX 2012 has extensive reporting capabilities like Excel, Word, PowerPivot, Management Reporter, and most importantly the SSRS reports. While there are many methodologies to generate reports, SSRS remains the prominent way to generate analytical and transactional reports. SSRS reports were initially integrated in AX 2009 and today it has replaced the legacy reporting system with AX 2012.

Through the recipes in this chapter, we will build the released products report. The released products report will list all the released products under each item group. This report will use the query datasource to fetch data from Dynamics AX and subsequently create an auto design based report. This report will then be deployed to the reporting services and will be attached to a menu item in AX so that it can be displayed inside the rich client.

Using a query as a datasource in a report

A query is the simplest way to fetch data for a report. Queries are beneficial as they are reusable and are easy to design. This recipe will guide you in creating a query in the AOT with the necessary optimization for a report datasource. The later part will guide you through creating a Visual Studio project for report development and use the query created to create a report datasource.

Getting ready

To work through this recipe, AX 2012 or AX 2012 R2 rich client with developer permission is required.

How to do it...

You can use a query as a datasource in the report, as follows:

1. Open the AX Development Workspace.
2. Navigate to **AOT** | **Queries**, right-click and select **New Query**.
3. Rename the query to `PKTReleasedProducts`.
4. Go to the query's datasource node, right-click and select **New Data Source**.
5. Rename the datasource to `InventTable` and set the `Table` property `Table` to `InventTable`.
6. There are two steps to select fields from **InventTable**.

7. Go to the **Fields** node under the **InventTable** datasource and set the **Dynamic** property to **Yes**. This will automatically add all the fields in the **InventTable** to the query. Now set the property back to **No**. This is an easy way to add fields to the query node, alternatively, the property can be kept **No** and the fields can be dragged-and-dropped from the actual table.

8. Drop all fields except **Item**, **ItemType**, and **Namealias**. This optimizes the query and consequently the fetch time:

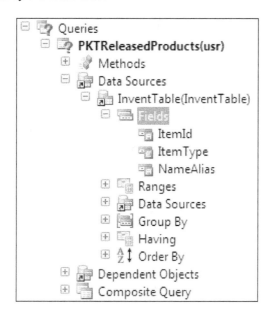

9. Save the query.

10. Open Visual Studio.

11. Navigate to **File | New | Project**.

12. In the new project dialog, click on **Microsoft Dynamics AX** and then **Report Model**.

13. Set the name as `PKTReleasedProducts`:

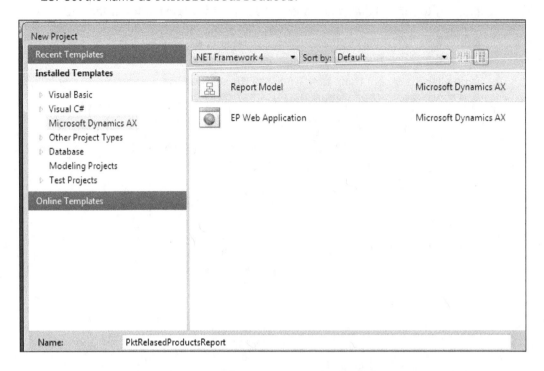

14. Now right-click on the project and click on **Add PKTReleasedProducts to AOT**.

15. On the reporting model, right-click, select **Add** and choose **Report**.

16. Rename the report as `PKTReleasedProductsReport`.

17. Go to the **Datasets** node and right-click on **Add Dataset**:

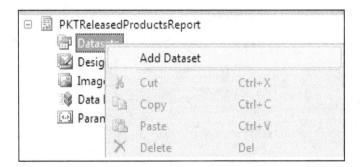

18. Name the dataset as `Products`.
19. Right-click on the **dataset** and open the properties.
20. Click on the ellipsis (**...**) button in the query.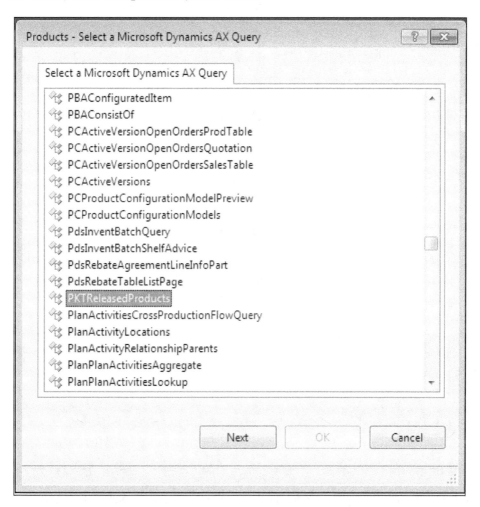
21. This opens a dialog with all queries in AOT:

22. Select the query that was created for the report **PKTReleasedProducts** and click on **Next**:

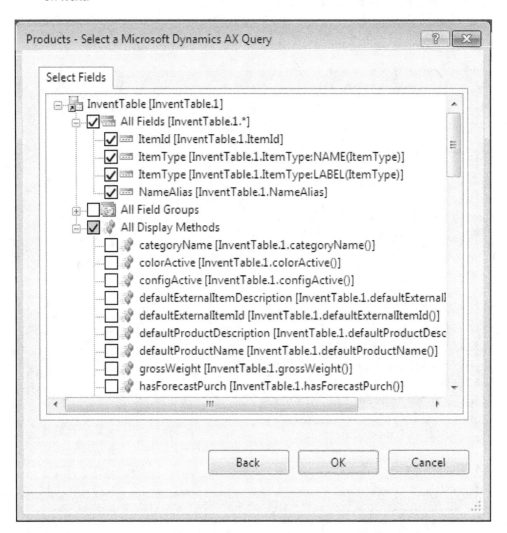

23. Select **All Fields,** since we dropped all the unwanted fields during the creation of the query.

24. Go to the **All Display Methods** node and select the **inventUnitId**, **itemGroupId**, and **itemName** methods and click on **OK**.

25. This will generate the fields list for the dataset. This completes the addition of the dataset to the report.

How it works...

Connecting VS to AX: When creating a new report project in Visual Studio, if there is no option such as Microsoft Dynamics AX then ensure that you have your reporting extensions installed. When you have multiple instances of Dynamics AX installed, the Visual Studio identifies the instance to connect from the client configuration. The active client configuration is used to establish the connection. The layer in which the report must be created is also fetched from the client configuration.

Metadata and data retrieval: With AX 2012, WCF-based system services have been introduced. This includes the metadata service, query service, and user session service. SSRS reporting extension uses the query and metadata services. The metadata service helps the report designer in Visual Studio to retrieve the metadata information of query, tables, and EDT while the query service is used to fetch the data.

Verify the query: In case of a complex query, a better approach would be validating the query before it is included in the report. Write a job in Dynamics AX that will use the query to retrieve the data and print the values to the infolog. This will help in nailing the problem when there is an issue with the report.

No Joins: The report supports multiple datasets but as in AX forms, these datasets cannot be joined and they remain independent.

Creating an auto design from a dataset

In this recipe, we will use the data set added in the previous recipe to create a simple auto design that will list all the items.

Getting ready

To develop reports using AX 2012 and AX 2012 R2, you need access to the rich client with development permission, a Visual Studio installation for report development, and the reporting extensions for Dynamics AX must be installed.

The SQL reporting services must be installed and running. You must have the permission to deploy the reports to the reporting server and must be able to access the reporting manager that lists all the reports in the system.

How to do it...

You can create an auto design from a dataset, as follows:

1. Right-click on the **Designs** node, select **Add** and then **Auto Design**. This creates a new auto design and name it as `Released Products`.

2. On the **Properties** node, set the property layout to `ReportLayoutStyleTemplate`.

3. Set the title property to `Released Products`:

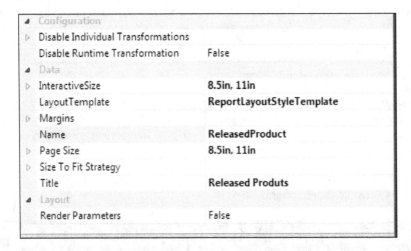

4. Right-click on the new **Released Product** auto design node, navigate to **Add | Table**:

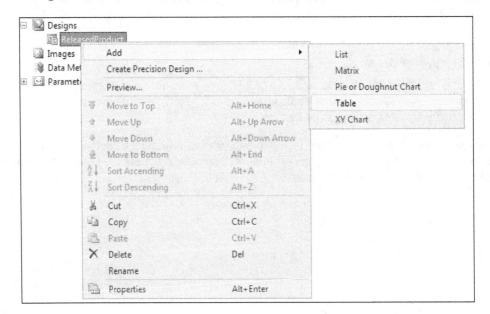

5. Set the following properties:

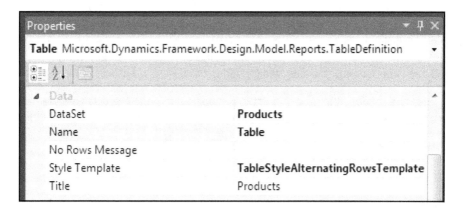

6. Notice that the fields have been added to the table design automatically.

7. Right-click on the **Auto design** and select **Preview**. This will show a preview of the report:

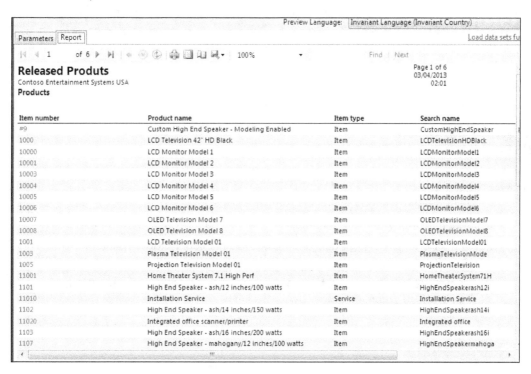

How it works...

Auto design is much easier to design and develop when compared to precision design. The default type of design (table, chart, and so on) for an auto design is defined in the property of the dataset. The default type determines what kind of control is added when the dataset is dragged-and-dropped into the auto design node.

The templates are responsible for printing the header, footer, and the company name on the report. They also manage the font and colors. Currently AX doesn't support printing the company image in the header through auto design.

The report preview accesses the default company in AX to show a report preview. So ensure the default company in AX has data; otherwise, you may not find data in the preview.

 The Standard SSRS reporting doesn't have a concept of auto design. This is only available in AX SSRS implementation.

Grouping in reports

The previous recipe results in a report where all the items are listed sequentially, but to make information more readable it must be structured. Structuring the data simplifies and helps in finding the detail that is needed. Here in this recipe, we will structure the report by grouping the items based on the item group making it easier to navigate.

How to do it...

Reports are grouped in as follows:

1. Go to the **Dataset** and select the **itemGroupId** field.
2. Drag-and-drop it to the **Groupings** node under the auto design **ProductsReport**.
3. This will create a new grouping node and add the field **itemGroupId** to the group.
4. Each grouping has a header row where even fields that don't belong to the group but need to be displayed in the grouped node can be added. The **itemGroupId** field is added automatically:

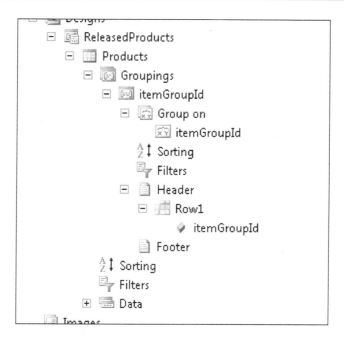

5. This groups the record and also acts like a header.

How it works...

The grouping can also be done based on multiple fields. Use the row header to specify the fields that must be displayed in the header. A grouping can be added manually but a drag-and-drop saves a lot of task such as setting the row header.

Adding ranges to the report

Ranges play a crucial role in reports as they try to limit the amount of data that appears and makes it much more interactive. In this part of the recipe, we will see how we can easily expose a query field as a range in the report.

How to do it...

The following steps will help you add ranges to the report:

1. Open the **PKTReleasedProduct** query in AOT.
2. Drag the field **Name Alias** to the **Range** node in AOT.

3. In the Visual Studio project right-click on **Datasets** and click on **Refresh**.

4. The parameter `Products_DynamicParameter` collectively represents any parameters that will be added dynamically through the ranges. This parameter must be set to `True` to make additional ranges available during runtime. This adds a **Select** button to the report dialog, which the user can use to specify additional ranges other than what is added:

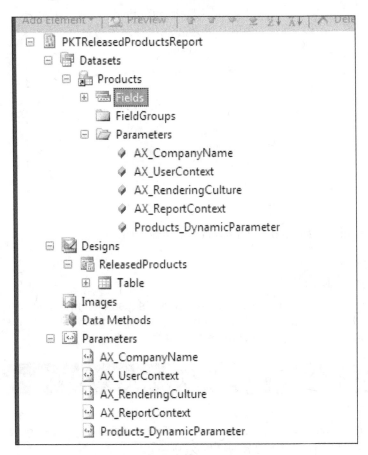

5. Right-click on the auto design **ReleasedProducts** and select **Preview**. The preview should display the range that was added in the query.

How it works...

The report dialog uses the query service UI builder to translate the ranges and to expose additional ranges through the query.

Dynamic parameter: Dynamic parameter unanimously represents all the parameters that are added at runtime. This adds the **Select** button to the dialog from where the user can invoke an advanced query filter window, which can be used to add more ranges and sorting. The dynamic parameter is available per dataset and can be enabled or disabled by setting the `Dynamic Filter` property to `true` or `false`.

The Report wizard in AX 2012 still uses the MorphX reports to auto-create reports using the wizard. The auto-report option that is available on every form uses the new AX SSRS report.

Deploying the report

SSRS being a server-side solution, after the development of the report it has to be deployed to the server. A report is not exposed to the users until it is deployed. This recipe will show how a report developed in Visual Studio can be deployed to the reporting server. There are multiple options to do it and the choice is left to the developer. PowerShell scripts are better when the reports are to be deployed by an AX administrator.

Getting ready

To be able to attempt the recipe. You need deploying rights to the SQL reporting services and permissions to view the report manager.

How to do it...

AX supports the following deployment options:

Deploy From	Steps to Deploy
Microsoft Dynamics AX	1. Reports can be deployed individually from a developer workspace in Microsoft Dynamics AX.
	2. In the AOT, expand the **SSRS Reports** node, expand the **Reports** node, right-click on the report, and then click on **Deploy Element**.
	3. The reports are deployed for all the translated languages.
Microsoft Visual Studio	1. Reports can be deployed individually from Visual Studio.
	2. In **Solution Explorer**, right-click on the reporting project that contains the reports that you want to deploy and then click on **Deploy**.
	3. The reports are deployed for the neutral (invariant) language only.

Deploy From	Steps to Deploy
Microsoft PowerShell	1. It is used to deploy the default reports that are provided with Microsoft Dynamics AX.
	2. It supports deploying multiple reports at the same time.
	3. Details on how to deploy the reports using PowerShell can be found at `http://msdn.microsoft.com/en-us/library/dd309703.aspx`.

To verify if the report is deployed, open the **Report Manager** in the browser and open the Dynamics AX folder. The report **PKTReleasedProduct** should be found in the list of reports.

The report can also be previewed from the reporting services. Open the reporting services and click on the name of the report to open the report preview.

How it works...

A report deployment is actually moving all the stuff related to the report to a central location, which is the server, from where they could be made available to the end user. The following list indicates the typical actions performed during deployment:

1. The RDL file is copied to the server.

2. The business logic is placed in the server location in the format of a DLL.

3. Deployment ensures that the RDL and business logic are cross-referenced to each other.

 The MorphX IDE from AX 2009 is still available. Any custom reports that are designed can be imported. This support is only for the purpose of backward compatibility.

See also

▸ The *Deploying language-specific reports to speed up execution time* recipe, in *Chapter 8, Troubleshooting and Other Advanced Recipes*.

Creating a menu item for the report

The final part of developing a report is to make it available inside AX for the users. Post deployment, the report can be linked to an **Output** menu item. This recipe will expose the report inside the rich client through a menu item.

How to do it...

A menu item for the report can be created as follows:

1. Navigate to **AOT** | **Menu Items** | **Output**, right-click and select **New Menu Item**. Set the following properties including the **LinkedPermissionType** setup shown in the screenshot:

Properties	Categories
Name	PktReleasedProducts
Label	Released Products
HelpText	
ObjectType	SSRSReport
Object	PktReleasedProductsReport
ReportDesign	ReleasedProducts
Parameters	
EnumTypeParameter	
EnumParameter	
ReadPermissions	Auto
UpdatePermissions	Auto
CreatePermissions	Auto
CorrectPermissions	Auto
DeletePermissions	Auto
LinkedPermissionType	SSRSReport
LinkedPermissionObject	PktReleasedProductsReport
LinkedPermissionObjectChild	ReleasedProducts
RunOn	Client
ConfigurationKey	

2. Open the menu item to run the report. A dialog is shown, the range **Search Name** added in the query appears followed by a **Select** button. The **Select** button is similar to the MorphX reports option where the user can specify additional conditions. To disable the **select** option go to the `Dynamic Filter` property in the dataset and set it to `false`.

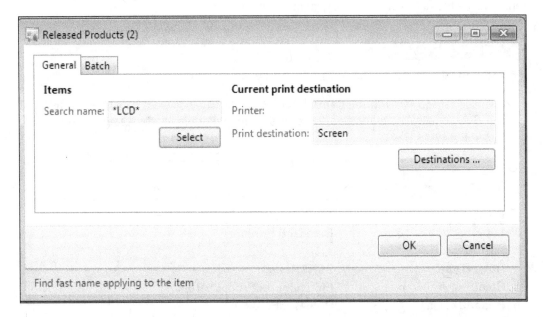

3. The report output should appear as follows:

| ◄ ◄ 1   of 1 ► ►| ⊕   ▮▼   100% ▼   Find   Next |

Released Produts

Contoso Entertainment Systems USA

Products

Page 1 of 1
3/4/2013
2:19 AM

Item group

Projectors

Item number	Product name	Item type	Unit
1507	Lamp for LCD Video Projector Model 01	Item	ea
1508	Lamp for LCD Video Projector Model 02	Item	ea
1501	LCD Video Projector Model 01	Item	ea
1502	LCD Video Projector Model 02	Item	ea
1509	LCD Video Projector with Batch Registration	Item	ea

Item group

Ind Exp

Item number	Product name	Item type	Unit
9018	LCD Monitor, 19", Speakers	Service	ea
9020	LCD Monitor, 20", no Speakers	Service	ea
9019	LCD Monitor, 20", Speakers	Service	ea

Item group

Television

Item number	Product name	Item type	Unit
10000	LCD Monitor Model 1	Item	Pcs
10001	LCD Monitor Model 2	Item	Pcs
10003	LCD Monitor Model 3	Item	Pcs
10004	LCD Monitor Model 4	Item	Pcs
10005	LCD Monitor Model 5	Item	Pcs
10006	LCD Monitor Model 6	Item	Pcs

How it works...

The report viewer in Dynamics AX is actually a form with an embedded browser control. The browser constructs the report URL at runtime and navigates to the report's URL. Unlike in AX 2009, when the report is rendering the data, it doesn't hold up using AX. Instead, the user can use the other parts of the application while the report is rendered in parallel. This is particularly beneficial for the end user as they can continue to proceed with other tasks as the report executes.

The permission setup is important as it helps in controlling the access permissions of a report.

See also

> ▶ *Adding reports to the role center* in *Chapter 6, Beyond Tabular Reports.*

> ▶ *Handling events post report completion* in *Chapter 8, Troubleshooting and Other Advanced Recipes.*

 To make changes faster and to view the changes on the reporting screen, use the vertical group option in Visual Studio. This puts the report model and the preview side-by-side, making it easier to review the changes as seen in the following screenshot:

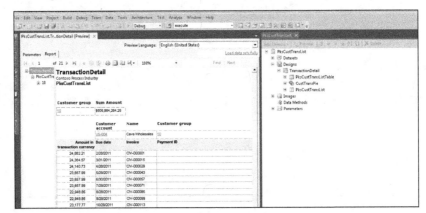

 Downloading the example code

You can download the example code files for all Packt books you have purchased from your account at http://www.packtpub.com. If you purchased this book elsewhere, you can visit http://www.packtpub.com/support and register to have the files e-mailed directly to you.

2
Enhancing Your Report – Visualization and Interaction

We will look into the following recipes in this chapter:

- ▸ Creating multiple data regions and charts in reports
- ▸ Creating a chart data region
- ▸ Creating a new layout template
- ▸ Expressions in layouts
- ▸ Aggregation in reports
- ▸ Adding an image in auto design
- ▸ Formatting reports
- ▸ Adding unbound parameters in reports
- ▸ Adding filters to data regions
- ▸ Adding a document map navigation to reports
- ▸ Adding a drill up/drill down navigation to reports

Introduction

A report is what stands out to exemplify the standard of a company. Hence, every report development has a huge focus on the fine finish of the reports. This chapter offers you the knowledge of different options that are available to enhance the visualization in reports, using a sample implementation. The chapter focuses on enhancing the visualization and interactivity in a report. A report case is chosen and passed through several transformations to make it visually appealing. The flow is such that the concept and practice are put side-by-side, so that by the time the chapter is finished, an extensive experience of the features is also achieved for the reader.

Creating multiple data regions and charts in reports

This recipe will show how data regions can be used to render data. A data region in simple definition is a subreport report that shares the parameters and datasets, and is present inside the report design itself. This and the following recipe will help you understand how multiple data regions can be created in SSRS. The first of the two data regions will display the detailed customer transactions, while the second data region will show a pie chart that shows the total value of the transactions against each customer group.

Getting ready

This and the other recipes in the chapter will be extending the report built in this section. Working through *Chapter 1, Understanding and Creating Simple SSRS Reports*, should make it easier to create SSRS reports. So following the guidelines learned from the previous chapter, create a simple SSRS report using the following steps:

1. Create a `PktCustTransList` query, which includes the `CustTable` and `CustTrans` tables. Remove the unwanted fields and retain only the fields that are shown in the following screenshot:

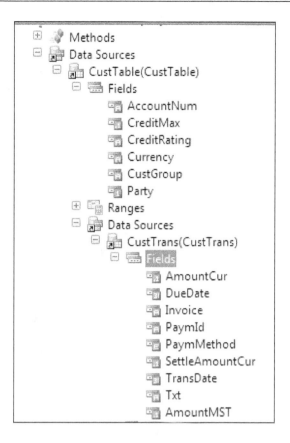

2. Open Visual Studio and create a new **Report Model Project** named `PktCustTransReport` and create a dataset that refers to the `PktCustTransList` query.

3. When selecting the fields in the query window, select all the fields and the `name` data method from `CustTable`.

How to do it...

Multiple data regions can be created as follows:

1. Drag the **CustTrans** dataset to the auto design node. This will create a `Table` design layout.

2. The grouping ability of the data regions helps in presenting the data effectively, by ordering and organizing them.

3. Drag the **CustGroup** field to the **Group on** node and then drag the **AccountNum** field to the **Group on** node from the dataset.

4. Expand the **Group on** node and navigate to the **Row** property and drag the field's **Currency**, **Party_Name** to the **AccountNum** group node.

5. Grouping helps in rendering the data in a summarized view. The order of the grouping property determines the order in which they are summarized. In this case, the grouping is done by the customer group followed by the customer:

6. Preview the report and see how multiple groupings look in action:

Customer group

10

	Customer account	Name	Customer group		Currency
	1102	Sunset Wholesales	10		USD

Invoice	Due date ⇕	Date		Amount	Description
100009	3/16/2012	1/16/2012		15,614.16	Sales invoice 100009
100035	3/1/2012	1/1/2012		125,059.83	Sales invoice 100035
100037	3/30/2012	1/30/2012		9,703.48	Sales invoice 100037
100038	3/30/2012	1/30/2012		9,281.59	Sales invoice 100038

How it works...

If you have been working with the legacy reporting system, your mind might tune in to find two records, one for the customer table and the other for the customer transactions. It works differently with SSRS, where the data is completely flattened. This means if the customer table has records `c1`, `c2` and the transactions table has `t11`, `t12`, `t21`, `t22` records, then the flattened dataset of an SSRS will have four records, where each line will hold `c1 t11`, `c1 t12`, `c2 t21` and `c2 t22`.

Grouping helps recreate relational data on a flattened dataset. For example, Customer – Customer Transaction. So here the grouping helps classify the transactions by customer and in turn acts as the header record.

Creating a chart data region

We will also incorporate our second data region through this recipe. The same report has two sections that summarize the same data in alternate ways.

In this recipe, we will create a chart data region. This chart data region will show the total value of transactions against each customer group. The report will show a summary through the chart, followed by details of the transactions. Creating charts was not possible in the legacy system, while with the new framework it is just a matter of a few clicks and setups, as you will see in this recipe.

Getting ready

This recipe is in continuation to the report developed in the *Creating multiple data regions and charts in reports* recipe, in this chapter.

How to do it...

A chart data region is created as follows:

1. Right-click on the **Designs | TransactionDetail** node and navigate to **Add | Pie or Doughnut Chart**.

2. Name it as `CustTransPie`.

3. From the dataset, select the **AmountMst** field and drop it in the **Data** node under the chart.

4. Set the following properties for the **AmountMST** control:

Property	Value
Caption	=SUM(Fields!AmountMST.Value)
Expression	=SUM(Fields!AmountMST.Value)
Point Label	="Group =" + Fields!CustGroup.Value

5. From the dataset select the **CustGroup** field and drop it in the **Series** node under the chart:

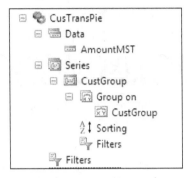

6. Start the preview, and the preview will show the chart followed by the table (The order is based on the position of data regions under the auto design.):

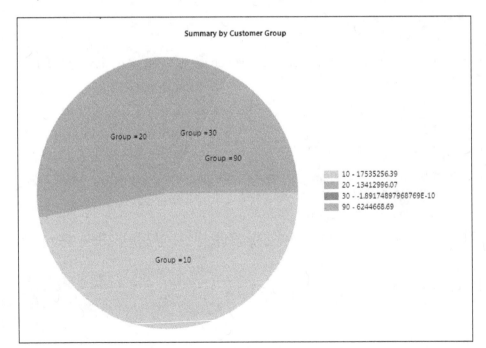

How it works...

Multiple data regions present the capability to offer different representations of data. They create smaller slices of the report that can present the related information in an isolated region. Each data region is attached to a dataset and they are mutually exclusive, except for the parameters. Parameters are shared between the data regions and there is no ability to define parameters per data region.

SSRS supports the following visualizations for data regions through auto design and a broader list through precision design, as discussed in *Chapter 6, Beyond Tabular Reports*:

- List data regions
- Table data regions
- Matrix data regions
- Chart data regions

You can also use views as a datasource. Just add a view to the query and then the view is ready to be used as a datasource. Due to huge data normalization done in AX 2012 with DirPartyTable, Financial Dimensions, and so on, using views can make it easier and accurate to retrieve data.

Creating a new layout template

Chapter 1, Understanding and Creating Simple SSRS Reports, discussed how using templates can standardize the report. Dynamics AX offers standard templates but there is also the capability to add a new template. This recipe will show how to create a custom layout template that can be used to standardize report aesthetics such font, size, color, and so on.

How to do it...

A new layout template can be created as follows:

1. Open Visual Studio and navigate to **View | Application Explorer**. This displays the entire AOT as in the AX environment in Visual Studio.

2. Navigate to the `Sharedlibrary` project under **Visual Studio Projects | Dynamics AX Model Projects**. Right-click and select **Edit**.

3. This project contains all the predefined templates. Right-click on the project and select **Add | Table** style template (Choose the template based on the data region such as table, list, and so on.).

4. There is no inheritance concept among templates, each template is independent and must define the entire formatting.

5. Double-click on the template to open the editor and rename it as `PktTableStyleFancyTemplate`.

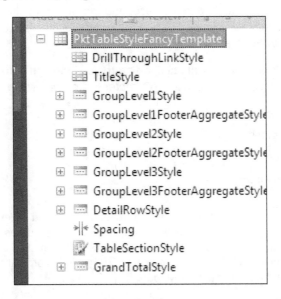

6. In the current report design, there are two levels of groupings defined, **CustGroup** followed by **AccountNum**.

7. To set the fonts for both the levels, the **GroupLevel1Style** and **GroupLevel2Style** nodes must be modified.

8. Expand **GroupLevel1Style** and double-click on the **FieldCaptionStyle** node to open the following form (Alternatively open the property window):

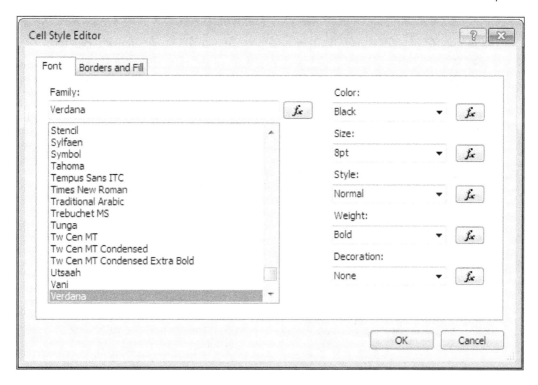

9. Set the following properties for both the nodes:

Property	Value
Font	Family	Verdana
Font	Size	8 pt
Borders and Fill	Style	Dashed

10. Repeat the same procedure for **FieldValueStyle** node and set the properties except for the last one which is not needed.

11. The template is set for the groupings. The next step is to set the template for the detailed rows.

12. Navigate to the **DetailRowStyle | FieldCaptionStyle** and set the following properties:

Property	Value
Font	Family	Verdana
Font	Size	8 pt

13. Repeat the same for **DetailRowStyle | FieldValueStyle**

14. Templates don't need deployment and they are available once they are created. Switch to the report node and select the table data region **CustTransTable**.

15. The drop-down will have the new template that was added, and set that as the template:

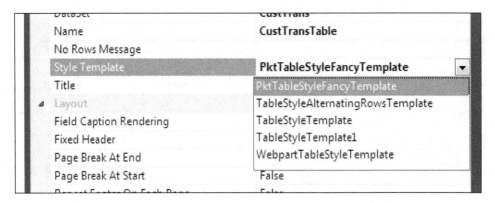

16. Right-click and preview to see that the fonts are different and the group nodes have a dashed line.

How it works...

Layout templates define the general layout settings such as company name, date, page number, and formatting for a report. The style templates are applicable for data regions and depending on the data region the type of template also varies. AX offers a set of predefined report layout and style templates.

These templates bring in the ability to present uniform look and feel across reports. The elements in a template are fixed depending on the type, so elements cannot be added or removed but can only have different formatting. The templates are useful only in case of auto design, while in the case of precision design they are not used.

Expressions in layouts

Expression is an interesting capability that SSRS supports. They can be used not just in expressions but in every possible property that needs customization at run-time. This recipe will get us introduced to expressions, by implementing the most interesting feature of printing the alternate lines in different colors. We will use the layout template created in the previous recipe to implement this.

How to do it...

Expressions can be implemented in the report, as follows:

1. On the template, select the node **DetailRowStyle | FieldValueStyle**.

2. For the **Background Color** property, choose the **Expression** list:

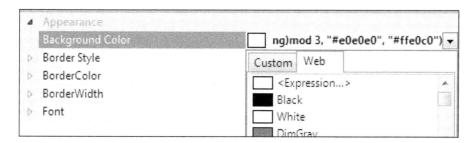

3. The expression window opens.

4. Type the following expression in the expression window:

   ```
   =iif(RowNumber(Nothing)mod 3, "#e0e0e0", "#ffe0c0")
   ```

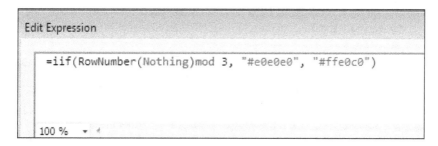

5. Save the template and go back to the `PktCustTransList` report for a preview.

6. The report should now appear with a different color on every third line when previewed.

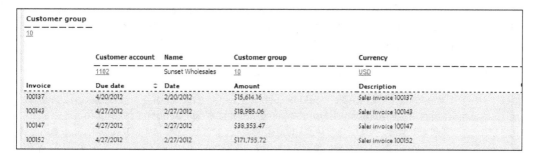

How it works...

Expressions are powerful means through which you can manipulate the content and the formatting style of the report data. These are widely used across the report model to retrieve, calculate, display, group, sort, filter, parameterize, and format data. They are not just limited to the ones listed but apply to many properties. A precise definition would be that anywhere in the report if a drop-down list displays **<Expression...>** then expressions can be applied.

It creates a wide scope for manipulation, by providing access to the standard functions, data methods, fields, labels, and more. This can be compared to an Excel cell where a formula is evaluated to produce the data. Expressions are evaluated when the report is run, so the results can be seen through preview.

Here are a few sample expressions:

Sample expression	Purpose
`=Fields!FirstName.Value`	Display the value from the `FirstName` field
`=IIF(Fields!LineTotal.Value > 100, True, False)`	This condition evaluates and returns a Boolean value
`=Year(Fields!OrderDate.Value)`	Display the year from the `date` field
`=Sum(IIF(Fields!State.Value = "Finished", 1, 0))`	Conditionally count the records
`=RowNumber(Nothing)`	Start counting from the outermost data region

Expression syntax is based on Visual Basic and any syntax error is highlighted by a red color in the expression window. To know more about expressions, please refer `http://msdn.microsoft.com/en-us/library/dd220516.aspx`.

Many novice report designers tend to use the `IIF()` function to test the parameter expression for a `True` or `False` result, and then explicitly return a `True` or `False` result from the function. Since all expressions can return Boolean results, although this technique will work, it's redundant to use the `IIF()` function for this purpose. For example, the following expression could be used in place of the previous example:

```
=IIF(Parameters!ShowQuantity.Value = True, False, True)
```

The following example would be used to test the result of a non-Boolean value. By wrapping an expression containing a comparison operator in parentheses, we can cause the expression to return a Boolean result.

```
=(Parameters!ReportView.Label="Retail")
```

Aggregation in reports

Totals are an obvious need in most of the reports. SSRS brings in easy and powerful aggregation capabilities. This recipe will discuss a couple of aggregation methods and how they can be applied at different levels.

How to do it...

Reports can be aggregated as follows:

1. In this recipe, two aggregations will be implemented:
2. Total value of transactions per customer.
3. Count of the total number of transactions per customer.
4. To define the total value of the transaction, navigate to the **Data | AmountMst** node.
5. Set the **Aggregation Function** property to **Sum.**
6. To display the count of records implement the following steps. Go to the **Groupings | AccountNum** node in the table data region.
7. Right-click on **Add** and select **Field**.

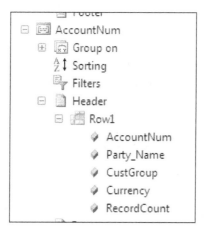

8. Set the following properties:

Property	Value
Caption	Transactions
Expression	=CountRows()
Name	RecordCount
Text Align	Left

9. Preview the report and notice that the aggregated values appear with the customer details. The transactions column indicate the number of records, while the other is the total value of the transactions.

How it works...

Aggregation provides the ability to calculate data based on various functions such as Count, Sum, Avg, Min, and Max. These are applicable to a data region or a dataset. The results of the aggregation can be displayed based on the data region.

When a certain field is to be displayed aggregated in the entire report, then aggregation can be configured in the property of the field in the dataset. Each field has a property called **Aggregate Function**, which must be configured in this case. If the aggregation is only for the specific data region, then it must be defined in the report control in the data region.

Aggregate function results can be displayed as a summary in the header/footer for the table and list data regions. While in the matrix report, the columns and rows can be aggregated to display a grand total.

Adding an image in auto design

This recipe will help you learn about using images in the report and how to use expressions to choose the images dynamically. A new column will be added to the report that indicates if the transaction date was before or after the due date. To indicate before and after, we will use a green check mark and a red cross for indication. A visual expression is easier to identify than just having a Boolean type value.

How to do it...

Images can be added in auto design as follows:

1. Identify the images that are going to be used and set them with right resolutions (**Syncfusion® Metrostudio** has been used to generate these images).

2. The images to be loaded:

3. Right-click on the **Images** node and select **Add a new image**.

4. Locate the path of the image in the **ImageSource** property for the **Images** node.

5. The image is imported, a thumbnail is visible and the system identifies the nature of the file automatically.

6. Repeat the same steps to add the second image.

7. In the table data region **CustTransTable**, expand the **Data** node and add a new image type field.

8. Set the following properties:

Property	Value
Caption	On Time
Source	Embedded
MIME Type	image/png
Expression	=IIF(Fields!DueDate.Value<>Fields!TransDate.Value, "Wrong", "Right")

9. The report is ready to display images. Start a preview to see the expression getting evaluated to display the appropriate image:

How it works...

Images are used in the scenarios to display the company logo or a product image. There are several ways to reference an image in a report such as embedded images, external images, and database. The tabular overview details the reference type and the usage:

Reference Type	Applicable to	Description
Embedded	Auto/Precision design	Image is part of the report or shared components.
Database	Auto/Precision design	Image is stored as binary data in a table field like product image.
External	Precision design	Image is referenced through a URL or location.

Adding a company logo is a common scenario but at the moment, only precision design supports it and auto designs cannot reference the company image in the report header.

See also

▶ The *Adding headers and displaying company images* recipe in *Chapter 4, Report Programming Model – RDP*.

Formatting reports

If you view the currency values in the report output from the previous recipes, the currency values are not aligned. In this recipe, these formatting changes will be made on the text control, to align properly.

How to do it...

Reports can be formatted as follows:

1. To set the alignment, modify the **Text Align** property to **Left** and the **Format string** property must be set to **Currency**.

2. For the **AmountMST** field in the table data region, modify the **Format String** property and set it as **Currency**. The revised report appears as follows:

Invoice	Customer account	Name	Customer group	Currency	Transactions	Sum Amount
	1101	Forest Wholesales	10	USD	5	$0.00
	Due date	Date	Amount	Description	On Time	
	1/1/2012	1/1/2012	($1,233,425.25)		✓	
	3/30/2012	3/30/2012	($2,654,444.33)		✓	
10013	8/29/2010	6/30/2010	$1,233,425.25	Invoice 10013	✗	
10027	5/11/2012	3/12/2012	$2,654,444.33	Invoice 10027	✗	

How it works...

The format string has a set of predefined formats that can be applied on a specific field such as **Date**, and **Number**.

 If you have set up custom values on different properties and want to set the original value, then just right-click on the property field and choose **Reset**. This will reset the selected property to its default value.

Adding unbounded parameters in reports

Parameters bring interactivity to reports. In the last chapter, we had discussed how a new parameter can be added to a dataset through a query. There can be scenarios where we may want to have a parameter that is not linked to the dataset but is needed for the purpose of reporting. These parameters are referred as unbound parameter. In this and the following recipe, we will discuss how to add a parameter and how to use it in the report. The following sections of the recipe should also give you a greater detailed understanding regarding reports.

How to do it...

Unbounded parameters can be added into reports as follows:

1. In this recipe, we will add two parameters, one of type Boolean and the other a String type. The following recipe will show how they will be put to use.

2. Go to the **Parameter** node in the report, right-click on **Add** and select **New Parameter**.

3. On the new parameter set the following properties:

Property	Value
Name	ShowPieChart
Prompt string	Show Pie chart
Data Type	Boolean
Default Value	True
Nullable	True
AllowBlank	True

4. Follow the same procedure and add a second parameter on the parameter node. Set the following properties:

Property	Value
Name	CustGroup
Prompt string	Customer Group
Data Type	String

5. Previewing the report should show two new parameters in the report dialog, but filling these values will not have any influences as these have not been linked to the report.

How it works...

Parameters are the means to get user inputs into reports. The parameters for an SSRS report can be found under the parameters node in the report.

There are two kinds of parameters here:

System parameters	These are parameters that start with `AX_` and are defined by the system for internal purposes, but can be made visible to the user based on the requirement, except for the `AX_UserContext` parameter.
User-defined parameters	Parameters that are defined in the dataset and any other parameters that are added are referred as user-defined parameters.

System parameter

System parameters are hidden by default and have a default value, which is defined through the expression. For example, the `AX_CompanyName` parameter has the following expression filled in by default:

```
=Microsoft.Dynamics.Framework.Reports.
    BuiltInMethods.GetUserCompany(Parameters!AX_UserContext.Value)
```

The system parameters consist of the following:

Parameter	Function	User Modification
`AX_CompanyName`	Indicates the company from which data is to be fetched.	Allowed
`AX_RenderingCulture`	Language in which the report is rendered, for example, English.	Allowed
`AX_ReportContext`	Indicates if the report is running on EP or client.	Allowed
`AX_UserContext`	User who runs the report.	Not Recommended
`AX_PartitionKey`	Defines the active partition for the report.	Not Allowed

User-defined parameters

Further there are two types under user-defined parameters, the bounded and unbounded parameter.

Bounded Parameters

Parameters that are connected to a dataset are identified as bounded parameters. If a dataset is linked to a query, then the parameters are automatically created from the fields that are added to the **Ranges** node in the AOT query.

Unbounded Parameters

These are parameters that are added manually and may or may not be connected to a dataset. These are used for the purpose of formatting or calculating methods.

Parameters and datasource types

As seen in the earlier chapter, AX SSRS supports different types of datasources such as Query, RDP, OLAP, and External Data Sources. The parameters that are defined, depend on the linked datasource. This chapter will describe the query-based parameters.

Query parameters

When a query is added as a dataset, the ranges defined for the query are automatically added to the **Parameters** node of the dataset and the report. The dataset parameters can be seen under the parameter node in the dataset. Fields cannot be added manually in the dataset parameters. Each parameter in the dataset refers to **Report parameter**, which can be seen through the **Report parameter** property:

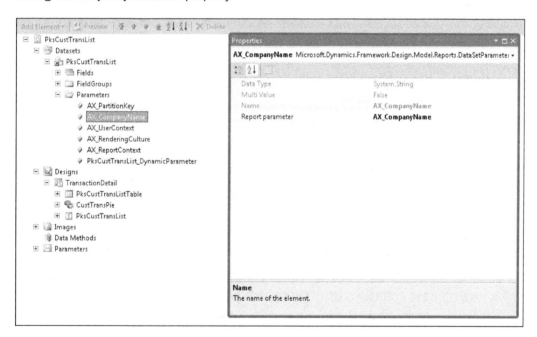

If multiple datasets are added and they refer the same type of field as a parameter, for example, `ItemId`, then both the dataset parameters are added to the report parameter. This results in a redundant report parameter for the same field type. In this case, delete one of the two report parameters and then modify the dataset pointer to point to the same report parameter.

Dynamic filters

As in line with the legacy system (AX 2009), it is possible to allow more parameters to be added by the user through the query framework. To enable this, set the **Dynamic filters** property to **Yes** on the datasource node.

 If you, by mistake, delete the **Dynamic parameter** from the **Report parameter** node, then you can retrieve it by right-clicking and selecting **Refresh** on the dataset.

See also

▸ The *Adding ranges to the report* recipe in *Chapter 1, Understanding and Creating Simple SSRS Reports*.

Adding filters to data regions

This recipe will use the parameters added in the previous recipe and influence the report. Of the two parameters added, the one with the Boolean type will be used to show or hide the chart data region, while the one with the String type will be used to restrict the data shown in the table data region.

How to do it...

Filters can be added to the data regions, as follows:

1. Select the **CustTransPie** chart data region and open its properties.

2. Click on the **Visible** property and open the expression editor. In the editor, enter the following expression. The expression helps to relate the visibility of the control based on the parameter:

   ```
   =IIF(Parameters!ShowPieChart.Value, True, False)
   ```

3. Navigate to the **Filters** node of **CustTransTable** and create a new filter.

4. On the new filter node, set the following properties:

Property	Value
Name	CustGroup
Value	=1
Expression	=IIF((Parameters!CustGroup.Value=Fields!CustGroup.Value),1,0)

5. The data region displays only the data for which the expression evaluates to 1.

6. Now that the report is finally over, select preview and activate the parameters tab. The parameters that were added are visible along with the standard parameters. Verify the parameters through the report preview.

7. The report is now ready to be deployed. The deployed report dialog should appear as shown:

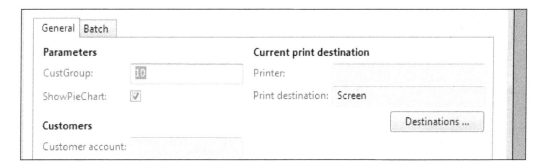

8. The deployed report will show up as seen here in the image.

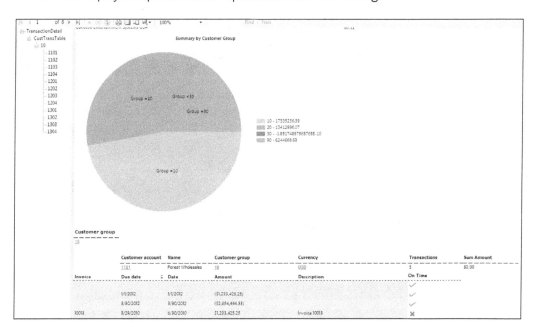

How it works...

Filters are present in the data region and are used to apply a filter on a specific data region. A filter works on the client side and operates on the flattened data. This is used in cases where the data needs to be restricted only to a certain data region and not the entire dataset. As you can see, the chart data is summarizing the entire data but the table data region shows the data only for the selected customer group.

Filters must be used cautiously and must not be considered as an alternative for a query range. The reason being that the system fetches the whole data from the datasource, after which it applies the filter:

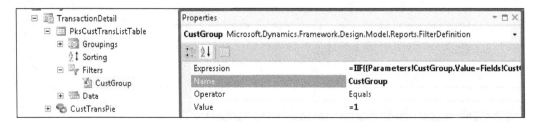

Adding a document map navigation to reports

In this simple recipe, we will see how we can create a powerful navigation system for the report. The document map navigation is an easy-to-use navigation style for reports.

How to do it...

A document map navigation can be added to the report, as follows:

1. The table data region already has the relevant table groupings, based on **customergroup** followed by **AccountNum**.

2. Choose the **CustTransTable** table data region and set the **Data Navigation Style** property to **DocumentMap**.

3. Now preview the report:

4. The navigation on the right-hand side is generated through the document map. This gives a summarized view and enables easy traversing to the right customer account without searching for the pages.

How it works...

The document map is an interesting design addition that offers an easier way to traverse the report. This can be compared to the table of contents generated in a Word document. To apply a document map to a data region, it is necessary to have grouping implemented.

Adding a drill up/drill down navigation to reports

In this recipe, we will get introduced to another navigation style for reports. This is used to collapse or expand data. Additionally, we will learn about the list type data region.

How to do it...

A drill-up/drill-down navigation can be added to the report, as follows:

1. In order to get a feel of this navigation, hide the previous design. Go to the **CustTransTable** table data region and set the **Visible** property to **false**.

2. Right-click on the **Auto design** node and navigate to **Add | List**.

3. On the new list data region **CustTransList**, drag the same set of fields as in the table data region.

4. Similarly add two levels of groupings, **CustomerGroup** followed by **AccountNum**.

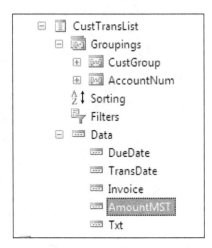

5. Select the data region **CustTransList** and set the property **Data Navigation Style** to **DrillDown**.

6. Now your report should appear with collapsible groups in the preview:

Customer group	10				
Customer account	1101				
Due date	Date	Invoice	Amount		Description
1/1/2012	1/1/2012		1,233,425.25		
3/30/2012	3/30/2012		2,654,444.33		
8/29/2010	6/30/2010	10013	1,233,425.25		Invoice 10013
5/11/2012	3/12/2012	10027	2,654,444.33		Invoice 10027
Customer account	1102				
Customer account	1103				
Customer account	1104				

How it works...

This is another navigation method as the document map. This displays collapsible groups in reports that can be expanded and closed by the user. This can be applied to Table, List and Matrix types of reports.

3

A Report Programming Model

We will look at the following 12 recipes in this chapter:

- ▶ Opening a report through a controller
- ▶ Modifying the report query in the controller
- ▶ Adding ranges from unbound parameters to the query
- ▶ Modifying the UI by caller
- ▶ Turning off the report dialog
- ▶ Setting up security for reports
- ▶ Calling multiple reports from a controller
- ▶ Debugging a report model
- ▶ Adding data methods in business logic
- ▶ Adding a URL drill-through action in reports
- ▶ Debugging business logic
- ▶ Unit testing business logic

Introduction

In the previous chapters, the report model has been discussed extensively. The coming chapters, including this, will discuss the report programming model in AX 2012 in greater detail. This chapter will give the reader a deeper understanding of how the reporting framework is modeled for report execution. Execution of a report is not only about designing the model but also involves receiving inputs and presenting it to the user. The recipes discussed in this chapter will assist in making better choices of how to use the reporting framework to present and get inputs for reports. The two important contracts, RDP and RDL, are compared in detail to create clarity for developers. The later sections have recipes that give details on how C#-based business logic can be designed, debugged, and tested in the report model.

Opening a report through a controller

A controller plays a key role in orchestrating the entire report life cycle. This recipe will be the first step in using a controller and will explain how a report can be invoked from a controller. The *How it works* section of this recipe will give you a detailed picture of the report programming model that will help you to understand the other recipes discussed in this chapter.

Getting Ready

To work with this recipe and the others explained here, it is required that you are familiar with the reports discussed in *Chapter 1, Understanding and Creating Simple SSRS Reports* and *Chapter 2, Enhancing Your Report – Visualization and Interaction*.

How to do it...

To implement the recipe discussed here and the ones following, create a report with the following specifications:

1. Create a query `PktRdlCustTransList` with a limited selection of fields, as detailed in *Chapter 1, Understanding and Creating Simple SSRS Reports*.
2. Create a new report in Visual Studio `PktRdlCustTransList` using the query.
3. Add an `Auto design` with grouping by `Customer Account`.

4. Go to the Parameters node in the report and add the following unbound parameters:

Name	Type	Property "Nullable"
FromDate	DateTime	True
ToDate	DateTime	True
ShowApproved	Boolean	True

5. Build and deploy the report to AX.

6. Create a class `PktRdlCustTransController` that extends the `SRSReportRunController` class.

7. Add a new main method as shown:

```
public static void main(Args args)
{
    PktRdlCustTransController srs;

    srs = new PktRdlCustTransController ();
    srs.parmReportName(ssrsReportStr(PktRdlCustTransList,
        CustTransList));
    srs.parmArgs(args);
    srs.startOperation();
}
```

8. The new controller class is now capable of running the report. Press *F5* to test run the report.

How it works...

Though we have added only a few lines of code to identify our report, the whole process flows without obstructions. This is orchestrated by the `SSRSReportRunController` class that is extended by the controller created in this recipe. The detailed description should help you understand the report programming model.

Report programming model

The report programming model in AX 2012 adopts mainly the MVC pattern to be able to decouple the user interface and business logic. An MVP pattern, in simple terms, improves abstraction and creates clarity on responsibilities; consequently, it brings down the growing complexity caused by mashing up the logic that drives the user interface and the business logic. The `Runbase` framework in AX 2009 is an example of how business logic and UI are put together in the patterns adopted by legacy systems.

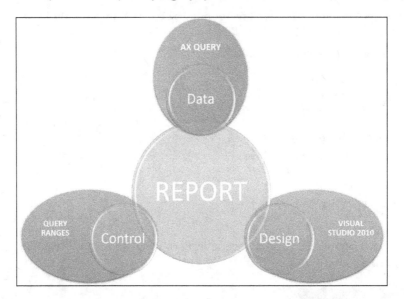

The MVC pattern, when applied to a reporting framework, would distribute the responsibilities as specified here:

- **View**: This represents the visualization of the report.
- **Model**: This represents the data that is generated by processing the parameters.
- **Controller**: This represents the parameters and UI builders that will be used to generate the report.

Model

A model for the SSRS report can be an **AOT query**, **Report data provider** (**RDP**), or business logic.

AOT query are queries modeled using the MorphX IDE, while RDPs are classes that extend `SRSReportDataProvider`. An RDP model is used where complex business logic is involved in computing the data to be rendered. The data is modeled from different sources before being sent to the report.

Controller

The controller implementation in a report is through a group of classes that are bound under the report controller.

- ▶ **Report controller**: This is the main controller that binds different contract classes and controls the execution of the report starting from parsing the report RDL, binding the contracts and UI builder classes to the report, rendering the UI, invoking the report viewer, and post-processing actions after the report is rendered. It is implemented by the base class `SSRSReportRunController` and can be extended to apply report-specific controls.

  The report controller uses different contract class, each aimed at different purposes. All contracts involved in a report are referenced through the report data contract.

- ▶ **Report data contract**: Implemented by `SRSReportDataContract`, this is the class that holds the different contracts used in a report. Each contract has its designated access method, such as `ParmQueryContract` and `ParmRDLContract`, in the report data contract class. Here is a list of contracts present in a report data contract:

Name	Purpose

`RDLDataContract`
 	
`SRSReportRDLDataContract`
	Contract provider that holds all the parameters related to the report, including the system parameters, such as company, report context, and user context

`RDPDataContract`	Contract provider for an RDP class. Holds the parameters related to the RDP class
`Query Contract`	Manages parameters for a query, including the dynamic filters and static ranges

`PrintingContract`
 	
`SRSPrintDestinationSettings`
	Provider manages the print settings, such as destination and format

- ▶ **Report UI builder**: This is another controller class that is responsible for building the UI, based on the related contracts. Implemented by `SRSReportDataContractUIBuilder`, this class extends the `SysOperationAutomaticUIBuilder` and can be modified for report-specific implementation, overridden to handle UI events, such as validate, and modified.

View

The report model, or the design is the representation of the View and it is designed through the Visual Studio extension for Dynamics AX. Designing a report model was discussed in the previous chapters.

The following diagram will help you to understand the flow, as it happens from the time a request to open a report is invoked, till rendering the report, and after rendering it.

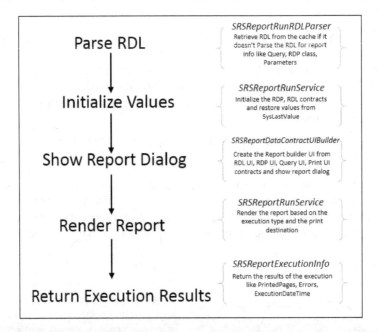

Parse RDL	*SRSReportRunRDLParser* Retrieve RDL from the cache if it doesn't Parse the RDL for report info like Query, RDP class, Parameters
Initialize Values	*SRSReportRunService* Initialize the RDP, RDL contracts and restore values from SysLastValue
Show Report Dialog	*SRSReportDataContractUIBuilder* Create the Report builder UI from RDL UI, RDP UI, Query UI, Print UI contracts and show report dialog
Render Report	*SRSReportRunService* Render the report based on the execution type and the print destination
Return Execution Results	*SRSReportExecutionInfo* Return the results of the execution like PrintedPages, Errors, ExecutionDateTime

Modifying the report query in the controller

Queries present the ability to add dynamic ranges. Some of the situations demand ranges or sorting orders to be filled in, making it easier for the user. A good example would be that when a report is opened from the customer form then the range `customer` is prefilled. This recipe will handle the scenario of modifying the queries through the controller class.

Getting Ready

This and the following recipes will use the `PktRDLCustTransList` report created in the first recipe.

How to do it...

1. In your controller class, override the method `prepromptModifyContract` and write the following code:

```
protected void prePromptModifyContract()
{
    Query query;
```

```
QueryBuildDataSource qbds;

CustTable custTable;

//if an argument is received then see if it is custTable
custTable = args ? args.record() as custTable : null;

if (custTable.RecId)
{
  //get the query associated with the report
  query = this.getFirstQuery();
  qbds  = query.dataSourceTable(tableNum(CustTable));
  qbds.addRange(fieldNum(custTable,
    AccountNum)).value(custTable.AccountNum);
}
}
```

2. Create a new menu item and add it to the `CustTable` form. Verify that the data source property on the button is set to `CustTable`.

3. Click on the button to see that customer name is prefilled in the range in the report dialog.

How it works...

The `prePromptModifyContract` method in the controller class is the designated location to place the code for modifying queries, before they are displayed in the dialog. So, any caller-based modification, locking of ranges based on the caller or addition of other data sources, can be done here. The code discussed here could be applied to the `preRunModifyContract` method as well, but this method is invoked after the report dialog; so the user never gets an option to modify or see the changes made to the query.

Adding ranges from unbound parameters to the query

The SSRS reports support using parameters that are not the part of a dataset. This recipe will attempt to use the unbound parameters, `FromDate` and `ToDate`, added in the report to set the ranges in the report query. These parameters are added in the report and are not connected to any dataset. The values in these controls will be received and set on the report query.

How to do it...

1. The first step is to create a contract and a UI builder class and bind them together. (Assuming you have created the parameters as discussed in the first recipe, *Opening a report through a controller*.)

2. Add a `UIBuilder` class that extends `SRSReportDatacontractUIBuilder`:

    ```
    class PktRdlCustTransListUIBuilder extends
      SrsReportDataContractUIBuilder
    {

    }
    ```

3. Add a contract class that extends `SRSReportRdlDataContract`:

    ```
    [
        SrsReportNameAttribute(ssrsReportStr(PktRdlCustTransList,
          CustTransList)),

        SysOperationContractProcessingAttribute
        (classstr(PktRdlCus
        TransListUIBuilder),
        SysOperationDataContractProcessingMode::
        CreateSeparateUIBuilderForEachContract)
    ]
    class PktRdlCustTransListRdlContract extends
      SrsReportRdlDataContract
    {
        TransDate     fromDate;
        TransDate     toDate;
        #define.FromDate('FromDate')
        #define.ToDate('ToDate')
    }
    ```

4. The next step is to show these values in the UI. If the report is previewed in Visual Studio, the `FromDate` and `ToDate` parameters appear as shown in the following screenshot. This may not be a convenient way for the end user to specify the date ranges.

FromDate	4/21/2013 10:01:10 AM	▾	☐ NULL
ToDate	4/21/2013 10:01:10 AM	▾	☐ NULL

5. To add the date fields to the report dialog, add the following method and call it from the overridden method `PktRdlCustTransListUIBuilder\build`.

```
class PktRdlCustTransListUIBuilder extends
    SrsReportDataContractUIBuilder
{
    DialogField dialogFromDate;
    DialogField dialogToDate;

    //identifier text for retrieving the value
    //from the parameter map in RDL data contract
    //The names must match the name provided in the report
    model
    #define.FromDate('FromDate')
    #define.ToDate('ToDate')
    #define.ShowApproved('ShowApproved')
}
private void addDateFields()
{
    dialog                          dialogLocal;
    PktRdlCustTransListRdlContract   transContract;
    dialogLocal   = this.dialog();
    transContract =
    this.getRdlContractInfo().dataContractObject()
    as PktRdlCustTransListRdlContract;

    dialogFromDate  = dialogLocal.
    addFieldValue(
    extendedTypeStr(FromDate),
    //set the value from the contract.
    //is equivalent of unPack and initialzie in ax 2009
    DatetimeUtil::date(transContract.getValue(#FromDate)),
    "@SYS5209");
```

```
        dialogToDate  = dialogLocal.
        addFieldValue(
        extendedTypeStr(ToDate),
        DatetimeUtil::date(transContract.getValue(#ToDate)),
        "@SYS14656");
    }

    public void build()
    {
        super();
        this.addDateFields();
    }
```

6. Run the report to see the result as shown in the following screenshot:

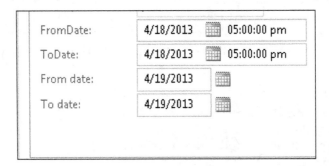

7. The report image shows four controls. This is the result of the framework adding two controls for the type `Datetime` and two controls being added by the extended class for type `Date`. To make only the controls added by the child class visible, comment the `super` in the `build` method. This turns out to be a disadvantage, as for every other control, such as the `showApproved` present in the report, a dialog field must be added explicitly in the same way as the `FromDate` and `ToDate` are added.

8. After the controls are added, these values must be saved in the contract to be set in the query. Override the `getFromDialog` method in the UI builder class and write the code shown. This will save the value to the contract.

```
public void getFromDialog()
{
    PktRdlCustTransListRdlContract   transContract;

    transContract   =
        this.getRdlContractInfo().dataContractObject()
        as PktRdlCustTransListRdlContract;

    transContract.setValue(#FromDate,
    DateTimeUtil::newDateTime(dialogFromDate.value(), 0));
    transContract.setValue(#ToDate,
    DateTimeUtil::newDateTime(dialogToDate.value(), 0));
}
```

9. This completes adding the fields of type `Date` to the UI, storing, and showing back the values from the data contract.

10. The values from the dialog should be set in the query to make it complete. This must be done after the user clicks on **OK** on the report dialog. The `preRunModifyContract` method on the controller is invoked after the user clicks on **OK**, so this method will be appropriate to use in this case.

11. Override this method with the code here:

```
protected void preRunModifyContract()
{
    #define.parameterFromDate('FromDate')
    #define.parameterToDate('ToDate')
```

```
SrsReportRdlDataContract        contract    =
this.parmReportContract().parmRdlContract();
Date   fromDate           =
   contract.getParameter(#parameterFromDate).
   getValueTyped();
date   toDate             =
   contract.getParameter(#parameterToDate).
   getValueTyped();
Query query                      = this.getFirstQuery();

// Modify the query contract based on fromDate & toDate.
SrsReportHelper::addFromAndToDateRangeToQuery(query,
fromDate,
toDate,
tableNum(CustTrans),
fieldNum(CustTrans, TransDate));
}
```

12. The last part is to ensure that the value of `FromDate` is less than `ToDate`. Any validations on the contract values can be placed in the `contract` class; override the method `PktRdlCustTransListRdlContract\Validate` with the following code:

```
public boolean validate()
{
   boolean isValid = super();
   fromDate = this.getValue(#FromDate);
   toDate = this.getValue(#ToDate);

   if(fromDate && toDate)
   {
      if(fromDate > toDate)
      {
         isValid = checkFailed("@SYS120590");
      }
   }

   return isValid;
}
```

How it works...

The two report parameters, `FromDate` and `ToDate`, that are added to the report directly are accessed through the controller. Since the report model only supports DateTime and not Date, the report dialog when previewed, shows a control of type `DateTime`. The `Datetime` field type in the UI may not be convenient way to enter inputs and the date value alone is required in this case. This can be done by adding custom controls of type `date` to the UI. Through blocking the `super` call, the controls are prevented from being added to the report dialog. Alternative date controls are added through the code and are bound to the report parameters. The values from these overridden controls are then added to the query. This way, we understand how we can create an unbound control and override the type of control that is rendered to the UI.

The classes created in this recipe are decorated with attributes. The attributes attached to the `contract` class create the necessary binding. The UI and the controller are bound by `SysOperationContractProcessingAttribute`, while the contract associated with a report is determined by `SRSReportNameAttribute`. As seen in the image in step 6, a control of `DateTime` type is shown. To be able to do this, it is important to understand the parameters, contracts, and how they are stored.

RDP versus RDL data contract

This chapter will largely use **RDL (Report Definition Language)** contract for controlling the report parameters. In this section, the major contract types are discussed to create clarity in understanding. Contracts are used to share the input values between the controller, UI builder, and the report at runtime. As described in the first recipe, there are many contracts for a recipe. The RDL and RDP contracts are very important, since they carry the user inputs. The RDP and RDL are compared here to give a detailed understanding. RDP contracts are discussed in detail in *Chapter 4, Report Programming Model – RDP*.

RDL data contract	RDP data contract
Holds system parameters and report model parameters	Holds contract specific parameters
Parameters are accessed by their identifier name, for example, `Contract.get("FromDate")`, `Contract.set("FromDate")`	Parameters are accessed by the corresponding parm method, for example, `Contract.ParmFromdate`
Contracts are stored in Maps	Stored in corresponding variable
Weakly typed	Strongly typed
Used in all reports	Only used for RDP based reports

RDL data contract	RDP data contract
Parameter map consists of all parameters including the RDP parameters	Holds reference only to its own parameters
Bound to a report	Can be shared across reports
Stores the system parameters, such as Company name and Report Context	System parameters are not accessible through this contract

An RDP report can have both RDL and RDP data contracts. Each data contract can have its own UI builders, but care must be taken that events are carefully delegated and handled.

Modifying the UI by caller

This recipe will discuss how controls in the report dialog can be added or removed based on the caller. For this purpose, the third parameter, ShowApproved, added in the first recipe will be used. CustTrans has a field, Approved, and the idea is to link this unbound parameter to this field in the dataset, so that the users can easily choose it in the report dialog, rather than adding it through the dynamic filters in the query.

How to do it...

1. The build method from the UI builder class will be the ideal choice to handle any changes to the UI. Create a method enableApprovedFlag() and call this method from the build method in the UI builder. This can alternatively be invoked from the postBuild method of the UI builder.

```
private void enableApprovedFlag()
{
    Dialog      dlg;
    TableId     tableId;
    PktRdlCustTransController transController;
    DialogField dialogApproved;

    dlg = this.dialog();
    //add the field since the super call is blocked in the
    build method
    //dialogApproved is a global variable
    dialogApproved  = dlg.
    addFieldValue(
    extendedTypeStr(NoYesId),
```

```
this.dataContractObject().getValue(#ShowApproved),
"Include Approved");

//if super is not blocked then get the dialog field using
this syntax
// dialogApproved  =
this.bindInfo().getDialogField(this.dataContractObject(),
//#ShowApproved);

transController = this.controller() as
  PktRdlCustTransController;

if (transController.parmArgs())
{
  tableId = transController.parmArgs().record().TableId;
  if (tableNum(CustTable) == tableId)
  {
    dialogApproved.visible(false);
  }
}
}
```

2. As learned in the recipe *Adding ranges from unbound parameters to the query*, the methods `getDialogField` in the UI builder (`PktRdlCustTransUIBuilder`) and `preRunModifyContract` in the controller classes must be modified to retrieve the value and to set the value in the query correspondingly.

3. Save and compile the classes and now run the report. When the report is invoked from the `CustTable` form, the report dialog will display the flag **Show approved**.

How it works...

The visibility of controls can be easily switched as shown here, helping in creating a dynamic and context-specific report dialog. If you wish a report parameter to be completely hidden, it is recommended to use the visible property in Visual Studio.

Turning off the report dialog

When no user interaction is required, the report can be run directly without the report dialog. This short recipe will show how this can be done.

How to do it...

1. In the `controller` class for the report, add the following code:

```
public static void main(Args args)
{
    PktRdlCustTransController controller;

    controller = new PktRdlCustTransController();
    controller.parmReportName(ssrsReportStr
        (PktRdlCustTransList, CustTransList));
    controller.parmArgs(args);
    //turn off dialog
    controller.parmShowDialog(false);
    controller.startOperation();
}
```

2. Run the report to see that the report opens up directly without any prompts.

Setting up security for reports

Security setup for a report is significant as it helps to apply the right control. As a developer, it is important to understand the right security approach during the development. Through this recipe, we will learn how to do a proper security setup for reports.

How to do it...

1. Go to the **Action** menu item and add a new menu item.
2. On the properties for the menu item, set up the following properties:

Property	Value
Name	PktRDLCustTransList
Object Type	Class
Object	PktRDLCustTransController
LinkedPermissionType	SSRSReport
LinkedPermissionObject	PktRDLCustTransList
LinkedPermissionObjectChild	CustTransList

How it works...

The LinkedPermission type properties control the security of a report. They tell the security framework where the security for this menu item must be inferred from. The framework tries to retrieve the associated report from the object attached to the entry points, which is a menu item in this case. When there is no controller class, the steps discussed here could be applied to the display menu item that invokes the report.

Calling multiple reports from a controller

A single controller can be used to invoke multiple reports. This recipe will discuss how to use the same controller for different reports and the security setup for multiple reports from a single controller.

How to do it...

1. Here, we have modified our method to choose two different reports, one developed in *Chapter 2, Enhancing Your Report – Visualization and Interaction*, and the other from this chapter.

```
public static void main(Args args)
{
  PktRdlCustTransController controller;

  controller = new PktRdlCustTransController();
  if (args && args.record())
  {
    switch (args.record().TableId)
    {
      case tableNum(CustTable)):

        controller.parmReportName(ssrsReportStr
        (PktRdlCustTransList, CustTransList));
      break;
      case tableNum(CustGroup)):

        controller.parmReportName(ssrsReportStr
        (PktCustTransList, TransList));
      break;
    }
  }
  controller.parmArgs(args);
```

```
controller.startOperation();

}
```

2. When the controller is connected to more than one report, the permission setup for the menu item differs. It involves creating a security permission object and linking it to the report controller.

3. Go to **AOT | Security | Code Permissions**. Right-click on **Code Permissions** and select **New Code Permission**.

4. Create a new permission object `PktCustTransReport` and expand to the node **Associated Objects**, select **Reports** and add the reports that are used in the controller.

5. Create an action menu `Item` and set the properties as shown in the following table:

Property	Value
Object Type	Class
Object	PktRDLCustTransController
LinkedPermissionType	CodePermission
LinkedPermissionObject	PktRDLCustTransList

How it works...

The code permission object `PktCustTransReport`, bundles all the reports and helps the menu item determine the security rights that must be assigned to a role that will use this report bundle. Use the main method in the controller class to select the appropriate report based on context.

Debugging a report model

One challenge that comes along with the new reporting model is debugging. Different approaches for debugging issues must be taken based on the context. This is a short recipe that will tell you the configurations to debug the report model and the possible methods where the debugging points would be appropriate to start.

How to do it...

1. For debugging the framework-related classes, the AX debugger can be used.

2. Under the **Development** option, make sure the **Execute business operations in CIL** flag is unchecked to ensure that you will be able to debug the code in the X++ debugger.

3. The following methods are ideal to place your debugger for examining the execution:

   ❑ **Controller**: The methods `PrePromptModifyReport` and `PreRunModifyReport`

   ❑ **UI Builder**: The method `build`

Making changes to the model and adding new classes

This subsection is about refreshing the code when you make changes to the model or framework classes.

1. When changes are made to the query by adding ranges or fields, then ensure that you open the Visual Studio. On the dataset, select **Refresh** and then redeploy the project.

2. The report model is cached inside AX to ensure faster operation. In the event of changing the report model or introducing a new UI builder or contract class, it is important to refresh the cached elements under **Tools | Caches | Refresh elements**.

3. If this still doesn't reload the changes, resolve the problem by attempting to re-login to AX. This would definitely refresh the cache.

How it works...

Unlike AX 2009, not every part of a report can be debugged by a unified approach, such as using the AX debugger. This specific recipe suggests how the report modeling framework, inside AX that comprises of the controller and UI builder, can be debugged.

Adding data methods in business logic

While the methods in AX can be accessed through the table methods exposed in the Query window, there can be small computational needs in every report. These small computations, if they cannot be implemented by expressions, could be handled by data methods. These are based on C# and can be used to leverage the C# framework capabilities for small computations. This recipe will showcase adding a data method to the report where the text in a selected field is turned into upper case.

How to do it...

1. On the **Data Methods** node of your report data model, right-click to add a new data method.

2. Rename the data method as changeCase.

3. Double-click on the new data method and a new C# Sharp Project with the name of the report can be seen added to the Solution.

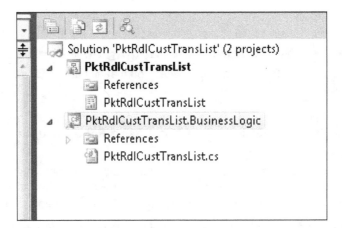

4. The cursor will point to a plain implementation method that appears similar to the following code:

```
[DataMethod (), PermissionSet (SecurityAction.Assert, Name
  = "FullTrust")]
public static string DataMethod1()
{
  throw new NotImplementedException("The method or
    operation is not implemented.");
}
```

5. The `[DataMethod]` attribute indicates that this is a data method. The default return type is string but this method can return any .NET supported types.

6. Rewrite the logic to convert the voucher number to upper case.

```
[DataMethod(), PermissionSet(SecurityAction.Assert, Name =
  "FullTrust")]
public static string changeCase(string value)
{
  return value.ToUpper();
}
```

7. Compile the code and it is ready to be used. Verify to see the report model showing the new parameters as subnodes.

8. To use the business logic that was created previously, expand the **Data** node in the Auto Design and add a new field.

9. Go to the property expression, open the expression dialog, and key in the following code line:

```
=changeCase(Fields!Voucher.Value)
```

10. This way, the expression is tied to the data method added.

11. Run the report and notice the new field showing the voucher number in upper case.

How it works...

Data methods on the report model provide the ability to manipulate and modify the report date. They can be used for:

▶ Implementing expressions

▶ Returning a `DataTable` that can be used as a dataset

▶ Building URLs for the drill through action connecting to a SubReport or a URL

It is wise to remember that these data methods are no alternative to the AX business logic. Avoid using data methods for implementing business logic or querying the AX database. Simple data methods can also be achieved using expressions, but the choice has to be made based on the requirement.

Data methods versus expressions

Chapter 1, *Understanding and Creating Simple SSRS Reports* and Chapter 2, *Enhancing Your Report – Visualization and Interaction*, detailed how the expressions window can be used to write simple logics but they are limited in the number of lines that can be used, are not reusable, and there is no possibility of including any external references from the .NET framework to compute. A data method overcomes these disadvantages.

Data methods can be invoked from expressions and they offer the flexibility to include external references, write bigger computations, and the compiler indicates any break in the code with greater detail. A data method can be accessed and called via an expression.

Adding a URL drill-through action in reports

A URL drill-through action is similar to the **View Details** option in forms. AX supports a URL mechanism that can be processed to open a form with the appropriate record highlighted.

How to do it...

1. The first step to implement a URL drill is to identify the URL builder that will be used for constructing the URL. The `SRSDrillThroughCommon` project consists of a list of helper classes for different modules.

2. Press *Ctrl+D* or navigate to **View | Application Explorer** to open the AOT.

3. Navigate to **C sharp projects** under **Visual Studio** and select `SRSDrillThroughCommon`.

4. Right-click and select **Edit**. This will add the project to the current report solution.

5. Search through the `drillThroughCommon` C# class for the prebuilt methods for the field.

6. In this case, the field is `Voucher` and the finance helper classes have a prebuilt function that can handle drill-through for vouchers.

7. Navigate back to `PktRdlCustTransList.BusinessLogic` and add the `SRSDrillThroughCommon` project as a reference.

8. Add the following namespace to the C# class:

```
using Microsoft.Dynamics.AX.Application.Reports;
```

9. Add this code to generate the URL for opening the Voucher Transactions from the voucher column in the report and build the solution:

```
[DataMethod(), PermissionSet(SecurityAction.Assert, Name =
    "FullTrust")]
public static string DrillVoucher(string     reportContext,
string     VoucherNum,
DateTime   ADate,
String     CompanyValue)
{
    return DrillThroughCommonHelper
    .ToLedgerTransVoucherForm(reportContext,
    VoucherNum,
    ADate,
    CompanyValue);
}
```

10. Move to the report model and right-click on the **field Voucher**. Navigate to **Add | URL Drill Through Action** and give it a name, such as URLDrillAction.

11. On the new node, the **Properties** node, select the expression and enter the following code:

```
=drillVoucher(!Parameters.AX_ReportContext.Value,
    !Fields.CustTrans.VoucherNum.value,
    !Fields.CustTrans.TrandDate.value,
    !Parameters.AX_CompanyName.Value);
```

12. Rebuild the solution and deploy the report to see the drill-through in action.

How it works...

A typical URL, to open a currency form, appears like `menuitemdisplay://currency/+47+%5B1:USD%5D`. This URL is processed by the `SysHelp::processStandardLink()` method to open the appropriate forms and highlight the selection.

AX automatically adds drill-through action to fields with foreign-key relations, such as customer and vendor. In the case of specific fields, such as `Voucher Number`, where finding the record involves more than one field or is different, a drill-through action needs to be added. AX has built-in classes that have helper classes that can handle the majority of the drill-through actions.

Debugging business logic

Business logic can be debugged using the Visual Studio debugger. Follow this recipe to activate the debugging.

How to do it...

1. Ensure that you are on the same server where the reporting services are installed.
2. Set the project configuration to point to debug mode and rebuild and deploy the solution including the report model and the included business logic.
3. This will deploy the necessary symbols for debugging.
4. Navigate to the **Tools | Attach to Process** window; make sure **Show Process from All users** and **Show Process from All sessions** are checked.
5. Under the displayed process, select `ReportServicesService.exe` and click on **Attach**.
6. Open the report through the report services in the web browser or in AX.
7. After specifying the parameter values in the dialog, the reporting services will activate the debugger.

How it works...

The business logic for a report is stored along with the report as a **DLL** (**Dynamic-Link Library**). These DLLs are deployed along with the RDL. To debug the data method, the debug files are loaded. If the files are not loaded, debugging is impossible. Prefer to use the unit testing approach defined in the following recipe.

Unit testing business logic

Debugging can be a time-consuming task as it is required to re-deploy the reports for every change that is done. An alternative way to reduce this cycle and make it easier to test is by creating Unit Test cases. Visual Studio has handy tools that can create Unit Testing projects. This recipe will implement unit testing for the drill-through action implemented in the recipe, adding a URL drill-through action in reports.

How to do it...

1. Select the `DrillVoucher` method in the business logic class, right-click and select **Create Unit Tests**.

2. A **Create Unit Tests** dialog will prompt with the `DrillVoucher` method selected by default. If additional methods are present, check them and click on **OK**.

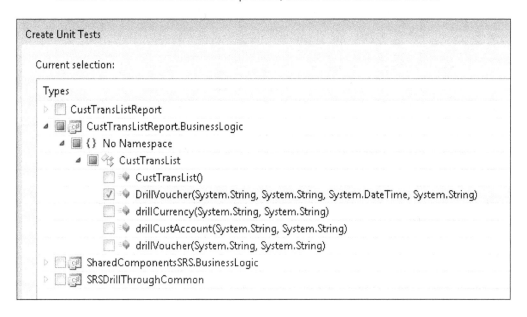

3. This will create a Unit Test project and a specific implementation to invoke the `DrillVoucher` method like this:

```
[TestMethod()]
public void DrillVoucherTest()
{
  string reportContext =
    "?RunOnClient=1&PrintMediumType=Screen"
  string VoucherNum = "ARPM000004";
  DateTime ADate = new DateTime(200, 02, 28);
  string CompanyValue = "USSI";
  //intialize if you want use assert
  //string expected;
  string actual;
  actual = CustTransList.DrillVoucher(reportContext,
  VoucherNum,
  ADate,
  CompanyValue);
  //intial approach would be test using
  //Ax Class SysHelp::ProcessStandardLink
```

```
    //Once the link is verified it can be added to the
    expected.
    //Assert.AreEqual(expected, actual);
}
```

4. Place the debugger anywhere in the method. On the tool bar, navigate to **Test |
   Debug | All Tests in Solution**. This will activate the debugger.

5. The business logic tested in the previous recipe is a drill-through URL; copy the
   returned URL from the Unit Test and run the following job in AX to see if it opens
   the right form and highlights the selection:

```
static void JobTestURL(Args _args)
{
    //Add the URL fetched through the unit test results
    SysHelp::processStandardLink
        ('menuitemdisplay://ledgertransvoucher/+3123+%5B63
        :ARPM000004%5D%5B2:02/28/2011%2000:00:
        00%5D%5B64:USSI%5D', null);
}
```

How it works...

The unit testing framework comes as part of Visual Studio and helps in testing code units.
Most of the process is automated here and requires minimal efforts to get it working, such
as passing the input parameters and validating the output parameters. This also helps in
achieving better coverage of the logic, since some logic never gets tested during the functional
testing. This Unit Test can be maintained or discarded after this testing; but prefer to discard
it as it can always be regenerated if necessary, unless you have huge prerequisites that are
difficult to recreate, such as inserting records.

4
Report Programming Model – RDP

In this chapter will discuss the following eight recipes:

- ▸ Creating a simple RDP report
- ▸ Testing RDP
- ▸ Creating a simple precision design
- ▸ Creating an advanced RDP report
- ▸ Creating a group view report
- ▸ Adding headers and displaying company images
- ▸ Using an existing temp table in RDP
- ▸ Preprocessing reports

Introduction

When designing reports, not all the data can be retrieved through queries. Many reports involve analysis and consolidation of data that comes through business logic. The **Report Data Provider** (**RDP**) enables the use of existing business logic in reports, but in an abstract manner.

In this chapter, we will discuss the working pattern of RDP and how to choose whether to use it in reports. The samples discussed in this chapter detail the different approaches and patterns for using RDP. This chapter will introduce you to precision design in **SSRS** (**SQL Server Reporting Services**) and will discuss the widely used tabular design in greater detail. Precision design offers a lot of flexibility and control in rendering a report.

Creating a simple RDP report

This recipe will create a simple RDP report, helping you to understand the concept of RDP. The report will take amount, interest rate, and years as input and will print the compounded interest calculated on the report.

Getting ready

To be able to do this recipe and the others involving RDP in this chapter, you need a basic understanding of X++, data contracts, and data attributes.

How to do it...

1. RDP uses a temporary table to store the data and so, the first step in RDP development is to identify the fields involved in the report and create them as a temporary table.

2. For the present scenario, a temporary table `PKTInterestCalcTmp` with the fields `Amount`, `Interest`, `Total`, and `Year` is created.

3. In the table, set the property `Table type` as `InMemory` to make it temporary.

4. After creating the table, the next step is to define the contract. The contract must contain all the parameters that are exposed to the user and those that are hidden. Here looking at the user inputs, they would be the initial amount, interest rate, and total number of years. Create the contract class using the code here:

```
[
    DataContractAttribute
]
class PktInterestCalcContract
{
    Amount  arcmount, interest;
    Yr      yr;
}


[
    DataMemberAttribute('Amount')
]
public Amount parmAmount(Amount _amount = amount)
{
    amount = _amount;

    return amount;
}
```

```
[
    DataMemberAttribute('Interest'),
    SysOperationLabelAttribute(literalStr("Interest")),
    SysOperationHelpTextAttribute(literalStr("Rate of
        Interest")),
    SysOperationDisplayOrderAttribute('1')
]

public Amount parmInterest(Amount _interest = interest)
{
    interest = _interest;

    return interest;
}


[
    DataMemberAttribute('Year'),
    SysOperationLabelAttribute(literalStr("Period")),
    SysOperationHelpTextAttribute(literalStr("Number of
        years")),
    SysOperationDisplayOrderAttribute('0')
]
public Yr parmYear(Yr _year = Yr)
{
    yr = _year;

    return yr;
}
```

5. The attribute `DataContractAttribute` at the class declaration indicates that this is a contract. If the contract requires a UI builder, that must also be defined in the class declaration.

6. Each parm method has the attribute `DataMemberAttribute` indicating that it is a contract member. This helps in having methods internal to the contract class, which don't have a decorator and are not accessible by other components, say the controller.

7. The remaining attributes in the contract methods, as seen in the previous code, are used for setting UI-specific values.

Attribute Name	Description
SysOperationLabelAttribute	Override the EDT label for the parm method
SysOperationHelptextAttribute	Override the Help text for the EDT parm method
SysOperationDisplayOrderAttribute	Order of the control in the report Dialog

8. The contract class is used by the UI builder for constructing the report dialog automatically, unlike in AX 2009, where the dialog field must be added for each field that is exposed to the user.

9. The next part involves creation of the RDP class. Create the RDP class using the code here. The SRSReportParameterAttribute decorator in the class declaration binds the contract and the controller.

```
[
    SRSReportParameterAttribute(classStr
        (PktInterestCalcContract))
]
class PktInterestCalcDp extends SRSReportDataProviderBase
{
    PktInterestCalcTmp interestCalcTmp;
}
```

10. The ProcessReport method is decorated with the SysEntryPoint attribute to be invoked from the services framework. The temporary table must be filled in this method.

```
[SysEntryPointAttribute(false)]
public void processReport()
{
    PktInterestCalcContract contract;

    Amount amount, total, oldTotal;
    Amount interestRate, interest;
    percent interestPct;
    yr      yr, yrCount = 1;


    contract = this.parmDataContract() as
        PktInterestCalcContract;

    amount      = contract.parmAmount();
    interestPct = contract.parmInterest();
    yr          = contract.parmYear();

    interestRate = interestPct / 100;
    oldTotal     = amount;

    while (yrCount <= yr)
    {
        interest = (oldTotal*interestRate);
        total    = oldTotal + interest;
```

```
        this.insertInTmp(yrCount, oldTotal, interest, Total);
        oldTotal = total;
        yrCount++;
    }
}

private void insertInTmp(
Yr          _yr,
Amount      _amount,
Amount      _interest,
Total       _total)
{
    interestCalcTmp.clear();
    interestCalcTmp.Year = _yr;
    interestCalcTmp.Interest = _interest;
    interestCalcTmp.Amount    = _amount;
    interestCalcTmp.Total     = _total;
    interestCalcTmp.insert();
}
```

11. Any method that is decorated with SRSReportDataSetAttribute will be used to identify the temporary tables returned by RDP. There can be more than one method with this attribute, but in this case there is only one table.

```
[
    SRSReportDataSetAttribute(tableStr(PktInterestCalcTmp))
]
public PktInterestCalcTmp getInterestCalcTmp()
{
    select interestCalcTmp;
    return interestCalcTmp;
}
```

12. This completes the designing of the RDP class. The next recipe will use this RDP class to create a simple precision design-based report.

How it works...

The RDP framework enables us to consolidate all data required across a report into a temporary table and then use that as a datasource to create the report. In this recipe an RDP class is created as a datasource; this will be used in the subsequent recipe to construct a report. The section below will give you understanding of how the whole RDP framework plugs in to AX-SSRS.

Report Data Provider (RDP)

The concept of RDP is very simple. A temporary table that has all the necessary fields involved in reporting is filled using a query or business logic. This temporary table is used as a data source and the report is rendered. RDP constitutes of the following components:

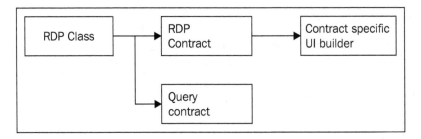

RDP class

The major component in an RDP class is the report data provider class. Any class that extends `SRSReportDataProviderbase`/`SRSReportDataProviderPreprocess` can act as an RDP. An RDP receives its inputs optionally through a contract or a query and implements the logic involved in filling the temporary table. The reporting services invoke the data provider through the query services framework to fetch the data.

RDP data contract

The RDP data contract is the contract class that holds all the parameters specific to an RDP class. The data contract is also used by the report UI builder to render the form controls for user inputs. A contract can use its own UI builder, which is bound through `SysOperationContractProcessingAttribute`. A data contract can include or extend other contracts, for example, `SalesFormLetterconfirmcontract` and `InventDimviewcontract`.

UI builder

Similar to an RDL contract, an RDP contract can also bind itself to an UI builder. If a report has both RDL and RDP contracts and each is bound to a UI builder, then the system invokes both in sequence. A report dialog is built by several UI builder classes, such as Query, PrintDestination, and the contract UI builders. These classes are responsible for adding the dialog fields, validations, grouping, and handling form control events.

The following figure can give you a clear view of how the report programming flow works with RDP:

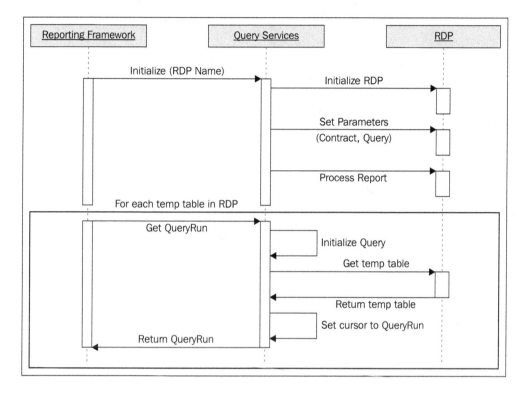

Choosing RDP for a report

A report can be designed to use RDP as the data source type in the following cases:

- ▶ Data to be rendered cannot be constructed as a query
- ▶ The business logic to be processed depends on a parameter
- ▶ Data can be rendered using existing business logic
- ▶ When more filters are to be added at runtime

 Fact: Do you know that the majority of the reports in AX 2012 are RDP-based reports?

See Also

- ▶ The *Adding ranges from unbound parameters to the query* recipe in *Chapter 3, A Report Programming Model*.

Testing the RDP

An RDP class can be tested even without hooking it to a report. This has the advantage of testing it faster and ensuring that it works reliably before connecting it to a report. This is an isolated test and helps validate the logic. The following recipe will show how to do the test on an RDP class.

How to do it...

1. Create a new job as in the code here:

```
static void TestInterestCalcRDP(Args _args)
{
  //initialize contract
  PktInterestCalcContract cont = new
    PktInterestCalcContract();
  PktInterestCalcDp    dp;

  //fill the contract
  cont.parmAmount(2000);
  cont.parmInterest(10);
  cont.parmYear(5);

  //instantiate
  dp = new PktInterestCalcDp();
  //pass the contract
  dp.parmDataContract(cont);
  //fill the table
  dp.processReport();
}
```

2. Change the temporary table used for this RDP to a persistent table by setting the property table type as `Regular`.

3. Run the job and verify that the data is filled in the table. If the RDP works well then data must be filled in the table created. After verifying, change the property of the table back to `InMemory`.

How it works...

This will be an effective way of testing your RDP even before the report is made. This can also be applied in a different instance where you don't want the RDP logic to be executed every time. When testing reports that have longer execution time, make the table permanent and execute the report once. Once the table is filled, the entire RDP logic can be commented. This allows only the reporting logic to be executed making it easier and faster to test.

Creating a simple precision design

Precision designs are flexible and offer abundant opportunities to customize your report by allowing you to decide the location, font, and much more.

Getting ready

This recipe will use the RDP class created in the recipe *Creating a simple RDP report*.

How to do it...

1. Open Visual Studio and create a reporting project. Add a report and call it `PktInterestCalcReport`.

2. Add a dataset and change the property `Data Source Type` to `Report Data Provider`. Click on the `Query` property button to show the list of the RDP class.

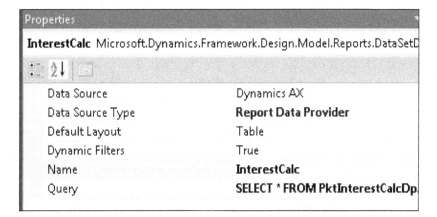

Properties	
InterestCalc Microsoft.Dynamics.Framework.Design.Model.Reports.DataSetD	
Data Source	Dynamics AX
Data Source Type	**Report Data Provider**
Default Layout	Table
Dynamic Filters	True
Name	**InterestCalc**
Query	**SELECT * FROM PktInterestCalcDp**

3. Select the RDP class created and click on **Next** to add the fields. Expand the dataset to see the fields from the temporary table and the parameters listed from the data contract.

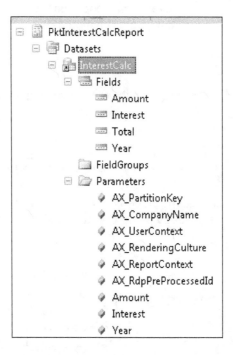

4. To start with the precision design, right-click on the **Design** node and select **Precision Design**.

5. After selecting the **Precision Design** node, set the following properties:

Property	Value
Name	InterestReport
Style Template	TableStyleTemplate

6. Right-click on **Precision Design** and select **Edit Using Designer....** This opens the designer. The left part of the designer holds the report data, which lists all the fields available for use in the report design. Right-click on the design area and select **Insert | Table**.

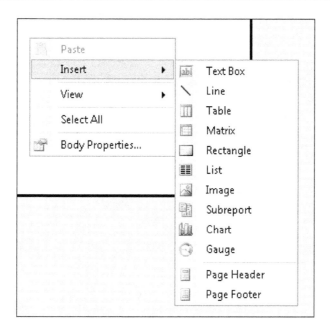

7. Drag the fields from the RDP table and drop them in the table.

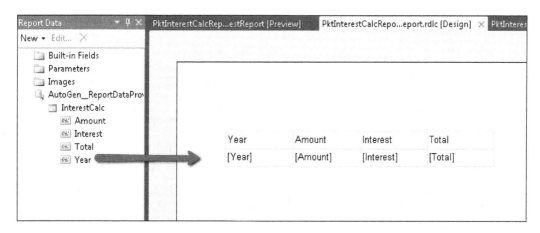

8. Save the report design and on the report model click on **Preview** to see the report as shown here in the following screenshot:

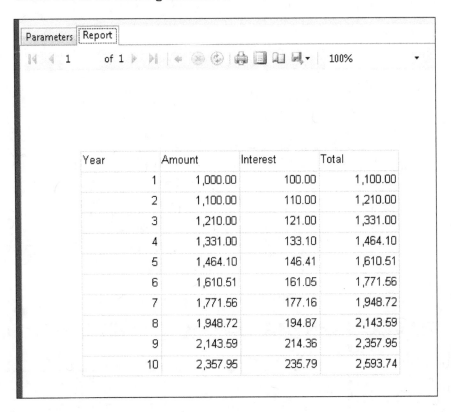

Year	Amount	Interest	Total
1	1,000.00	100.00	1,100.00
2	1,100.00	110.00	1,210.00
3	1,210.00	121.00	1,331.00
4	1,331.00	133.10	1,464.10
5	1,464.10	146.41	1,610.51
6	1,610.51	161.05	1,771.56
7	1,771.56	177.16	1,948.72
8	1,948.72	194.87	2,143.59
9	2,143.59	214.36	2,357.95
10	2,357.95	235.79	2,593.74

9. Now deploy the report and create a menu item to use the report in AX.

How it works...

This report shows how RDP can be used as a data source. The RDP doesn't necessarily require a query or contract; the key part is the content in the temporary table.

> Fact: Did you know that actually SSRS has no concept called an Auto Design?

Creating an advanced RDP report

The RDP report that was completed in the first part was simple. This recipe will implement an RDP class that is more practical in nature. The goal is to build a report for the customer desk where the user can key in the manufacturing date and find the batches manufactured on that date. On selection of a batch or batches, print a report with the batch and its transactions to track its history. This report will be implemented in the next two recipes. The first recipe will involve creating the RDP class for the business functionality, while the later recipe discusses the report design part.

How to do it...

1. As seen in the last RDP recipe, the first step is to identify the fields involved in the report and create a table for them. Let us create a table `PktInventBatchTransTmp` with the fields indicated here:

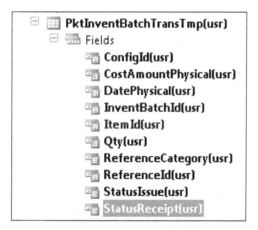

2. The contract class is to be created next. The parameters required are the manufacturing date and batch number. Create a data contract as shown:

```
[
    DataContractAttribute,
]
class PktInventBatchTransContract
{
    InventDimViewContract       inventDimViewContract;
    InventBatchProdDate         prodDate;
    InventBatchId               batchId;
}
```

```
[DataMemberAttribute('Batch')]
public InventBatchId parmBatchId(InventBatchId _batchId =
  batchId)
{
  batchId = _batchId;

  return batchId;
}

[DataMemberAttribute('ProdDate')]
public InventBatchProdDate parmProdDate(InventBatchProdDate
  _prodDate = prodDate)
{
  prodDate = _prodDate;

  return prodDate;
}
```

3. The next step is to fill the data in the temporary table. A select statement (**DML** (**Data Manipulation Language**)) can be used to fetch the data, but using a query would mean that the report ranges (parameters) can be extended later. So design a query `PktInventBatch` as seen in the following screenshot:

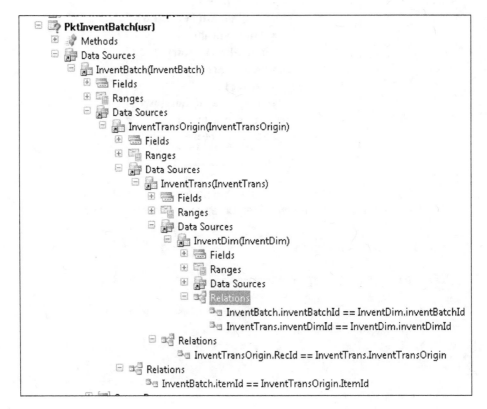

4. RDP must be created with a binding to the contract. The query created can also be bound to be exposed in the report dialog.

    ```
    [
      //bind query - shows in the report dialog
      SRSReportQueryAttribute(queryStr(PktInventBatch)),
      //bind the contract
      SRSReportParameterAttribute(classStr
        (PktInventBatchTransCotract))
    ]
    class PktInventBatchTransDP extends
      SRSReportDataProviderBase
    {

      PktInventBatchTransTmp tmpBatchTrans;

    }
    ```

5. The `processReport` method must be designed to receive the parameters from the contract and set them on the query. This query must be executed further to insert the data in the tables.

6. The `processReport` method, as seen here, will get the RDP query and set the range from the contract for the batch ID and the production date. This is followed by the execution of the query to insert the records in the temporary table.

    ```
    [
    SysEntryPointAttribute(false)
    ]
    public void processReport()
    {
      Query                  query;
      QueryRun               queryRun;
      QueryBuildRange        batchRange, dateRange;
      QueryBuildDataSource   qbds;

      InventBatch            inventBatch;
      InventTrans            inventTrans;
      InventTransOrigin      transOrigin;

      InventDimViewContract     viewContract;

      batchContract = this.parmDataContract() as
        PktInventBatchTransContract;

      query = this.parmQuery();
      qbds = query.dataSourceTable(tableNum(InventBatch));
    ```

```
//set the range
batchRange = SysQuery::findOrCreateRange(qbds,
  fieldNum(InventBatch,
InventBatchId));

batchRange.value(batchContract.parmBatchId());

if (batchContract.parmProdDate())
{
dateRange = SysQuery::findOrCreateRange(qbds,
  fieldNum(InventBatch,
ProdDate));
dateRange.value(SysQuery::value
  (batchContract.parmProdDate()));
}

queryRun = new queryRun(query);

while (queryRun.next())
{
  if (queryRun.changed(tablenum(InventBatch)))
  {
    inventBatch = queryRun.get(tableNum(InventBatch));
  }

  if (queryRun.changed(tablenum(InventTransOrigin)))
  {
    transOrigin =
      queryRun.get(tableNum(InventTransOrigin));
  }

  inventTrans = queryRun.get(tableNum(InventTrans));

  this.insertTmpTable(inventBatch, transOrigin,
    inventTrans);
  }

}
```

7. This method, `insertTmpTable`, is invoked from the process report to simply insert the records in to the temporary table.

```
private void insertTmpTable(
InventBatch          _inventBatch,
InventTransOrigin    _transOrigin,
```

```
InventTrans              _inventTrans,
InventDim                _inventDim
)
{
  tmpBatchTrans.clear();
  tmpBatchTrans.ItemId                   =
    _inventTrans.ItemId;
  tmpBatchTrans.InventBatchId            =
    _inventBatch.inventBatchId;


  tmpBatchTrans.ReferenceId              =
    _transOrigin.ReferenceId;
  tmpBatchTrans.ReferenceCategory        =
    _transOrigin.ReferenceCategory;

  tmpBatchTrans.StatusIssue              =
    _inventTrans.StatusIssue;
  tmpBatchTrans.StatusReceipt            =
    _inventTrans.StatusReceipt;
  tmpBatchTrans.DatePhysical             =
    _inventTrans.DatePhysical;
  tmpBatchTrans.Qty                      =    _inventTrans.Qty;
  tmpBatchTrans.CostAmountPhysical       =
    _inventTrans.CostAmountPhysical;

  tmpBatchTrans.insert();
}
```

8. This method is used by the reporting extension to retrieve the data.

```
[
  SRSReportDataSetAttribute(tableStr
    (PktInventBatchTransTmp))
]
public PktInventBatchTransTmp getinventOnhandTmp()
{
  select  tmpBatchTrans;
  return  tmpBatchTrans;
}
```

9. All the artifacts to enable the RDP are complete.

10. There is one UI-related change that needs to be incorporated; that is, when a manufacturing date is chosen, the batch displayed must be from the same date. This change requires a UI builder that must be bound to the contract. The approach is to override the `postRun` method in the UI builder and build a local lookup method for the batch ID field.

11. The UI builder `PktInventBatchTransUIBuilder` must be designed as shown here:

```
class PktInventBatchTransUIBuilder extends
SysOperationAutomaticUIBuilder
{
   DialogField batchDialog, dateDialog;
}

public void build()
{

   super();

   batchDialog = this.bindInfo().getDialogField(
   this.dataContractObject(),
   methodStr(PktInventBatchTransContract, parmBatchId));

   dateDialog = this.bindInfo().getDialogField(
   this.dataContractObject(),
   methodStr(PktInventBatchTransContract, parmProdDate));
}

public void postRun()
{
   super();

   //setup the event routing
   batchDialog.registerOverrideMethod(
   methodStr(FormStringControl, lookup),
   methodStr(PktInventBatchTransUIBuilder, batchLookup),
   this);
}

public void batchLookup(FormStringControl _control)
{
   Query               query;
   SysTableLookup      sysTableLookup;
   QueryBuildDataSource qbds;

   sysTableLookup =
     SysTableLookup::newParameters(tableNum(InventBatch),
     _control);
   sysTableLookup.addLookupfield(fieldNum(InventBatch,
     InventBatchId));
```

```
query = new Query();
qbds = query.addDataSource(tableNum(InventBatch));
//if no date is specified show all batch
if (datedialog.value())
{
qbds.addRange(fieldNum(InventBatch,
  prodDate)).value(queryValue(datedialog.value()));
}

sysTableLookup.parmQuery(query);
sysTableLookup.performFormLookup();
}
```

12. Decorate the class declaration of the contractor class to bind the UI builder.

```
[
    DataContractAttribute,
    SysOperationContractProcessingAttribute(classStr
      (PktInventBatchTransUIBuilder),
    SysOperationDataContractProcessingMode::
      CreateUIBuilderForRootContractOnly)
]
class PktInventBatchTransContract
{
    InventDimViewContract       inventDimViewContract;
    InventBatchProdDate         prodDate;
    InventBatchId               batchId;
}
```

13. This completes the design of the RDP.

14. Now test the RDP.

15. As performed on the last recipe, write a test job and validate the RDP.

16. This completes all coding-related modifications for the report. The next recipe will model a report using this RDP.

How it works...

The RDP class designed here uses a query to iterate through the data and insert it into the temporary table. The query is bound to the report through the query attribute in the class declaration of the RDP. However, if the business logic doesn't demand a lot of dynamic behavior, prefer to use DML (select statements) to fetch the information. This can speed up the report process.

When designing a temporary table for an RDP, remember to add replacement keys for any surrogate key and add relations to the table to enable drill through.

 RDP classes can be used for multiple purposes and need not be restricted to only reporting. The `TrailbalanceDP` class is used by the trial balance report and form.

Creating a group view report

We have started using precision design. The most prominently used reporting technique in precision design is tabular grouping. Grouping helps render the data hierarchy, and precision design leverages the capability many fold when compared to Auto design in this aspect. The RDP class created in the previous recipe will be used here as the source of data.

How to do it...

1. Create a new precision design. Set the property name as `BatchTransReport` and the style as `TableStyleAlternatingTow`. Double-click on **Design** to open the designer.

2. On the designer area, right-click on the report page and navigate to **Insert | New Table**.

3. A header and a detailed row appear. Drop the header by selecting the header row and right-clicking on the header row and selecting **Delete rows**.

4. Place the cursor in the column to see an icon like this 🔲. Click on this icon to get the list of fields and select the required field.

5. To add a new column, right-click and insert the column to the right.

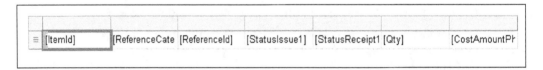

6. This shows all the detail lines. To add a grouping on batch, go to the grouping tab at the bottom (if grouping is not visible, navigate to **Report | Grouping** from the menu). Click on the downward arrow on the right-corner row that says **(Details)**.

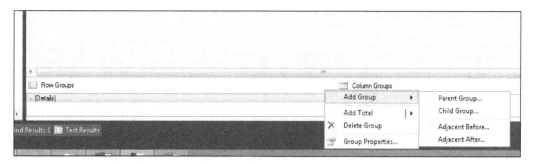

7. Navigate to **Add Group** | **Parent Group...** and on the prompted dialog select
   `InventBatchId`. This sets the grouping based on the selected field.

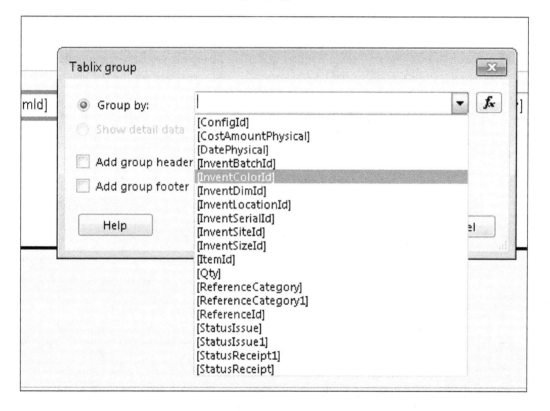

8. A new column, `InventBatchId`, is added to the design. Preview the report.

000001	M2002	Purchase order	000002	None	Purchased		117,000.00	64,350.00
000002	M2002	Production line	B-000015	Sold	None		-60,469.41	-33,258.18
	M2002	Purchase order	000002	None	Purchased		61,962.48	34,079.36
000003	P5000	Production line	B-000005	Sold	None		-646,190.90	-545,746.66
	P5000	Production line	B-000006	Sold	None		-342,461.88	-289,229.43
	P5000	Production line	B-000003	Sold	None		-123,550.24	-104,345.53
	P5000	Production line	B-000004	Sold	None		-969,404.84	-818,720.07
	P5000	Production	B-000001	None	Purchased		2,081,607.86	1,758,041.69
000004	P5000	Production	B-000002	None	Purchased		1,958,057.62	1,653,696.16
	P5000	Production line	B-000003	Sold	None		-1,958,057.62	-1,653,696.16
000005	P5006	Production	B-000003	None	Purchased		1,400.00	516,097.12
	P5006	Sales order	000332	Sold	None		-1,400.00	-516,097.12
000006	M5001	Purchase order	000001	None	Purchased		143,000.00	127,270.00

9. This view takes up one column for the batch, reducing the space for details. A better idea would be displaying the batch at the top. Also, the labels for the detail lines are missing. In the steps to follow, let us work this out.

10. Select the header for the `InventBatchId` column, right-click and choose **Delete Columns**. On the delete dialog, choose the option `Delete columns only`. This option will retain the grouping but delete only the fields.

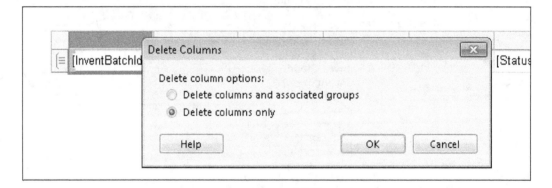

11. On the table row, select the row and right-click on it. Navigate to **Insert Row | Outside**. The group preceding this will add a new row. Add two rows; one will be for the labels and the other for the group header displaying the batch.

12. To create labels on the row immediately preceding the data fields, double-click on the cell, right-click and select **Create Placeholder**. A property window for the cell opens. Click on the ▣ icon next to the `value` field and enter the expression `Labels!@ sys13647`. Repeat this for each column header. (Identify the label ID from the label editor in the rich client before entering it.)

13. Of the two rows inserted, the one at the top will be used to display the group header. Select the first cell and enter the label for `InventBatchId` in the same manner as explained previously. On the topmost row, the first cell is used for the expression label for the batch. Select all the remaining cells and right-click and select **Merge Cells**. In the merged cell, click on the ▣ icon and select the field **Invent Batch**.

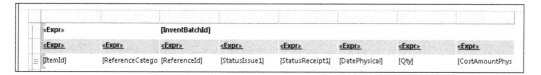

14. This will display a batch at the top, followed by the transaction with labels. You can collectively change the font, color, and size of each cell by selecting all of them. The sample discussed here uses Segoe UI font, 8pt for values and grey color background for the header cells. The precision design gives the comfort of setting up the properties collectively by multi-selection.

15. Set the property **Can Shrink** in the cells to `true`. This will allow automatic report sizing.

16. To add totals to each group on the **Grouping** node at the bottom, select **Group1** and click on the small arrow at the end. Navigate to **Add Totals | After**. This will insert a new row at the bottom and add the two sum fields for `Quantity` and `CostAmountPhysical`. Delete the `Quantity`, since we don't need it and instead, modify the expression to set the label as `Total`. This will print the label after each group.

17. To add the grand total, insert a row outside the group present at the bottom. Right-click on the cell beneath the group total and select **expression**. In the **expression** window, enter the expression Sum(Fields!CostAmountPhysical.Value) and similarly, set the label expression as Grand Total.

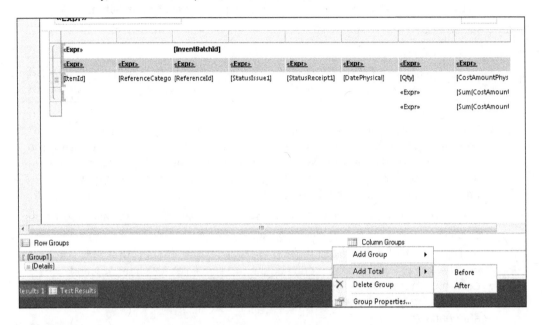

18. The following screenshot shows how the final report should appear:

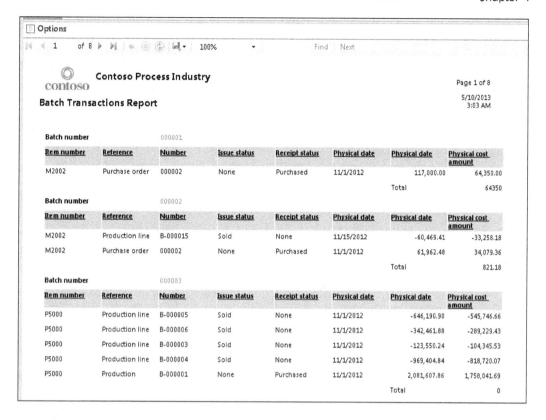

How it works...

Precision design allows the detailed modeling of the report, offering more flexibility and control. However, when the design is simple, prefer using Auto design. The company images on the header can only be added using precision design. So you may have to make this choice even for simple reports.

When using expressions in precision design, take special care to ensure that they are right, since the compiler doesn't indicate where these errors occur and might result in opening of every expression window. Though precision design might look exhaustive at the first look, it is more convenient and easier to control than Auto design.

Use the document outline view to see the controls in a precision design to identify the names of the controls in the design. The document outline view can be opened by _Ctrl+w, U_.

Adding headers and displaying company images

Images and headers help the report to get a professional appearance. This interesting recipe will guide you to build a report with company images and headers.

How to do it...

1. To insert the header right-click and navigate to **Insert | Header** and on the header, add the textbox each for the company name, page, date, and report name. On the expression fields of these controls, add the following code:

Company name	`=Microsoft.Dynamics.Framework.Reports.`
	`DataMethodUtility.GetFullCompanyNameForUser(`
	`Parameters!AX_CompanyName.Value,`
	`   Parameters!AX_UserContext.Value)`

Report name	`="Batch Transactions Report"`

Page	`=System.String.Format(Labels!@SYS182566, "" &`
	`   Globals!PageNumber & "", "" &`
	`   Globals!TotalPages & "")`

Date	`=Microsoft.Dynamics.Framework.Reports.DataMeth`
	`   dUtility.`
	`ConvertUtcToAxUserTimeZoneForUser(Parameters!A`
	`   _CompanyName.Value, Parameters!`
	`   AX_UserContext.Value, System.DateTime.UtcNow,`
	`   "d", Parameters!AX_RenderingCulture.Value) &`
	`   vbCrLf & Microsoft.Dynamics.Framework.`
	`   Reports.DataMethodUtility.`
	`ConvertUtcToAxUserTimeZoneForUser(Parameters!A`
	`   _CompanyName.Value, Parameters!`
	`   AX_UserContext.Value, System.DateTime.UtcNow,`
	`   "t", Parameters!AX_RenderingCulture.Value)`

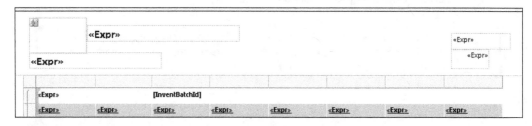

2. Adding the company image starts with defining a query. Create a query `PktComanyImage` and add the table `CompanyImage`. Come back to your Visual Studio report and add the query as `datasource`. Set the `Dynamic Filter` property to `false`. Save the report and open the designer.

3. In the designer, the new `datasource` will appear in the report data view. On the page header, create a new field of the type image. On the prompting window, select the imagesource as database and point the `value` field to the `image` field from the `companyImage` DataSource and set the MIME type, based on the image you have added. Resize the image and place it before the company name. Save and preview it to see the image.

4. Deploy the report and create a menu item to see the report working.

How it works...

The company image query that was created for this report can be reused for other reports that require a company image to be printed. If there are images that are specific to this report, then the field can be directly added to the temporary table field used by the RDP. You can also use embedded images in precision designs as seen in the *Chapter 2, Enhancing Your Report – Visualization and Interaction*.

Precision design allows copying of controls from one report/report design to another report/ report design. So copy the header fields if the same alignment is required in other reports.

Debugging RDP

The most preferable mode to debug an RDP report would be the test job discussed in the recipe *Testing the RDP*, However, if you prefer to debug it, on the `processReport` method of your RDP class, type the keyword breakpoint. Open the debugger even before opening or previewing the report by running the `axdebug.exe` file in the client installation. Once the execution reaches the debugging point, the debugger will be activated.

See Also

▸ The *Adding an image in auto design* recipe in *Chapter 2, Enhancing Your Report – Visualization and Interaction*.

Using an existing temp table in RDP

Temporary tables are used in AX in existing business logic and as a DataSource to forms. The reporting framework provides the ability for these temporary tables, filled outside in a form or business logic to be copied to the RDP without re-implementing the business logic. The reporting framework offers the ability to do this through a set of helper classes, SRSTmpTableMarshaller and SRSTmpTblMarshallercontract.

This recipe will simplify and make it easy to understand the temporary table pattern. This pattern helps in designing RDP reports faster when the temporary table and logic to fill it already exists.

How to do it...

1. To better understand the Marshaller and its usage, we will use the interest calculation example. In this example, the interest calculation is done in a form using a temporary table. The simulation in the form must be printed to a report. We will use the Marshaller to pass the prefilled table to the RDP.

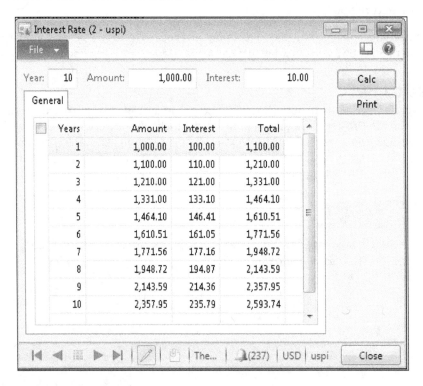

2. The user enters the values in the **Amount:**, **Interest:**, and **Years:** input boxes and clicks on **Calc**. The simulation is shown in the form. When the user clicks on the **Print** button, the temporary table must be passed to the RDP and rendered in the report.

3. The first step begins with creating a contract. Since the temporary table already exists, this step can be surpassed. There is no further input from the user to be received. So our contract class needs no parm methods except the one for holding `RecID` from DataSource. So the `SRSTmpTableMarshallerContract` contract can be directly used as the contract for RDP. (In situations where you have your own contract class, the `SRSTmpTableMarshallerContract` contract must be used as a nested data contract. See *Inventory Dimension in Reports* recipe in *Chapter 7, Upgrading and Analyzing Reports*.)

4. The RDP for a pre-populated temp table is much simpler. The only logic to be performed is to retrieve the data from the DataStore. The `processReport` method of the RDP appears as here:

```
[SysEntryPointAttribute]
public void processReport()
{
    SrsReportRunPermission   permission;

    SrsTmpTblMarshallerContract contract =
      this.parmDataContract() as SrsTmpTblMarshallerContract;
    breakpoint;

    tmpTableDataRecId    = contract.parmTmpTableDataRecId();
    permission           = new SrsReportRunPermission();
      permission.assert();

    //Temp Table Object that was returned from
      SRSTmpTblMarshaller
    tmpCalc =
      SRSTmpTblMarshaller::GetTmpTbl(tmpTableDataRecId);
    //drop the temp table from data store since it is copied
    //to the local buffer
    SRSTmpTblMarshaller::deleteTmpTblData(tmpTableDataRecId);
    CodeAccessPermission::revertAssert();
}
```

Bind the contract class `SRSTmpTableMarshallerContract` in the class declaration and create a data return method as in the previous RDP classes.

5. The controller class owns the responsibility of storing the temp table. Create a controller class and override the `prerunModifyContract` method with the following code:

```
public void preRunModifyContract()
{
    RecId recid;
    PktInterestCalcTmp tmp;

    SrsTmpTblMarshallerContract contract;

    new SRSReportRunPermission().assert();

    tmp.setTmpData(this.parmArgs().record());

    //store the data in data store and retrive the recid
    recid =
        SRSTmpTblMarshaller::sendTmpTblToDataProvider(tmp);
    CodeAccessPermission::revertAssert();

    //set the recid in contract to be used in RDP
    contract = this.parmReportContract().parmRdpContract() as
        SrsTmpTblMarshallerContract;
    contract.parmTmpTableDataRecId(recid);
}
```

6. In the main method, switch off the dialog since no user input is needed.

```
public static void main(Args args)
{
    PktMarshallCalcController control;


    control = new PktMarshallCalcController();
    control.parmArgs(args);
    control.parmReportName('PktMarshallCalc.InterestReport');
    control.parmShowDialog(false);
    control.startOperation();
}
```

7. All the code artifacts are ready. Design the report to look similar to the one in the first recipe of this chapter. The final part is to hook the controller to the `clicked` event in the button. Override the print button and call the controller.

```
void clicked()
{
   PktMarshallCalcController cont;
   Args args;
   super();

   args = new args();
   //pass the temptable buffer from the form
   //to the contract class
   args.record(PktInterestCalcTmp);
   PktMarshallCalcController::main(args);
}
```

8. Click on the **Run** button to run the report.

How it works...

The contents of the temporary table are transferred to the container and stored in a table in SQL called the DataStore. The data is identified by the `recid` of the record in the DataStore. This `recid` is stored in the contract and passed to the RDP. The RDP again retrieves the data from the DataStore by using the recid when required. Once data is retrieved, it must be explicitly deleted from the DataStore. The deletion is performed in the `processReport` method in the RDP class.

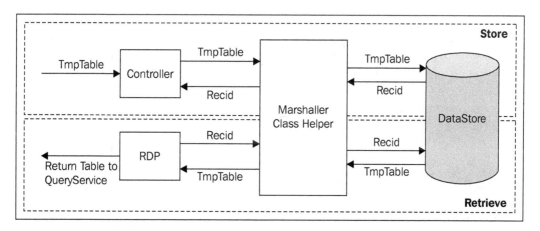

Preprocessing reports

SSRS uses the **WCF (Windows Communication Foundation)** to connect to the AOS for data access. This connection has a threshold limit and it might fail if a report takes a long time to execute. The report server execution waits for the RDP to process the data and return it. In the event where the RDP takes too long a time to execute the reporting, the service might fail. Preprocessing is a strategy to beat this issue. This recipe will help you understand how to enable preprocessing for any RDP report.

How to do it...

When a report processes a huge amount of data or is found to take considerable time during the execution, then you can decide to incorporate preprocessing. Follow these steps to enable preprocessing:

1. Extend the RDP class from the `SrsReportDataProviderPreProcess` class.

2. Set the following properties in the temp table used by the RDP:

Property	Value
Table Type	Regular
CreatedBy	Yes
CreatedTransactionId	Yes

3. The crucial portion of the RDP is inserting records in the table with the scope. In order for the tables to automatically generate `TransactionId` in the beginning of the process report, set the user connection as shown here. This sets a scope and generates `TransactionId`, which is valid only for that scope, for example `AgreementConfirmationDP`.

   ```
   Public void processReport()
   {
      InventBatchTransTmp.setConnection(this.parmUserConnectio
         n());
   }
   ```

4. Open the report in Visual Studio and refresh the DataSource to include the new `CreatedTransactionId` field. To do this, in Model Editor, right-click on the dataset and then click on **Refresh**.

5. In Solution Explorer, right-click on the **Solution** and click on **Deploy Solution** to deploy the new report.

How it works...

The AX reporting framework delays the invocation of the reporting framework until the data is processed. After the data is processed and inserted, the reporting framework is invoked, preventing the time-outs. The hindrance here is that the RDP uses a temporary table. Converting this to persistent introduces a different sort of problem with two different instances of the report potentially inserting conflicting of data.

AX reporting framework solves this problem by making the table persistent and introducing a scope field called `TransactionId`. The `TransactionId` field allows the reporting framework to identify the records created for the session. In the case of preprocessed reports, the data is inserted in the table and the details of the preprocessing are stored in the table `SRSReportPreProcessDetail`. The `recid` of the record is passed as `preprocessid` to the report framework and the data is fetched using this scope from the table.

Clean up

The data in these tables are cleaned up after the report runs automatically.

See also

▶   The *Handling long running reports in AX* recipe in *Chapter 8, Troubleshooting and Other Advanced Recipes*.

5
Integrating External Datasources

This chapter will cover the following recipes:

- ► Adding a datasource through business logic
- ► Using an XML feed as a datasource
- ► Building a parameter lookup using business logic
- ► Building a report through an external datasource
- ► Adding a parameter for an external datasource query
- ► Creating a customer summary OLAP report
- ► Adding a parameter lookup for OLAP
- ► Designing an OLAP table report with SQL Report Builder
- ► Designing a map subreport with SQL Report Builder
- ► Creating a subreport in auto design
- ► Creating a subreport in precision design

Introduction

One among the main lookout features from the transformation to SSRS reports is their ability to support multiple sources for rendering data. ERP is not a single corporate system but is one among many. With the data involved in making decisions spread across several multiple systems, it is important that the reports are able to pull data from different sources; for example, when a company switches to a new ERP system, the legacy system is still kept alive for transactional data references. This chapter will focus on offering recipes that involve different sources of data, such as XML feeds, SQL databases, and OLAP that can be used as a datasource for the report.

Adding a datasource through business logic

This recipe will show how a simple datasource can be created and used as a source of data through the business logic option in the reports.

Getting ready

This recipe requires that you have access to Visual Studio with the Dynamics AX reporting extension.

How to do it...

1. Create a new reporting project `PktExchRateReports` in Visual Studio.

2. Add a report `PKTExchRateDataTable`.

3. Right-click on the **Data Methods** node and create a new method:

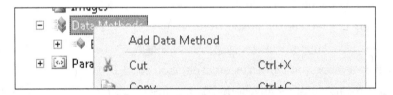

4. Double-click the node; this adds a new C# project to the solution and a C# class with the classname same as the report name.

5. Replace the empty data method with business logic as shown here:

```
[DataMethod(), PermissionSet(SecurityAction.Assert, Name =
"FullTrust")]
    public static DataTable ExchangeRateDataset(string _stest)
    {
        DataTable dt;

        dt = new DataTable();
        dt.Columns.Add("Category", typeof(string));
        dt.Columns.Add("Base Currency", typeof(string));
        dt.Columns.Add("Currency", typeof(string));
        dt.Columns.Add("Base Rate", typeof(double));
        dt.Columns.Add("Rate", typeof(double));
```

```
dt.Rows.Add("Australia", "USD", "AUD", 1, 1.03);
dt.Rows.Add("Asia", "USD", "SGD", 1, 1.26);
dt.Rows.Add("Europe", "USD", "EUR", 1,0.77);
dt.Rows.Add("Middle East", "USD", "AED", 1, 3.67);

return dt;
}
```

6. Save and build the solution. This will refresh the data method in the report model.

7. Open the report model, select the **Datasets** node and create a new dataset. On the new dataset property set the **Data Source Type** to Business logic:

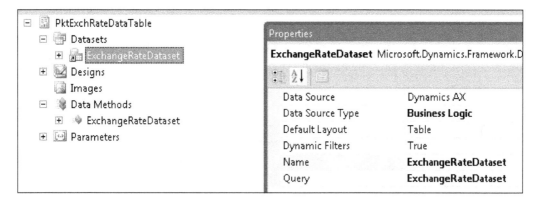

8. Now click the ellipsis (**...**) button on the **Query** property and select the business logic that was just created. Click on the exclamation mark on the left corner to validate data retrieval. This action will add the fields from the data table and the parameters of the method (if any will be added as parameters):

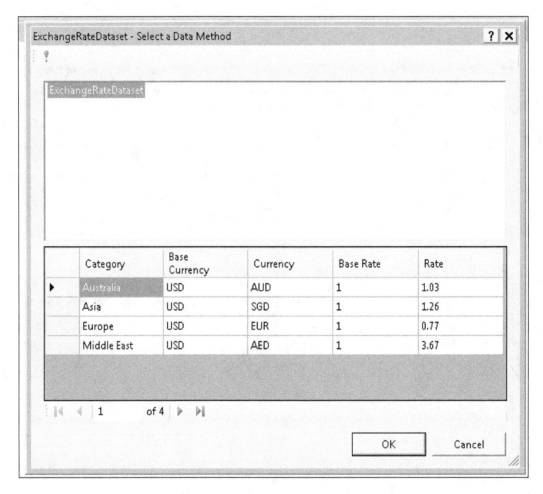

9. Drag the dataset to the report design. Apply templates, align the controls, and specify labels for rendering.

10. Save and preview the report:

Exchange Rates Local

Contoso Process Industry

ExchangeRateDataset

Base Currency

USD

Category	Currency	Base_Rate	Rate
Australia	AUD	1.00	1.03
Asia	SGD	1.00	1.26
Europe	EUR	1.00	0.77
Middle East	AED	1.00	3.67

11. The report can now be deployed and put to use.

How it works...

Any data method that returns a datatype of `System.data` can be added as a dataset to the report. The data table filled in the data method is used by SSRS to identify fields of the table. If there are parameters for the data method, then they are added as parameters for the dataset. The program logic creates a data table instance and adds columns with the datatype followed by inserting rows in the table. The row details are hardcoded in the table in this recipe.

See also

▶ The *Expressions in layouts* recipe in *Chapter 2, Enhancing Your Report – Visualization and Interaction*

▶ The *Adding data methods in business logic* recipe in *Chapter 3, A Report Programming Model*

Using an XML feed as a datasource

In the previous recipe the entire data for the report was hardcoded, while in this recipe we will continue to use the data table as a datasource but the data for this report will come through an XML feed. XML is retrieved at runtime, parsed and filled in a data table that is then rendered in the report.

Getting ready

This recipe requires the machine, in which you practice, to be connected to the Internet. The XML feed (`http://themoneyconverter.com/rss-feed/USD/rss.xml`) used in this report is downloaded at runtime.

How to do it...

1. On the existing project `PKTExchRateReports` add a new report `PKTExchRateFromWeb`.

2. Add a new data method and double-click on it to create the business logic.

3. Replace the empty method with the logic given here:

```
[DataMethod(), PermissionSet(SecurityAction.Assert, Name =
"FullTrust")]
    public static DataTable ExchangeRateData()
    {
        DataTable dt;

        dt = new DataTable();
        dt.Columns.Add("Category", typeof(string));
        dt.Columns.Add("Base Currency", typeof(string));
        dt.Columns.Add("Currency", typeof(string));
        dt.Columns.Add("Base Rate", typeof(string));

        XDocument xdoc = XDocument.Load("http://themoneyconverter.
com/rss-feed/USD/rss.xml");

        var q = from c in xdoc.Descendants("item")

        select new {
            title    = c.Element("title").Value,
            pubDate  = c.Element("pubDate").Value,
            desc     = c.Element("description").Value,
            cat      = c.Element("category").Value
        };
```

```
foreach (var obj in q){

    dt.Rows.Add(obj.cat,
                obj.title.Substring(0, 2),
                obj.title.Substring(4, 3),
                obj.desc);
    }

    return dt;

}
```

4. Before adding this as a datasource, it is important to ensure that this method works well, since any runtime issues might prevent it from using this data method as a datasource.

5. Create a unit test method (see the *Unit testing business logic* recipe in *Chapter 3, A Report Programming Model*) and run the test to ensure execution at runtime.

6. Add the data method as a datasource followed by adding it to the report design;

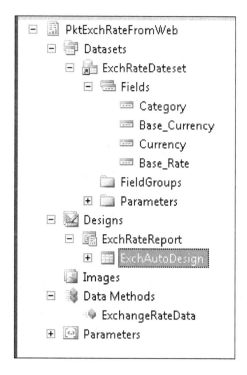

7. Remember to set the templates, and adjust fonts and labels before you run the report. The report preview will be as seen here:

Exchange Rates from Xml Feed
Contoso Process Industry

Category	Currency	Rate
Africa	EG	1 United States Dollar = 6.98753 Egyptian Pound
Africa	GH	1 United States Dollar = 1.99331 Ghana Cedi
Africa	GM	1 United States Dollar = 35.98998 Gambian Dalasi
Africa	KE	1 United States Dollar = 85.16999 Kenyan Shilling
Africa	MA	1 United States Dollar = 8.51679 Moroccan Dirham
Africa	MG	1 United States Dollar = 2,189.87071 Malagasy Ariary
Africa	MU	1 United States Dollar = 31.22997 Mauritian Rupee
Africa	NA	1 United States Dollar = 9.90858 Namibian Dollar
Africa	NG	1 United States Dollar = 158.64999 Nigerian Naira
Africa	SC	1 United States Dollar = 11.80002 Seychellois Rupee
Africa	TN	1 United States Dollar = 1.63346 Tunisian Dinar
Africa	UG	1 United States Dollar = 2,581.79994 Ugandan Shilling
Africa	XA	1 United States Dollar = 501.84148 Central African Franc

How it works...

The data table is initialized with columns followed by the logic to access the XML feed. The XML feed is downloaded at runtime and parsed. Parsing is done using **Language Integrated Natural Query** (**LINQ**) to XML in C# (LINQ offers a robust retrieval mechanism by abstracting the source of data) and is inserted into the data table.

It is good to keep in mind that the method must return a type of `System.table`; otherwise, it will fail to show up as a datasource. The unit test can be used to debug the logic at design time without much hooking involved to services such as reporting service for debugging.

The spin-off recipes

This business logic idea can be further extended to create and insert data in tables at runtime using other sources such as web services, JSON API, and even AX queries.

 Do not modify the design in a report model when the precision design editor is open. Close the precision design editor before modifying the report model; otherwise the changes are not stored.

Building a parameter lookup using business logic

In the last two recipes there was no user interaction, but real-time scenarios will demand that user input should be taken. Adding a parameter doesn't make it usable as the user might be left clueless as to what are the possible values as no lookup is available for the external data. This recipe will show how a dataset can be used just for the purpose of creating parameter lookups. The parameter here will be the **category** field that indicates the geographical location of the country. Apart from adding a parameter, this recipe will also discuss how to show the report parameter lookup from the business logic. The report built through this recipe will provide a parameter **category** and the lookup for the parameter through which the user can view the exchange rate data only for the selected category.

Getting ready

This recipe requires the machine, in which you practice, to be connected to the Internet. The XML feed (`http://themoneyconverter.com/rss-feed/USD/rss.xml`) used in this report is downloaded at runtime.

How to do it...

1. Create a report `PKTExchRateDataLookup` in the project `PktExchRateReports`.

2. Create a data method using the code here; this data method receives a `string` parameter **category**, and then applies it to the **category** field in XML:

```
[DataMethod(), PermissionSet(SecurityAction.Assert, Name =
"FullTrust")]
    public static DataTable ExchangeRateDataFilter(string
category)
    {
        DataTable dt;

        dt = new DataTable();
        dt.Columns.Add("Category", typeof(string));
        dt.Columns.Add("Base Currency", typeof(string));
        dt.Columns.Add("Currency", typeof(string));
        dt.Columns.Add("Base Rate", typeof(string));

        XDocument xdoc = XDocument.Load("http://themoneyconverter.
com/rss-feed/USD/rss.xml");
```

```
            var q = from c in xdoc.Descendants("item")
                    where (c.Element("category").Value == category ||
                          string.IsNullOrEmpty(category))

                    select new
                    {
                        title = c.Element("title").Value,
                        pubDate = c.Element("pubDate").Value,
                        desc = c.Element("description").Value,
                        cat = c.Element("category").Value
                    };

            foreach (var obj in q)
            {

                dt.Rows.Add(obj.cat,
                            obj.title.Substring(0, 2),
                            obj.title.Substring(4, 3),
                            obj.desc);

            }

            return dt;

        }
```

3. Rebuild the solution.

4. The next step is to build a lookup for this parameter. Create a new data method and place the business logic as shown here:

```
public static DataTable CategoryData()
    {
        DataTable dt;

        dt = new DataTable();
        dt.Columns.Add("Category", typeof(string));

        XDocument xdoc = XDocument.Load("http://themoneyconverter.
com/rss-feed/USD/rss.xml");
        XNamespace space = xdoc.Root.GetDefaultNamespace();

        IEnumerable<string> q = xdoc.Descendants("item").
Descendants("category").Select(pn => pn.Value).Distinct().
ToList();
```

```
        foreach (string category in q)
        {
            dt.Rows.Add(category);
        }

        return dt;
    }
```

5. Rebuild the solution. Add both the business logic as datasets. The parameter that was added in the data method **ExchangeRateDataFilter** should now be seen in the parameter node of the dataset and the report parameter:

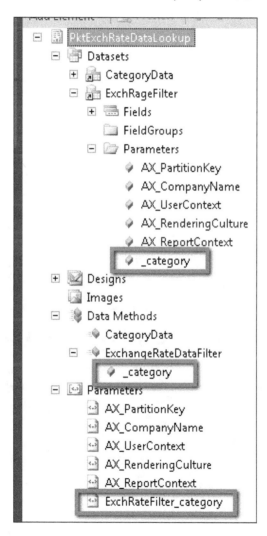

6. On the report parameter node **Parameters**, select the parameter **ExchRateFilter_ Category** and on the property **Values**, click on the button. A dialog box opens up. Fill the dialog box with the values shown here. This hooks up the **category** dataset to the lookup:

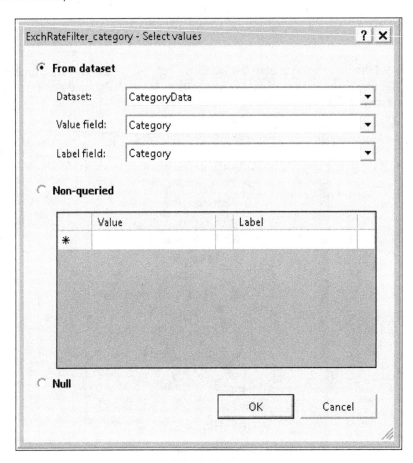

7. Preview the report after setting the templates, fonts, labels, and alignments. On the preview pane you should notice that the category shows the geographical classification:

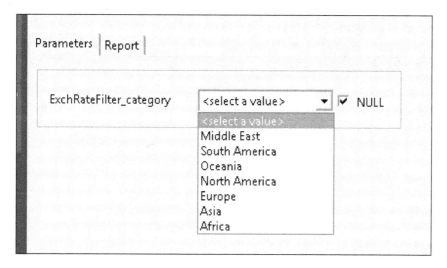

How it works...

When the report is executed the values for the lookup appear through the dataset **category** and once the user selects a value this is passed as a parameter to the business logic that returns the data for the report.

Business logic

The business logic for an exchange rate filter uses LINQ to read data. The difference here from the business logic used in the previous recipe is the additional `where` condition that determines if the node has a category that is equal to the parameter received. The OR condition in the logic is to deactivate this conditional check when the parameter is `null` so that it will retrieve all the data from XML.Lookup.

The business logic for **category** lookup uses LINQ to identify all the distinct values from the XML. Since there can be more than one node in the XML with the same category. The **category** dataset that is created using the business logic is used as a lookup source. This should give you an idea of how a lookup can be built using business logic.

Building a report through an external datasource

In this recipe we will create a report that connects to an OLTP datasource and retrieves data through an SQL query. We will learn how to add a generic report datasource that can be used across all reports. The report here will retrieve the employee information from the `AdventureWorks` sample database.

Getting ready

In order to do this you will need the `AdventureWorks` database installed in the SQL server. This is available for free download from Microsoft available at `http://technet.microsoft.com/en-us/library/ee873271.aspx`.

How to do it...

1. Open Visual Studio and create a project `AdventureWorkDatasoure`. This project is created to hold the new report datasource in AX.

2. In the project add a new element of type **Report datasource**:

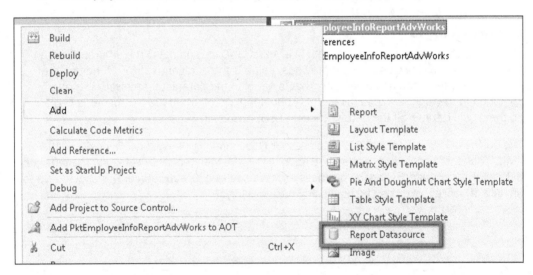

3. Open the **Report Datasource** and set the following properties:

Property	Value
Name	AdventureWorks
Connection String*	Server=AX2012R2A;Database=AdventureWorks2008R2; Integrated Security=SSPI
Provider	SQL

 '*****' – The database name and server name must be modified according to your setup.

4. Save this project.

   The reason to add it as a separate project is that you can later easily identify the project that holds the report datasource to change its properties; for example, connection string. This report datasource is now ready to be used across all reporting projects.

5. Create a new project `PktEmployeeInfoReportAdvWorks`.

6. Add a new dataset and on the property **Data Source**, the new datasource that was added must be visible along with other datasources:

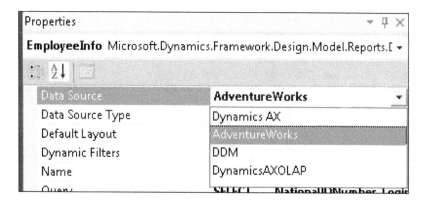

7. Select this as a datasource and click on the ellipsis (**...**) button in property **Query**. This opens a new editor window.

8. Key in the following `select` statement. Prefer to design your query in the SQL Server Management Studio before you apply it here:

```
SELECT        NationalIDNumber, LoginID, JobTitle, BirthDate,
MaritalStatus, Gender, HireDate, VacationHours, SickLeaveHours
FROM HumanResources.Employee
```

9. Click on the exclamation button ! to validate the query:

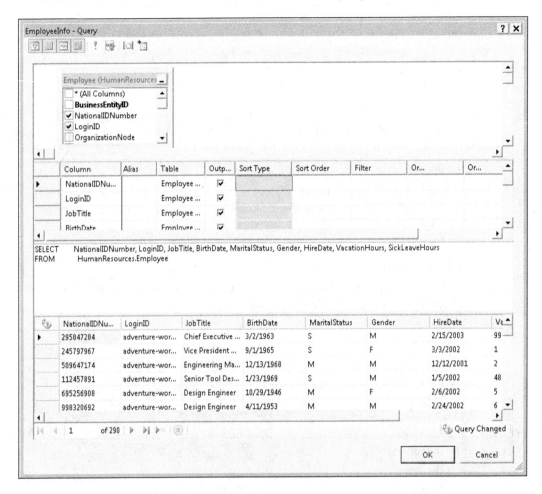

10. Click on **OK** to see the fields added to the new dataset.

11. Now drag it onto the auto design node. Set the template and appropriate labels to present the report.

12. Run the report preview:

EmployeeInfo

Contoso Process Industry

EmployeeInfo

Page 1 of 6
6/5/2013
6:14 AM

National ID Number	LoginID	Job Title	Birth Date	MaritalStatus	Gender	HireDate
10708100	adventure-works\frank1	Production Technician - WC50	8/24/1965 12:00:00 AM	S	M	3/27/2003 12:00:00 AM
109272464	adventure-works\bonnie0	Production Technician - WC10	10/11/1980 12:00:00 AM	M	F	2/2/2004 12:00:00 AM
112432117	adventure-works\brian3	Vice President of Sales	7/8/1971 12:00:00 AM	S	M	3/18/2005 12:00:00 AM
112457891	adventure-works\rob0	Senior Tool Designer	1/23/1969 12:00:00 AM	S	M	1/5/2002 12:00:00 AM
113393530	adventure-works\hung-fu0	Production Technician - WC20	11/23/1965 12:00:00 AM	S	M	2/7/2004 12:00:00 AM
113695504	adventure-works\alice0	Production Technician - WC50	2/27/1972 12:00:00 AM	M	F	1/8/2003 12:00:00 AM
121491555	adventure-works\wendy0	Finance Manager	11/12/1978 12:00:00 AM	S	F	1/26/2003 12:00:00 AM
1300049	adventure-works\nicole0	Production Technician - WC40	5/10/1980 12:00:00 AM	M	F	3/26/2003 12:00:00 AM
131471224	adventure-works\andreas0	Quality Assurance Technician	4/29/1983 12:00:00 AM	M	M	3/6/2003 12:00:00 AM
132674823	adventure-works\jeffrey0	Production Technician - WC10	8/12/1950 12:00:00 AM	S	M	3/23/2002 12:00:00 AM
134219713	adventure-works\ranjit0	Sales Representative	10/31/1969 12:00:00 AM	S	M	7/1/2006 12:00:00 AM
134969118	adventure-works\dylan0	Research and Development Manager	3/27/1981 12:00:00 AM	M	M	3/12/2003 12:00:00 AM
138280935	adventure-works\carole0	Production Technician - WC30	11/19/1977 12:00:00 AM	M	F	1/20/2003 12:00:00 AM
139397894	adventure-works\shu0	Sales Representative	4/10/1962 12:00:00 AM	M	M	7/1/2005 12:00:00 AM
141165819	adventure-works\gary1	Facilities Manager	3/21/1965 12:00:00 AM	M	M	1/3/2004 12:00:00 AM
14417807	adventure-works\guy1	Production Technician - WC60	5/15/1976 12:00:00 AM	M	M	7/31/2000 12:00:00 AM
152085091	adventure-works\sameer0	Production Technician - WC50	7/27/1972 12:00:00 AM	M	M	3/15/2003 12:00:00 AM
153288994	adventure-works\houman0	Production Technician - WC50	9/30/1965 12:00:00 AM	M	M	2/26/2003 12:00:00 AM
153479919	adventure-works\io1	Janitor	5/25/1948 12:00:00 AM	M	F	4/7/2004 12:00:00 AM

How it works...

The report uses the `Reportdatasource` connection string to establish connection with the report datasource. Ensure the necessary permission for the database is set up and is accessible. The query that is specified in the editor is an SQL query and not from AX. It is a good practice to design the query in the management studio and verify it before specifying it here. The editor in the database can be used to select fields, join tables, specify conditions, and validate them.

Global values, such as company name and report name can be used only in headers and footers in a precision design.

Adding a parameter for an external datasource query

This recipe will extend the previous recipe to add a parameter that will influence the data retrieved through the SQL query.

Getting ready

This recipe requires that you have the AdventureWorks database installed and you have read access to the SQL server. This is a continuation of the report developed in the recipe *Building a report through an external datasource* in this chapter.

How to do it...

1. Open the project and the report associated with the project.

2. Select the dataset and open the query editor window to modify the query as follows:

   ```
   SELECT          NationalIDNumber, LoginID, JobTitle, BirthDate,
   MaritalStatus, Gender, HireDate, VacationHours, SickLeaveHours
   FROM            HumanResources.Employee
   WHERE           (NationalIDNumber LIKE @Id)
   ```

3. Click on **OK** to see the parameter reflected in the **Parameters** node in the dataset and report parameters in the report model. A new pop-up will show up asking for the parameter; you can key in a valid ID or **%.**

4. Optionally, you can attach a lookup to the parameter by creating an additional dataset that filters the NationalIdNumber from the table as was done in the recipe *Building a parameter lookup using business logic*.

5. Save and preview the report.

How it works...

An SQL statement uses a like condition to make it work more like a search rather than trying to look for a match. The parameter to retrieve all the employees is not * as in AX, and should be %.

Creating a customer summary OLAP report

OLAP helps create interesting data mash-ups that can show trends, distributions, and various other dimensions summarized for the top-level management. Dynamics AX offers many different ways to represent OLAP reports, such as SQL Report Builder, Power View, and Excel but when it comes to exposing the reports over the web or deploying them to a role center, SSRS reports are an ideal choice. In this recipe we will get into the details of creating a simple OLAP report that will summarize the total transaction values across a customer group quarterly in a year.

Getting ready

To be able to implement this recipe you need the OLAP configured for Dynamics AX. You must have a basic understanding of OLAP and an ability to write MDX queries.

How to do it...

The goal of this recipe is to display the total value of transactions for a customer group represented quarterly in the year 2012.

1. The first step is to create an MDX query and the best place to do this is in the management studio. Open the Analysis service MDX query editor.

2. On the Microsoft Dynamics AX query editor run the following query and ensure that it works fine:

    ```
    SELECT {[Measures].[Accounts receivable amount - transaction
    currency]} on columns,
    nonempty(
    [Transaction date].[Quarter].[Quarter].Members*
    [Customer].[Customer group].[Customer group].Members*
    [Customer].[Customer group name].[Customer group name].Members,
    {([Measures].[Accounts receivable amount - transaction
    currency])})
    on rows
    FROM [Accounts Receivable Cube]
    WHERE( [Transaction date - fiscal calendar].
    [Year].&[USPI]&[2012],[Company].[Company].&[USPI])
    ```

3. The query editor lists all the available cubes and their dimensions and measures. As you execute the query, the results can be viewed at the bottom:

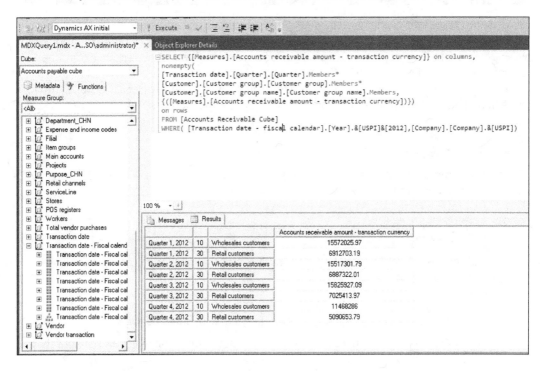

4. Create a new reporting project in Visual Studio and add a report `PKTCustgroupSalesSummary`.

5. Add a dataset and set the property **Data Source Type** as `DynamicsAxOLAP`.

6. Now copy the MDXquery from the management studio and paste it in the report query editor that is opened by clicking the ellipsis (**...**) button in the **Query** property:

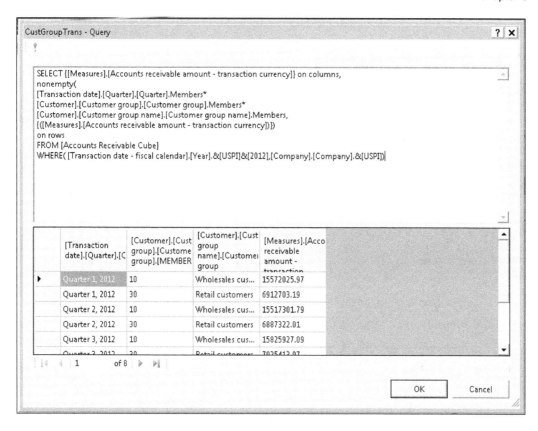

7. Click on the exclamation button to validate the query. This should display the data in the data editor window at the bottom. Click on **OK** to add the dataset:

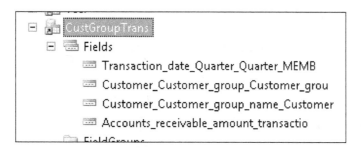

8. Add a precision design node **CustGroupSummary** and double-click to open the designer.

9. Insert a new design and add the following fields:

Customer Group	Name	Amount
[Customer_Customer_grc	[Customer_Customer_group_n;	[Accounts_receivable_amount_transacti

10. Add a **Parent Group** field on **Row Groups**:

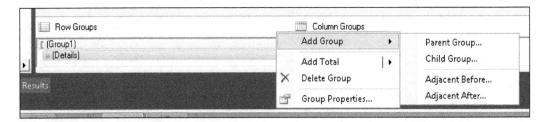

11. Select **Transaction_date_Quarter_Quarter_MEMB** in the **group by** option dialog.

12. Preview the report after adding labels and setting the fonts:

Customer Group Sales Per Quarter
Contoso Process Industry

Page 1 of 1
6/5/2013
1:44 PM

Quarter	Quarter 1, 2012	
Customer Group	**Name**	**Amount**
10	Wholesales customers	15572025.97
30	Retail customers	6912703.19

Quarter	Quarter 2, 2012	
Customer Group	**Name**	**Amount**
10	Wholesales customers	15517301.79
30	Retail customers	6887322.01

How it works...

The MDX query used in this report uses the account receivable cube that comes along with a standard AX. It tries to represent the total amount in transaction currency for each quarter against each customer. The `nonempty` function ensures that the query doesn't return any blank values.

See also

▶ The *Creating a group view report* recipe in *Chapter 4, Report Programming Model – RDP*

[Do you know you can copy and paste controls from a precision design in one report to another precision design?]

Adding a parameter lookup for OLAP

The previous recipe was a simple implementation of a static MDX query; this recipe will further extend it to influence it through parameters. We will parameterize both transaction year and company under the `where` condition. Users will be able to do a lookup for these parameters that are again attached to MDX queries.

Getting ready

To be able to implement this recipe you need the OLAP configured for Dynamics AX. You must have a basic understanding of OLAP and the ability to write MDX queries. This recipe extends the report build through the recipe *Creating a customer summary OLAP report* in this chapter.

How to do it...

1. The MDX query used in the existing report has two conditions hardcoded; one for the company and the other for the year. Modify the query as shown here to parameterize the hardcoded values:

```
SELECT {[Measures].[Accounts receivable amount - transaction
currency]} on columns,
nonempty(
[Transaction date].[Quarter].[Quarter].Members*
[Customer].[Customer group].[Customer group].Members*
[Customer].[Customer group name].[Customer group name].Members,
```

```
{([Measures].[Accounts receivable amount - transaction
currency])})
on rows
FROM [Accounts Receivable Cube]
WHERE( STRTOMEMBER(@EndDate), strtomember("[Company].[Company].&["
+ @Company + "]"))
```

2. Clicking on **OK** in the query editor will prompt for the values. Fill in a valid value to proceed; for example, `[Transaction date - fiscal calendar].[Year].&[USPI]&[2012]` , USPI:

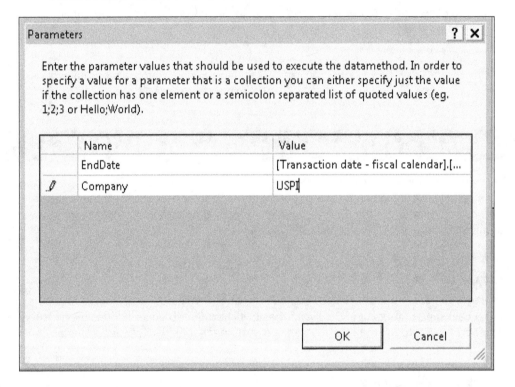

3. This adds the parameter to the dataset and report. Any error in the MDX query will fail to add it as a datasource, so double-check it with the MDX query editor and make sure the right parameter values are entered. Entering wrong parameter values also stops adding the query to the dataset.

4. The two parameters `@EndDate` and `@Company` are now added to the **parameters** node:

5. The next step involves creating the lookup for these parameters. Use the following MDX queries to create a report dataset to look up the company:

```
WITH

MEMBER [Measures].[ParameterCaption] AS '[Company].[Company].
CURRENTMEMBER.MEMBER_CAPTION'

MEMBER [Measures].[ParameterValue] AS '[Company].[Company].
CURRENTMEMBER.UNIQUENAME'

MEMBER [Measures].[ParameterLevel] AS '[Company].[Company].
CURRENTMEMBER.LEVEL.ORDINAL'

MEMBER [Measures].[Key] AS '[Company].[Company].CURRENTMEMBER.
PROPERTIES("Key")'

SELECT { [Measures].[ParameterCaption], [Measures].
[ParameterValue], [Measures].[ParameterLevel],[Measures].[Key]}
```

```
ON COLUMNS ,
Except( [Company].[Company].ALLMEMBERS,{[Company].[Company].
[Unknown],[Company].[Company].[All]})
ON ROWS
FROM  [Accounts Receivable Cube]
```

6. On the **report parameters** node for the parameter **CustGroupTrans_Company**, set the following values for the parameter dialog box that opens by clicking on the **values** property button. This links the dataset Company to this parameter for lookup purposes:

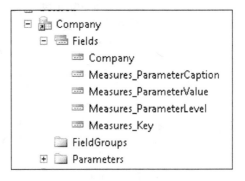

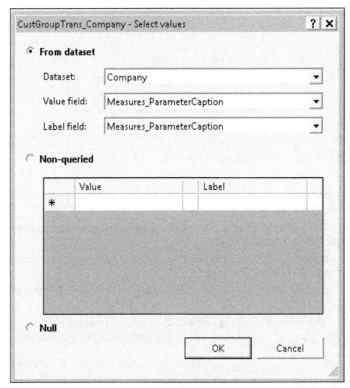

7. To set a default value for the company parameter modify the property **Default value** to the expression `=Parameters!AX_CompanyName.Value`.

8. For the parameter **EndDate**, create a dataset by using the following query:

```
WITH
MEMBER [Measures].[ParameterCaption] AS '[Transaction date -
fiscal calendar].[Year].CURRENTMEMBER.MEMBER_CAPTION'
MEMBER [Measures].[ParameterValue] AS '[Transaction date - fiscal
calendar].[Year].CURRENTMEMBER.UNIQUENAME'
MEMBER [Measures].[ParameterLevel] AS '[Transaction date - fiscal
calendar].[Year].CURRENTMEMBER.LEVEL.ORDINAL'
MEMBER [Measures].[Key] AS   '[Company].[Company].CURRENTMEMBER.
Properties("Key")'
SELECT
{
    [Measures].[ParameterCaption], [Measures].[ParameterValue],
[Measures].[ParameterLevel]
}
ON COLUMNS,
{
    [Transaction date - fiscal calendar].[Year].[All],
    FILTER
    (
        [Transaction date - fiscal calendar].[Year].MEMBERS,
        INSTR( [Transaction date - fiscal calendar].[Year].
CURRENTMEMBER.UNIQUENAME,"&[" + [Measures].[Key] + "]"  ) > 0
        AND
        INSTR( [Transaction date - fiscal calendar].[Year].
CURRENTMEMBER.UNIQUENAME,"&[1900]") = 0
    )
} ON ROWS
FROM [Accounts receivable cube]
WHERE STRTOMEMBER("[Company].[Company].&[" + @Company + "]")
```

9. This dataset used to look up the year for the parameter **EndDate** has another parameter **company** as seen in the MDX query. On the dataset for this MDX query expand the **Parameters** node, select the **company** parameter, and then set the property **Report parameter** to `CustGroupTrans_Company parameter`. This way the **company** parameter is attached to the value set for the **company** parameter in **CustGroupTrans** resulting in showing the years applicable for the selected company.

10. Bind the dataset to the parameter **EndDate** by modifying the **values** property as shown here to show up as lookup:

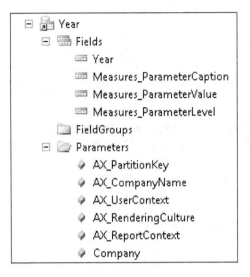

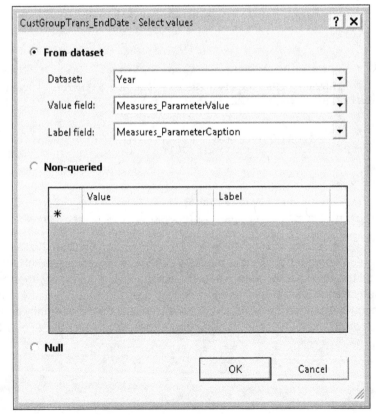

11. Preview the report and verify that the lookups show properly. Notice that the **Year** value changes based on the company selected. This is because of the binding created between the parameters in **CustGroupTrans** and **Year** datasets:

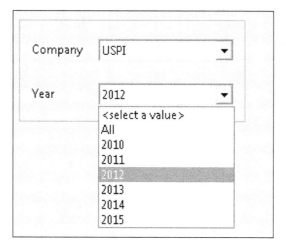

How it works...

▸ **The Company parameter**: The parameter **company** uses the default value that comes from the system parameter AX_company. The user can alternatively choose the value from the lookup that comes from the company dataset.

▸ **The EndDate parameter**: The lookup dataset uses a query that also has a parameter **company**. This is because the lookup should only show values that are applicable for a company selected by the user. So a binding is created between this parameter and the **company** parameter. This dependency causes the **EndDate** parameter to be activated only after the company parameter value is set.

▸ **The main query**: The main query has two conditions, the company and EndDate (actually holds a year value and not a date). Both have different formats; this has mainly to do with how they are represented in the cube. Each dimension in cubes has different attributes such as Member_Name, UniqueName, and Ordinal. To construct the **company** parameter, the Member_Name attribute is sufficient so the parameter lookup values for the **Value** field and the **Label** field are both set to Measures_Parameter Caption. For **EndDate**, the complete value must be constructed so the parameter lookup value for the **Value** field is set to Measures_ParamterValue and the **Label** field is set to Measures_parameterCaption.

Designing an OLAP table report with SQL Report Builder

The reports that we have designed so far use the Visual Studio based report development tools. This section will show how the SQL Report Builder can be used to build ad-hoc reports to be viewed and published back to the reporting services. The SQL Report Builder is not an AX-based solution but it is a generic reporting tool that can be used for generating reports. Designing reports using Report Builder is so convenient and user friendly that sometimes the end users themselves can design the reports. In the coming recipes we will see how with no coding or model changes the reports are developed with the help of built-in wizards.

This recipe will specifically show how the **Customer** group cube report that was made using SSRS in the *Creating a customer summary OLAP report* recipe could be designed and published using the SQL Report Builder.

Getting ready

This recipe requires that you have installed and have access to the reporting services manager and the Report Builder.

How to do it...

1. Open the reporting services on the browser and click on the **Report Builder** icon at the top:

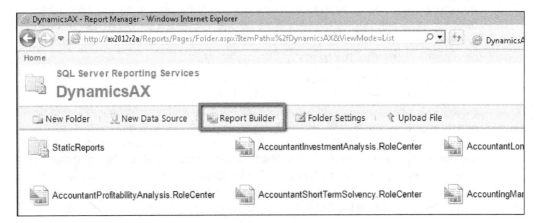

2. This opens up the Report Builder editor. In the wizard that shows up, select **Table or Matrix Wizard** and click on **Next**:

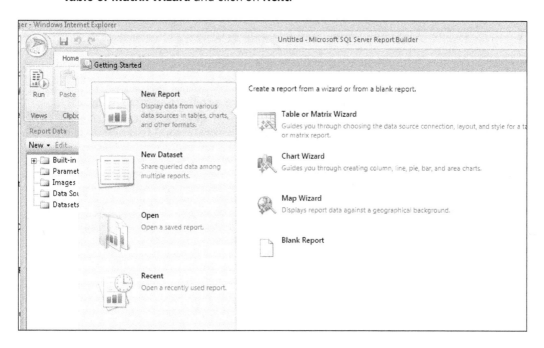

3. The next tab is where the dataset must be defined. Select **Create a dataset** and click on **Next**. The following tab is to choose the source of the report data. Click on **New**:

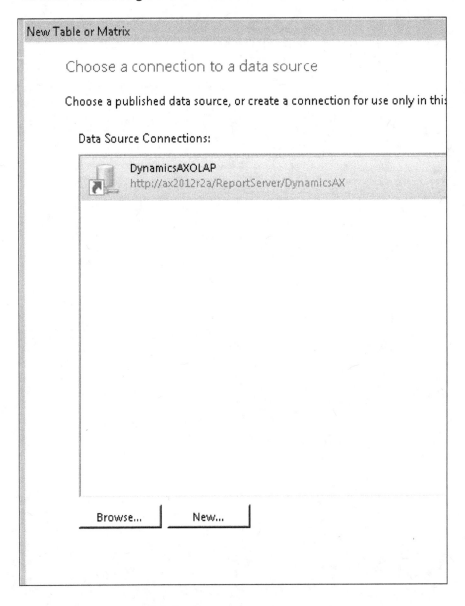

4. In the next screen for the **Data Source** property give a name such as AxOLAP and set **Select connection type** to Microsoft SQL Server Analysis Service and click on **Build**:

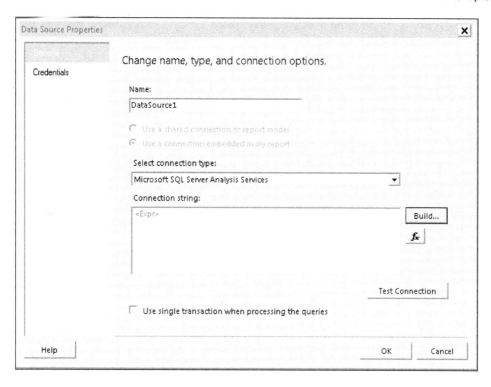

5. On **Connection Properties** type the name of the server and choose the database. Click on **OK** to return back and press the **Next** button in the wizard:

6. The wizard displays the query designer. Since we will use the **Account receivable cube**, use the datasource selector to select the cube:

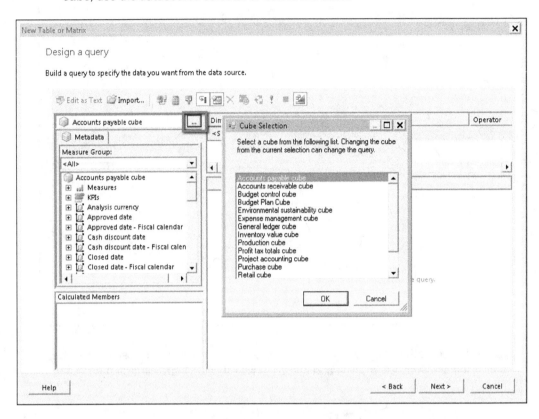

7. On the top dimensions row set the values as seen in the following screenshot by using the lookups in the columns:

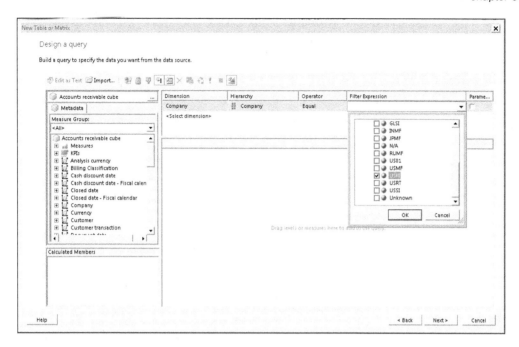

8. After completing this, on the empty space drag **Customer group name**, **Customer name**, and **State** from **Customer Dimension** from the left pane. Similarly, traverse to the **Dimension Transaction Date** node and drag the **Transaction date.Year-Quarter-Month-Date** to the empty space:

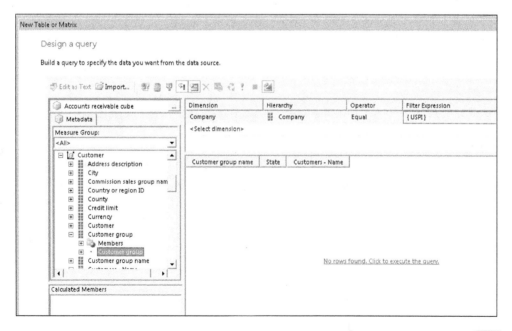

9. The next step is to go to **Measures** at the top in the left pane, expand **Customer transactions** and drag **Accounts receivable amount currency** to the columns. The query automatically executes and shows the data returned in the screen:

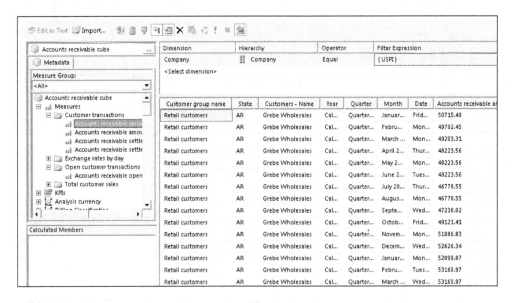

10. Click on **Next** and from the available fields' drag-and-drop the fields as shown here:

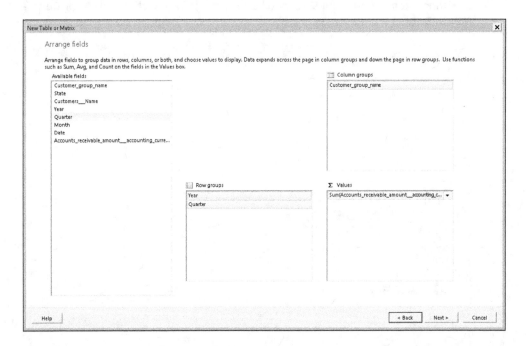

11. Click on **Next**; the layout designer provides options to select **Total** and **Subtotal**:

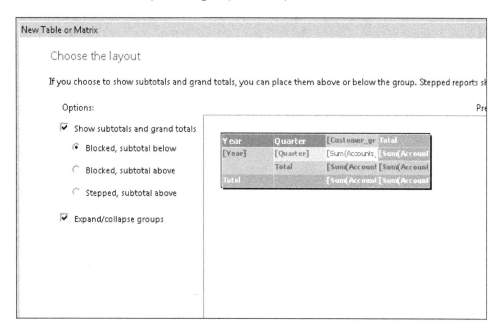

12. In the subsequent screen select the theme and click on **Finish** to see the fully-designed report in the editor:

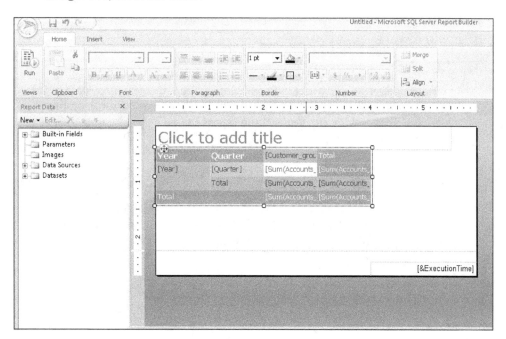

13. Click on **Run** to see the report preview:

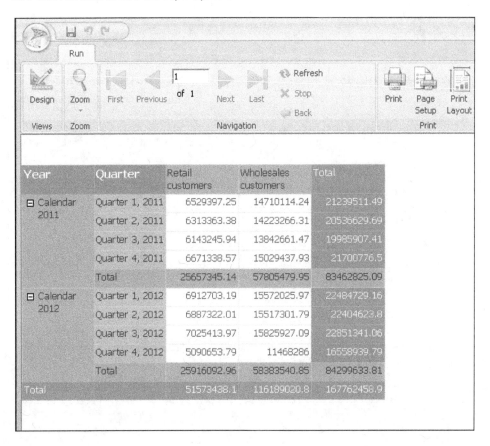

14. To save the report, publish this to Report Server. From the menu navigate to the **File | Save As** option and choose the location in the Report Server, preferably the DynamicsAX folder. Once saved, the report can be accessed through the reporting services.

How it works...

The SQL Report Builder also doubles as an easier way to verify a cube query before creating it using SSRS. The Report Builder can also be used against the OLTP database but the label transformations and security might not be put to action, so care must be taken in using it.

Designing a map subreport with SQL Report Builder

The AX SSRS extension, though has improved the capability of AX reports, is still to catch up with the actual SSRS. The features such as maps and a few other graphical additions to reports are yet to make way into it. However, there is a way to bring nice map reports to AX through the SQL Report Builder. This recipe will extend our previous recipe to add a map data that will then be added as a subreport.

Getting ready

This recipe requires that you have installed and have access the Report Server Manager and Report Builder. This recipe is a continuation to the recipe *Designing an OLAP table report with SQL Report Builder* in this chapter.

How to do it...

1. Continue with your last report by stretching the boarders of the report to make some space to insert a new control.

2. On the **Insert** ribbon bar, navigate to **Map** | **Map Wizard**:

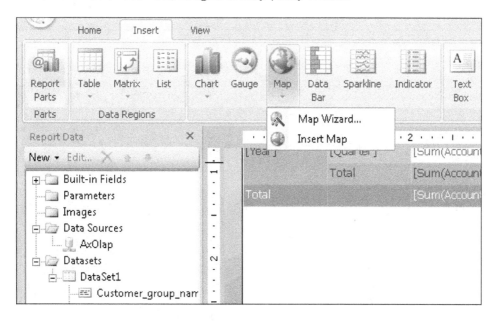

3. In the wizard, choose **USA by State Exploded** and click on **Next**:

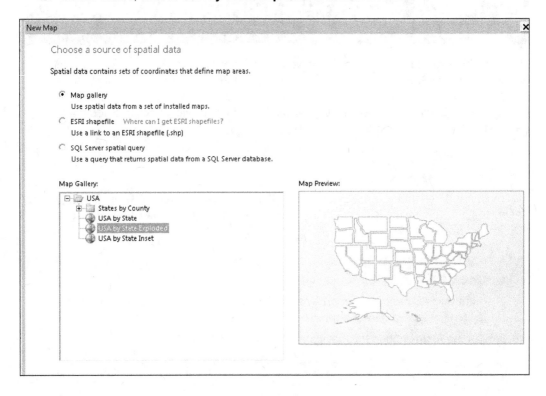

4. Let us use the same dataset that was added; so set the option to choose the already added datasource and click on **Next**:

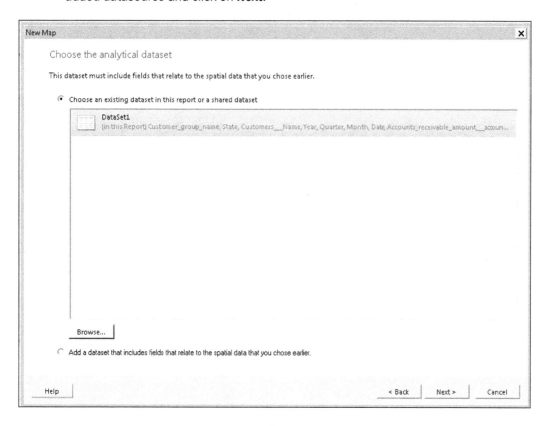

5. The next step is to relate the spatial data and the analytical data, in the following tab choose **Spatial data** which identifies a geographical location. Select **STUSPS** in the **Match** field and pick up the **State** field from the dataset fields:

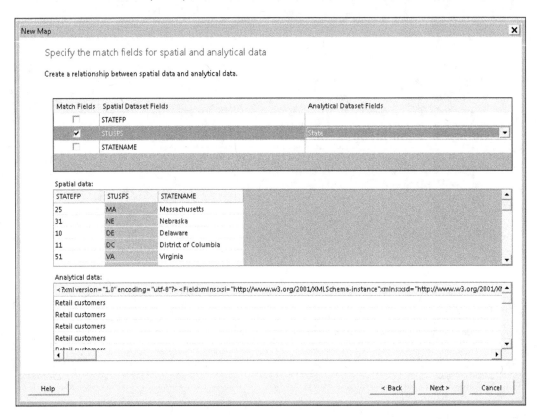

6. On the next tab choose a theme, preferably **Generic**, and choose the amount field sum for visualization, and then set the color rule to your preferred choice. Click on **Finish** to complete the wizard:

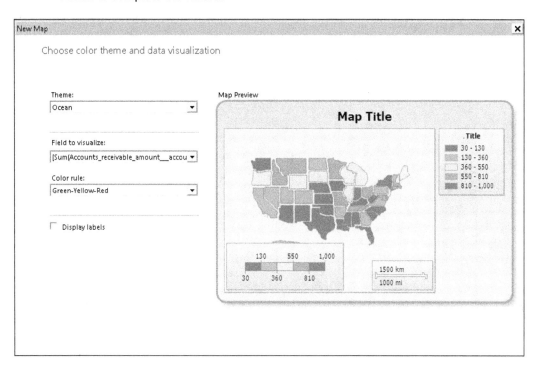

7. The map in inserted in the report. Before we make it a subreport it is necessary to drop all the extra add-ons on the map such as **Title** and **Scale**. So select each of them and uncheck the **Show** option:

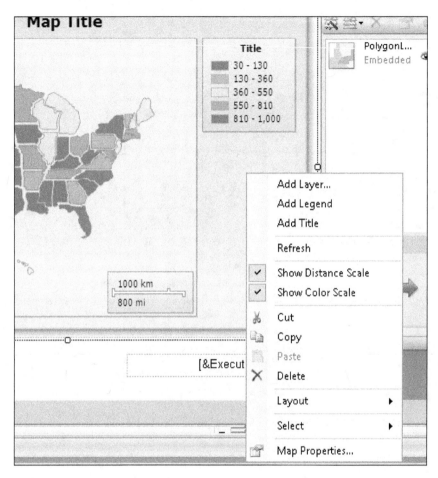

8. In the map area right-click and select **Viewport Properties**. On the properties set the **fill** and **border color** to none and **border size** to 0 pt. The map should appear plain as shown here. Resize it to a smaller size so that it can be inserted as a subreport:

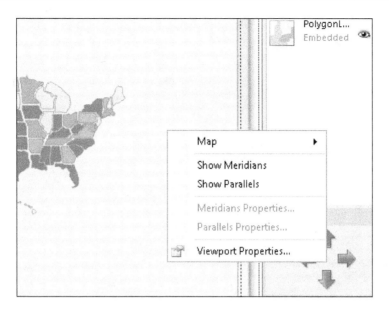

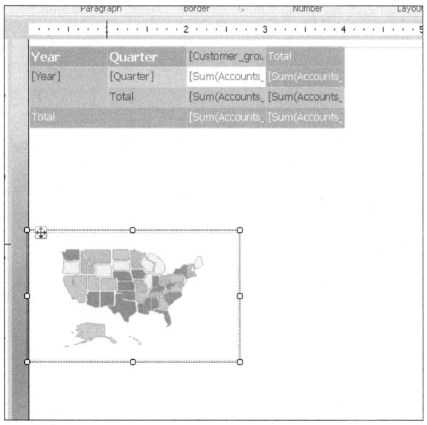

9. Now on the tabular design select the **Sum** field as seen here and insert a row **Inside group – Below**:

10. Read just the table design by stretching the columns and rows to build some space for the map. Cut the map and paste in the new column. This automatically makes the map a subreport:

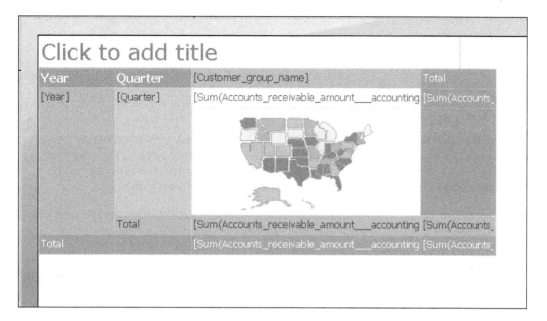

11. Run the report:

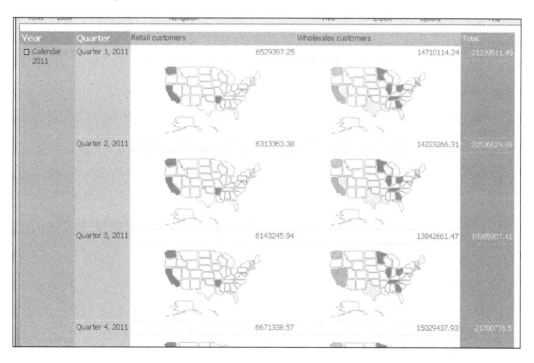

12. To save the report publish this to Report Server. From the menu navigate to the **File | Save As** option and then choose the location in the Report Server; preferably the `DynamicsAX` folder. Once saved, the report can be accessed through the reporting services.

How it works...

A subreport reflects the data inside the slice in which it is placed. The **subreport** option is automatically applied to the map when it is dragged and dropped into the existing table. The main report passes the relevant parameters, the subreport to render the right data, all these settings are taken care automatically by the Report Builder in this case.

These reports once published can be reused and made accessible to all users. To open the reports inside the rich client modify the report viewer (`SRSReportViewer`) to pass the URL and the report name through the `SRSReportRunAdapter` class.

Creating a subreport in auto design

Subreports can be compared to the **View Details** option in the Dynamics AX rich client forms. It is another way of adding drill-down information to reports. In this recipe we will see how to add subreports to auto design. The approach here is to create a report that shows the list of customer groups, and when the user clicks on a customer group then a subreport with all the customers belonging to the group will be created.

Getting ready

This recipe requires that you have access to Visual Studio and Dynamics Reporting Extension installed before you start.

How to do it...

1. Create a reporting project in Visual Studio and add a report `PktCustGroup`.
2. To the report `PktCustGroup` add a dataset through an AX query to list all the customer groups.
3. Drag the dataset to the auto design and create a design.
4. Preview the report node.
5. Add another report to the project `PktCustReport`.
6. To the report add `CustTable` AX query to list all the customers.
7. Drag the dataset to the auto design and create a design.

8. In the **Parameters** node create a new parameter called **CustGroup** of type `String`:

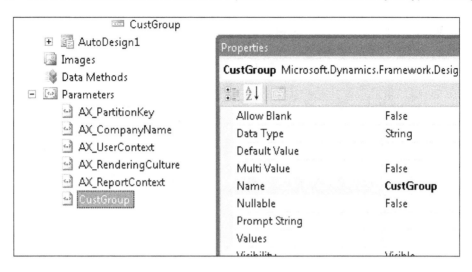

9. In the **Designs** node expand the node **Filters**, create a new filter, and set the following properties:

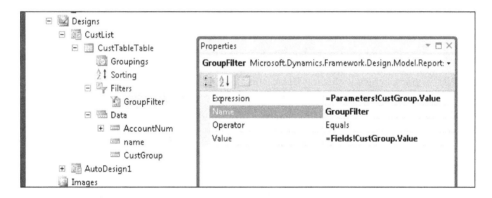

Property	Value
Name	`GroupFilter`
Expression	`=Parameters!CustGroup.Value`
Operator	`Equals`
Value	`=Fields!CustGroup.Value`

10. Save and preview the report.

11. Open the report `PktCustGroup`, on the **Designs** node expand the **Data** node and right-click on the field **CustGroup** and navigate to **Add | Report Drill Through Action**.

12. This will add a new node **ReportDrillThroughAction**; open the properties of the node and click on the button on the property **ReportDesign**. This will list all the reports in the same project. Expand **PktCustReport**, select the **Designs** node and click on **OK**:

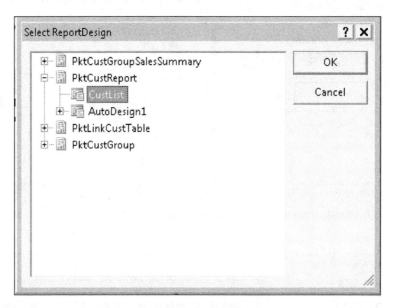

13. All the parameters including **CustGroup** that was created in **PktCustReport** will be added as subnodes. Navigate to each subreport and set it to the system parameter of the current report in the value field except for the parameter **CustGroup**:

14. For the parameter **CustGroup**, set the **value** field to the expression `=Fields!CustGroup.Value`.

15. Save and preview the report.

16. On the report preview as you navigate to the **CustGroup** the cursor will change to indicate a link. Clicking on the link will open the customer list filtered by the customer group.

How it works...

The reports that are linked must be in the same project to make it work. The filter that is added to the **CustList** report will restrict the design to show only records whose **Customer** group value is equal to the parameter as the filter is mapped to the parameter. This parameter value is filled with the **CustGroup** field value in the **CustGroup** report. When a user clicks on the link, the corresponding field value is automatically passed as parameter to the subreport.

The link field (**CustGroup**) doesn't need to match with the **Parameter** field. This means the drill through could be implemented for the field **Name** as well since the link is governed by the expression that is set up for the parameters under **ReportDrillThroughAction**.

Creating a subreport in precision design

This recipe is to create a subreport in precision design. To implement this recipe let's use the cube report that was designed in the recipe *Creating a customer summary OLAP report* in this chapter.

Getting ready

This recipe extends the OLAP report developed in *Creating a customer summary OLAP report* in this chapter and uses the report added in the recipe *Creating a subreport in auto design* in this chapter.

How to do it...

1. Add the report `PktCustgroupSalesSummary` (OLAP report) to the project `PktCustReport`, used in the previous recipe. This is because subreports and main report must exist in the same project.

2. Open the precision design software and navigate to the field for customer group. Select the field, and then right-click and choose **Textbox Properties**:

3. On the **Properties** dialog box, select the **Action** tab, and then choose **Go to Report** under the **Enable as a hyperlink** pane:

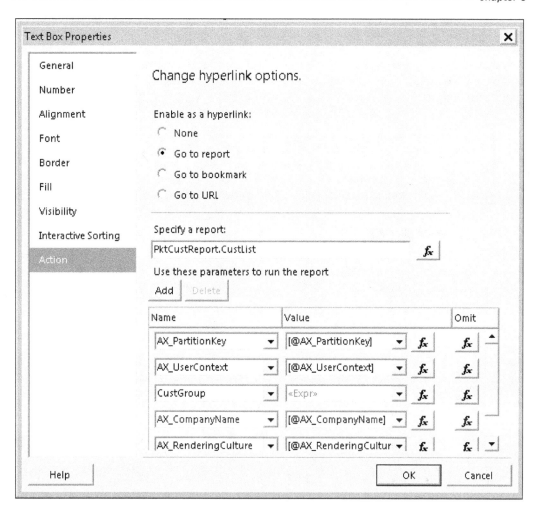

4. In the field **Specify a report manually**, fill the values with **PktCustReport.CustList** since no lookup is available in auto design.

5. Click on the **Add** button to add parameters. On the **Name** field, type the parameter name used in **PktCustReport** and on the **Value** field use the expression button and select the appropriate values from the report **PktCustgroupSalesSummary**.

6. Rebuild the project.

7. Deploy and preview the report.

How it works...

Sometimes, in the preview option, the links may not work resulting in an error. Go ahead and deploy the project to the Report Server, and verify it in the Report Server to ensure that it works.

 Precision design can be created from auto design. This can be helpful as it is easier to add fields to an auto-design. Also, creating report drill through actions is manual in precision design but automatic in auto design. So when an auto design is converted to precision design the drill through is automatically translated from the auto design.

See also

► The *Adding a drill up/drill down navigation to reports* recipe in *Chapter 2, Enhancing Your Report – Visualization and Interaction*

6
Beyond Tabular Reports

This chapter will cover the following recipes:

- ▶ Creating a matrix report
- ▶ Creating a multicolumn matrix report
- ▶ Creating a column chart
- ▶ Creating a line chart
- ▶ Gauges in reports
- ▶ List and rectangle controls in reports
- ▶ Adding reports to the role center

Introduction

The legacy reporting system in Dynamics AX had very limited capabilities of how you can render data. Something as simple as adding an image and placing it right was a mammoth task, while things such as graphs and charts were not imaginable. SSRS takes away this pain and makes it easy to represent data in different formats. SSRS reports help create easier and convenient representation of data graphically that is easy for the end user to assimilate. This chapter will discuss recipes that cover the different kinds of controls other than the table layout discussed so far that can be used to represent data, such as matrix, charts, and gauges. The reader will be familiarized with the different controls and how they can be put to use in reports through this chapter.

Creating a matrix report

A matrix is an interesting representation format with a two-dimensional view of the data, allowing capabilities to consolidate by row and column. This recipe will discuss how to add and use a matrix data region in reports. Also discussed is the totaling capabilities in matrix reports.

How to do it...

This recipe is broken down into two sections. In the basic report design section we will build a simple RDP that will be used in this recipe as well as in other recipes found in this chapter and the actual recipe is in the second section.

Basic report design

1. Before we start on this recipe we will build an RDP class that can be used as a source for all the recipes in this chapter. This RDP will be used as the source of a dataset for all the following reports.

2. Create a query as seen here. The `InventItemGroupItem` table uses the `exists` join and is added for the purpose of limiting the sales lines data to certain item groups.

3. The goal of the RDP is to run across the sales line in the system and then retrieve the item, item group, and the shipping date confirmed. The shipping date confirmed is also split into multiple parts such as years, months, and days.

 This RDP can be time consuming if you have a huge database of sales orders, so limit your data to certain item groups or a certain period as required in the RDP's `processReport` method.

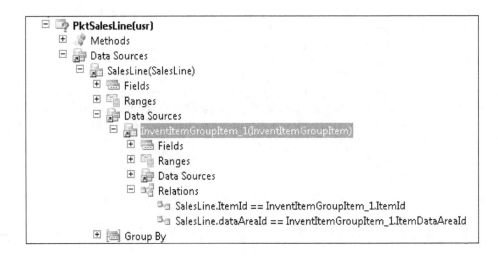

4. This RDP will fill a temporary table shown here:

5. The RDP shown here will fill the temporary table by running through all the sales lines in the system.

 The general approach for analysis like this is to use OLAP so that it is faster and provides multiple dimensions of consolidations but using an OLAP to demonstrate these report controls might stop several from practicing. This is because the majority of AX developers are not BI experts. Keeping this in mind this RDP has been used to demonstrate the examples.

```
[
    //bind query - shows in the report dialog
    SRSReportQueryAttribute(queryStr(PktSalesLine))
]
class PktItemSalesHistoryDP extends SRSReportDataProviderBase
{
    PktItemSalesHistoryTmp salesHistoryTmp;
}


[
    SRSReportDataSetAttribute(tableStr(PktItemSalesHistoryTmp))
]
public PktItemSalesHistoryTmp getItemSalesHistoryTmp()
{
    select  salesHistoryTmp;
    return  salesHistoryTmp;
}
```

```
private void insertTmpTable(SalesLine _salesLine)
{
    Qty                qty;
    date               shipDate;
    InventItemGroupItem groupItem;

    qty             = _salesLine.QtyOrdered;
    shipDate        = _salesLine.ShippingDateConfirmed;
    groupItem       = InventItemGroupItem::findByItemIdLegalEnti
ty(
                                        _salesLine.ItemId,
                                        _salesLine.
DataAreaId);

    salesHistoryTmp.clear();
    salesHistoryTmp.ItemId          = _salesLine.ItemId;
    salesHistoryTmp.ItemGroupId     = groupItem.ItemGroupId;
    salesHistoryTmp.Price           = _salesLine.salesPrice;
    salesHistoryTmp.Amount          = _salesLine.SalesPrice * Qty;
    salesHistoryTmp.Qty             = qty;
    salesHistoryTmp.Year            = year(shipDate);
    salesHistoryTmp.MonthOfYearId   = mthOfYr(shipDate);
    salesHistoryTmp.Days            = dayOfMth(shipDate);
    salesHistoryTmp.insert();
}


[
SysEntryPointAttribute(false)
]
public void processReport()
{
    Query       query;
    QueryRun    queryRun;
    SalesLine   salesLine;
    InventItemGroupItem itemGroup;

    query = this.parmQuery();

    queryRun = new queryRun(query);

    while (queryRun.next())
    {
        salesLine = queryRun.get(tableNum(salesLine));
        this.insertTmpTable(salesLine);
    }
}
```

Creating a matrix report

1. Create a report in Visual Studio named `PktMatrixReport` and add the RDP provider as a dataset.

2. Set the **Dynamic filter** property to `false`.

3. Create a new precision design and name it `matrixDesign`, and then double-click to open up the editor.

4. Right-click and insert a new matrix data region:

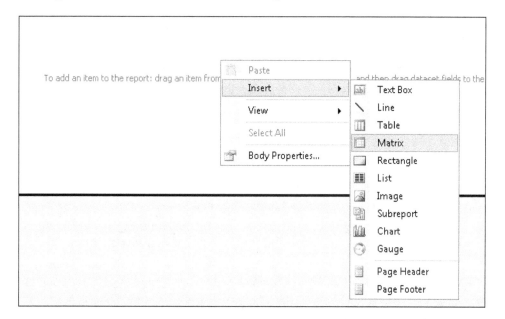

5. Use the field selector to set the fields as shown in the following screenshot. Choosing **Qty** in the data section will automatically add the Sum function to it:

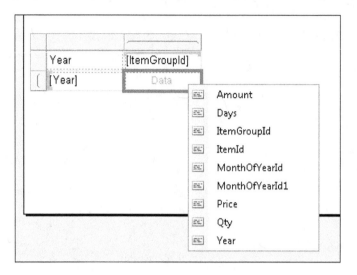

6. To add the total quantity for each row, on the **Row Groups** option at the bottom, click on the small arrow and then navigate to **Add Totals | After**.

7. To add the total quantity for each column, on the **Column Groups** option at the bottom, click on the small arrow and then navigate to **Add Totals | After**.

8. There are three total boxes in the design. Each represent the row total, column total, and the grand total. Grand total tallies the sum of rows and sum of columns.

9. As you can see in the following screenshot that the grand total block in the title row is colored and the font is also set to bold. This will give a better appearance for the matrix:

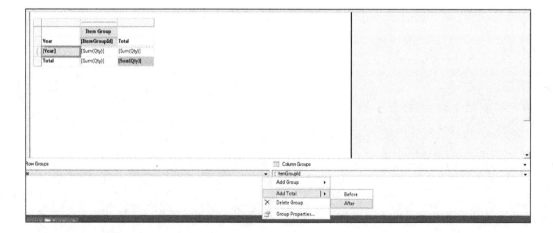

10. The header for the row is present but there is no similar header for the column group. So right-click on the first column and navigate to **Insert Row | Outside Group – Above**. This will give a header for the column. Enter the expression string **ItemGroupId** using the label ID or the static text. The design appears as shown here:

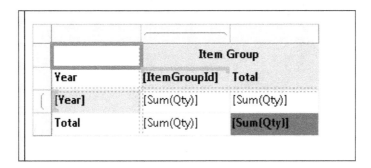

11. Save the report and preview it:

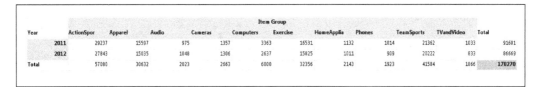

Year	ActionSpor	Apparel	Audio	Cameras	Computers	Exercise	HomeApplia	Phones	TeamSports	TVandVideo	Total
2011	29237	15597	975	1357	3363	16531	1132	1014	21362	1033	91601
2012	27843	15035	1048	1306	2637	15825	1011	909	20222	833	86669
Total	57080	30632	2023	2663	6000	32356	2143	1923	41584	1866	178270

How it works...

A matrix data region is actually a Tablix control behind the hood. The Tablix control combines the behavior of table, list, and matrix reports. Though the UI has table, matrix, and list controls, they are the same controls under the hood; they open up with a different configuration. The matrix data region has both row and column group, whereas a table control has only column group. Matrix helps create summary type reports.

Creating a multicolumn matrix report

This recipe will show how a multicolumn matrix can be implemented. Here we will expand our report to see how we can dissect it into detail where the rows are further split by months following years and the columns will also show the average price other than the quantity.

Getting ready

This recipe requires that you complete the recipe *Creating a matrix report* in this chapter.

How to do it...

1. Create a new design as in the previous recipe or extend the design created in the previous recipe with the steps detailed here.

2. From the **Report Data** toolbar, drag the control **MonthOfYearId1** to the **Row Group** control next to **Year**. When you drop it a blue bar appears and it must face the **Year** column as shown here:

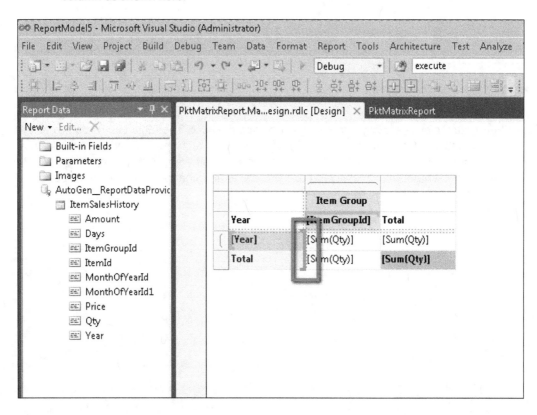

3. From the **Report Data** toolbar drag the control **Price** to **Column Group** next to **Qty**. A vertical blue bar appears and it must face the **Qty** column as seen here:

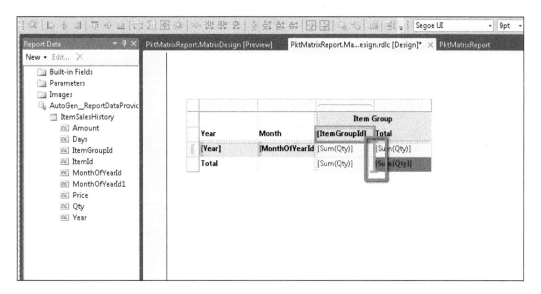

4. The price field, by default, gets placed in as a Sum operation. Change it to Average by right-clicking on the cell and choosing **Expression**. In the expression field modify the sum and set it to average.

5. Since price can have decimal values it is important to set the decimal ranges; otherwise, it ends up in an improper formatting. Right-click on **price control** and choose **Textbox properties**.

6. On **Textbox properties** set the **Formatting** to **Number** and ensure Decimal places is set to 2:

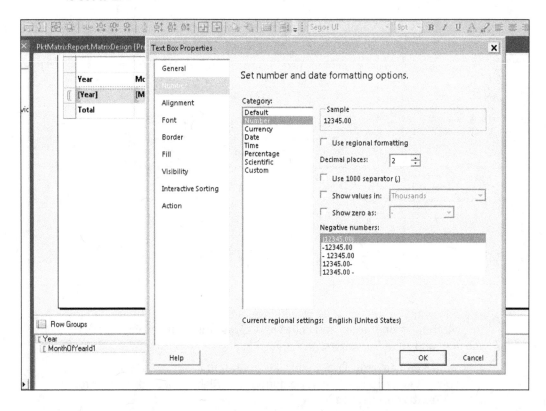

7. If you are extending the previous recipe drop the column totals before doing this; otherwise, directly move to the column group at the bottom and click on the arrow button and then navigate to **Add Totals | After**. This will add the totals for the quantity and price fields.

8. The report design appears as shown here. Save the report and preview it.

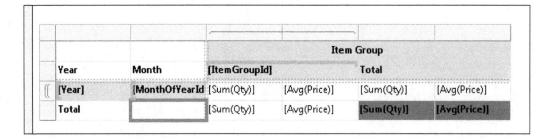

9. The first screenshot shows preview with limited data (the **Load dataset fully** option is not activated):

Year	Month	Item Group			
		ActionSpor	Total		
2011 April		26	57.13	26	57.13
	August	39	61.74	39	61.74
	December	63	59.34	63	59.34
	February	29	60.35	29	60.35
	January	78	56.79	78	56.79
	July	39	59.22	39	59.22
	June	47	60.81	47	60.81
	March	45	59.28	45	59.28
	May	33	58.94	33	58.94
	November	39	57.43	39	57.43
	October	34	59.99	34	59.99
	September	42	61.05	42	61.05
2012 April		35	59.70	35	59.70
	August	28	63.43	28	63.43
	December	45	61.05	45	61.05
	February	36	62.28	36	62.28
	January	47	57.99	47	57.99
	July	28	58.85	28	58.85
	June	48	59.79	48	59.79
	March	51	58.74	51	58.74
	May	44	59.08	44	59.08
	November	30	64.54	30	64.54
	October	26	63.74	26	63.74
	September	34	62.28	34	62.28
Total		966	59.88	966	59.88

10. The second screenshot shows the preview with the full dataset loaded:

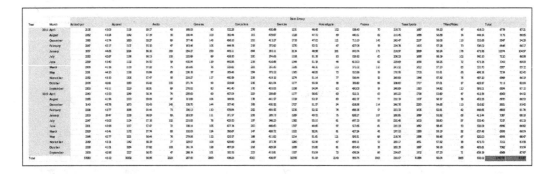

How it works...

Here in this report, the summary is broken down by years and months while the columns summarize multiple values than just one value. In this way, a matrix can be used to build detail-drilled summary reports.

The report preview option in Visual Studio always loads a limited sampled data and doesn't bring the entire data behind the system. This is not realized in the case of small datasets. When using big datasets, as in the case in this chapter, you will notice that data changes every time. In this case, to confirm if everything is loaded, activate the **Load data set fully** option available in the right corner of your preview window.

Creating a column chart report

This recipe will guide you to create chart-based reports in Dynamics AX. Charts are interesting pictorial representations of data and the SSRS reports support a multitude of chart types. It is v to switch between chart types in SSRS. In this recipe we will create a column chart that represents the total sale of quantity over a couple of years.

Getting ready

Complete the RDP defined in the *Getting ready* section of the recipe *Creating a matrix report* in this chapter.

How to do it...

1. Since the RDP class can return a large number of item groups, it is ideal to limit it to two item groups to test this recipe. This will make it faster and easier to work through this recipe.

2. Modify `processreport` in the RDP to add ranges for the item group in the query.

3. In Visual Studio create a new report `PktColumnChartReport` and link the RDP class to it. Remember to set the **Dynamic filter** property in the dataset to `false`.

4. Create a new precision design and name it `ChartDesign`.

5. Open the editor, right-click and then navigate to **Insert | Chart**. In the prompting dialog window that shows the different chart types available, choose the **Column** chart:

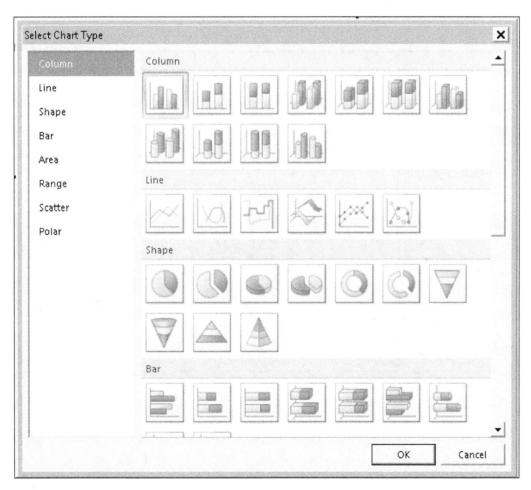

6. Resize the chart to a required size and double-click on the chart area. This will show additional square boxes around the chart image for category, series, and data as seen in the following screenshot. Drag the following fields to the specified region accordingly:

Field	Drop area
Year	Category
ItemGroupId	Series
Qty	Data

7. As fields are dropped in the chart area you can see the report changing at design time. Though this may not reflect the exact data, it will give you a feeling of how it looks at runtime.

8. Modify the chart title and the axis title. Save the report design.

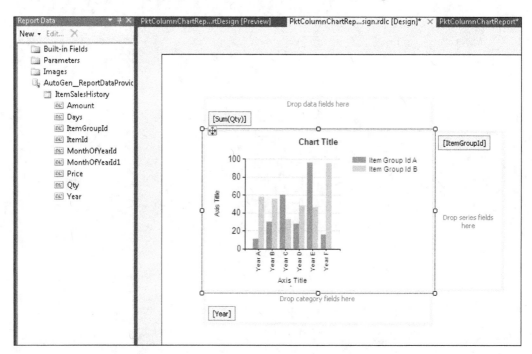

9. The report preview appears as seen here:

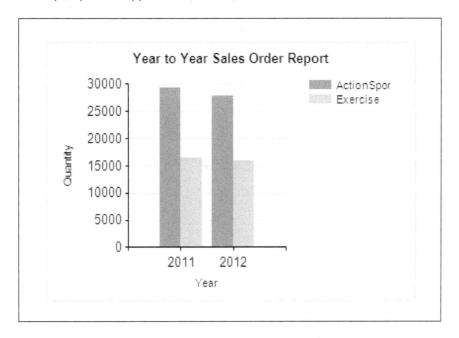

How it works...

The report seen here is a multi-series chart, which means the category is applied across the series. A static series is where we represent a single series item; for example, item group. In this case if the item group is not restricted, then each year would be showing up for all the item groups in the system. Care has to be taken in what is added to the series so that the comparison makes sense to the user.

See also

▶ The *Creating a chart data region* recipe in *Chapter 2, Enhancing Your Report – Visualization and Interaction*

Creating a line chart

This recipe will discuss another chart-based report. Here we will try to show the monthly quantity trend for the item groups over the years. The line chart is the best option to reveal trends. This recipe will also focus on the aesthetical properties of charts, such as color and axis design.

Getting ready

This recipe requires the *Creating a column chart report* recipe in this chapter to be completed beforehand.

How to do it...

1. Create a new precision design for the report. Call it `line design`.

2. Open the editor and insert a new chart.

3. Double-click on the chart area to open up the field editor. On the field editor drop the following fields as specified:

Field	Drop area
Year, MonthOfYearId	Category
ItemGroupId	Series
Qty	Data

4. The next few steps will deal with how the aesthetics of a chart can be made better. On the **General Properties** window, set **Palette** to `SeaGreen`. This will apply a different set of colors for each series.

5. To set up markers for the series on the value points, right-click on the chart area and select **Series Properties**. On the **Markers** tab set the type of marker as `Square`.

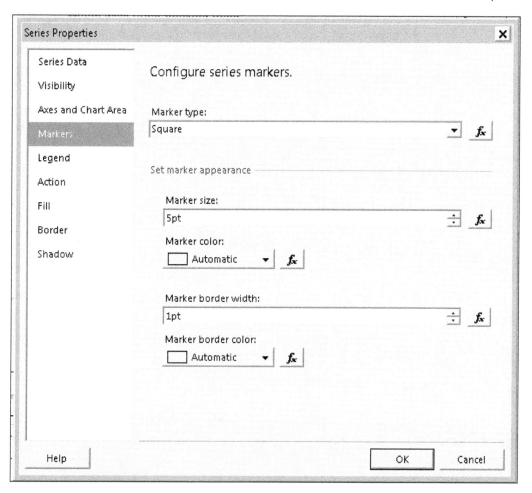

6. The axis may not show all the labels for the category axis. To make sure that it shows all the months as labels right-click on an axis and open the **Axis** properties form. In the property form on the **Axis** options tab under **Set axis** scale and style, set the interval to 1. This will ensure that all the labels are visible.

7. Right-click on the **Legend** option and choose **Legend properties**. On the **General** tab under the **Legend** position choose from the circular radio buttons the position of the legend:

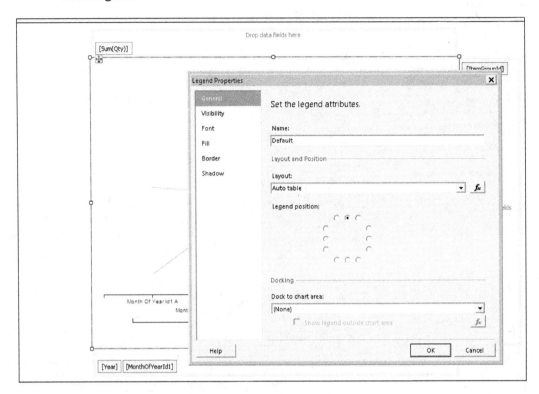

8. To disable the quantity axis right-click on any axis, uncheck **Show Value Axis**, and then the design should be similar in style to the screenshot here:

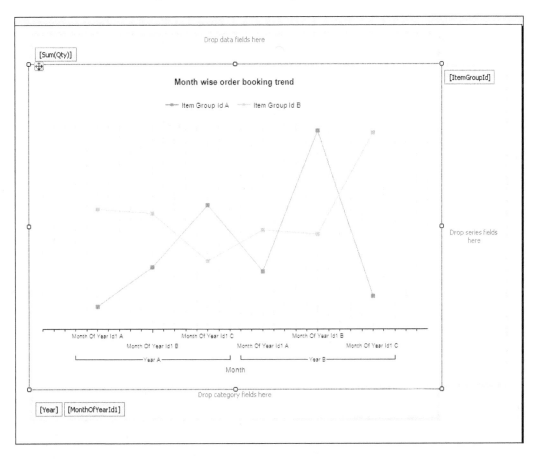

9. Save the report and preview it.

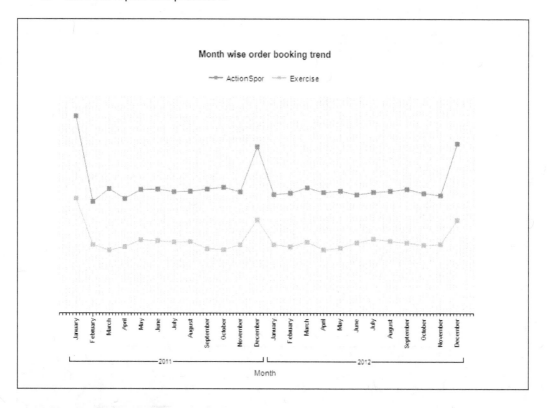

This recipe details how the appearance of a report can be controlled through the various associated properties. This recipe discusses only limited options while there are tons of more options that you can explore.

There's more...

Though the chart design shown here is from precision design, auto design also supports charts.

Chart reports in auto design

In auto design the category, series, and data appear as group nodes as seen here. The chart type can be changed from the **Properties** node of the chart control. The fields can be dragged into it to from the datasets.

Precision design is more flexible and convenient than auto design for the following reasons:

- ▸ Modify and preview the chart in design time
- ▸ Clarity to understand the field and its corresponding axis
- ▸ Extent of customization and visibility of the available charts
- ▸ More control on where and how the data is rendered, such as the marker and legend

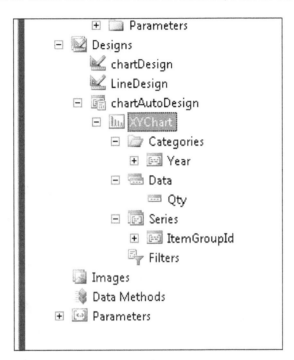

 Prefer using precision design over auto design when it comes to charts.

Gauges in reports

Gauges are one-dimensional data regions that can display a single value in your dataset. A gauge can be used as a KPI, in table or matrix cells, to indicate single values. This recipe will show how a gauge can be added in a matrix cell to indicate the average price.

Getting ready

Complete a report design as specified in the recipe *Creating a multicolumn matrix report*. The report design must appear as seen here:

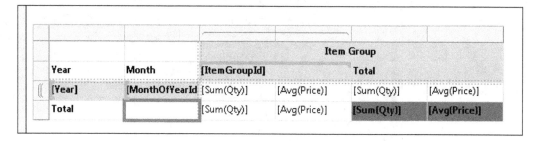

How to do it...

1. Open the precision design created in the *Create a multicolumn matrix report* recipe.

2. Select the `ItemGroupId` field, and then right-click and navigate to **Insert Column | Inside group – Left**.

3. In the newly created column drag the **Gauge** control from the **Report Items** in the toolbox. Select **Radial** and choose the design highlighted in the following screenshot:

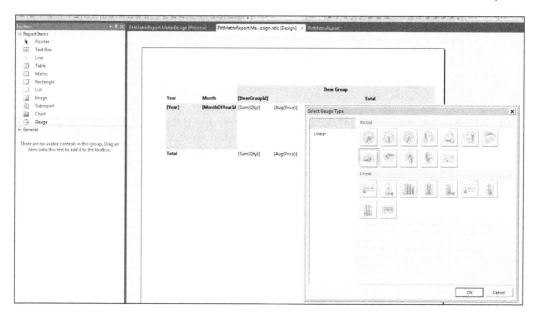

4. Stretch the box to allow resizing the **Gauge** control; notice that the **Gauge** control increases as the box expands. Stretch it to a visible limit.

5. Double-click on the gauge control and on the **Drop data fields here** box that appears over the gauge, drop the field `Price` by dragging it from report data. By default this value might appear as `Sum(Qty)`, convert it to `Avg(price)`:

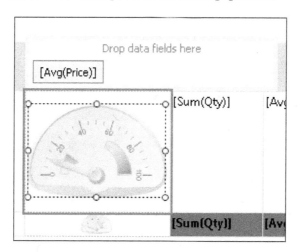

6. Right-click on the **Gauge** control and select **Pointer Properties**. In the **Properties** form on the **Pointer** options tab, click on the expression button in the `Value` field and convert `sum` to `avg` in the expression editor.

7. The **Gauge** control, by default, shows red on the max value but in the case of average price the higher the value, the better it is. To modify, select the range in red color, and then right-click and open **Range** properties. In the **Range properties**, set **secondary color** to `Green` from the default color:

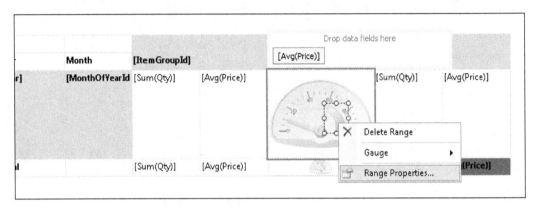

8. To add a new range, right-click inside the **Gauge** control and select **Add Range**. A new range gets added to the lower corner:

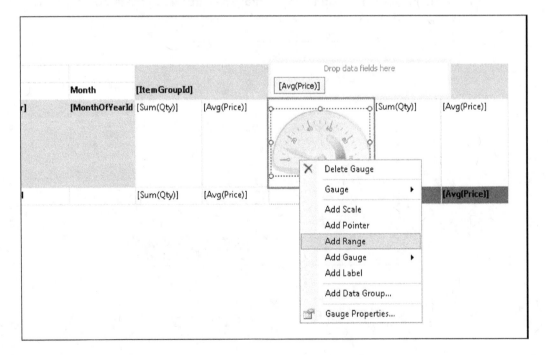

9. Select the range and open **Range Properties** by right-clicking on the new range. In the **Range properties** form set **Start range at scale value** and **End range at scale value** to 1 and 20 respectively and also change the fill color to Red. Any number of ranges can be added in a similar way with different scale values.

10. The final design appears as seen here:

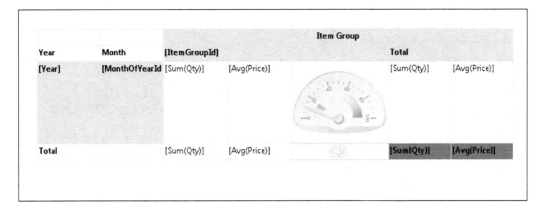

11. Save and preview the report.

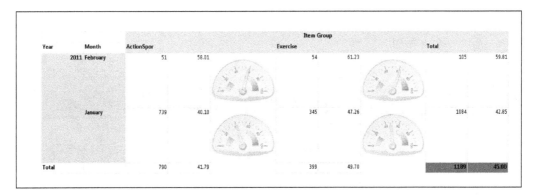

List and rectangle controls in reports

List and rectangle are container controls in SSRS. The rectangle control is used for flow control while the list data region is like an array control. The list region can help create very interesting representations of the report. This recipe in the process to build a summary sheet for each item group will discuss the idea of list and rectangle controls.

How to do it...

Carry out the following steps to create the list-based report:

1. Create a new report with the RDP named `PktItemSalesHistoryDP`, and add a new precision design.

2. On the editor window insert a list region. Right-click on the control and select **Tablix** properties. In the property window set **dataset** to the RDP dataset `ItemSalesHistory`.

3. The **Row Groups** window at the bottom must indicate a **Details** row. Click on the arrow in the corner and open **Group Properties**:

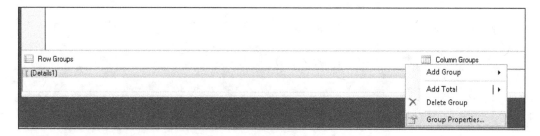

4. In **Group Properties** add a new grouping by **ItemGroupId**:

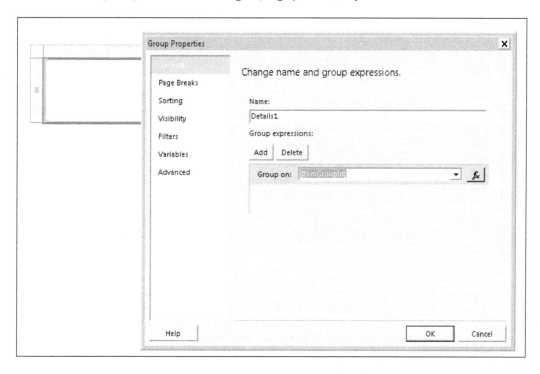

5. Stretch the list data region to fit the entire report. From the toolbox drag the textbox control and set the field to ItemGroupId. Also, enter the text title as Summary Sheet before ItemGroupId as seen in the following screenshot:

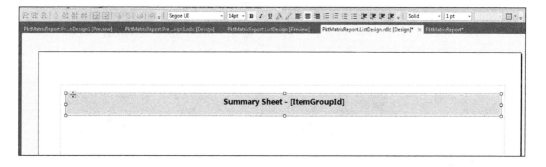

6. Increase the font size, set the alignment to center and the back color using the text toolbar.

7. From the toolbox again drag a rectangle control to the list box. Inside the rectangle control add quantity and price sum. Also, add labels, header text, and back color. The rectangle should reflect the total quantity and the amount for the item group:

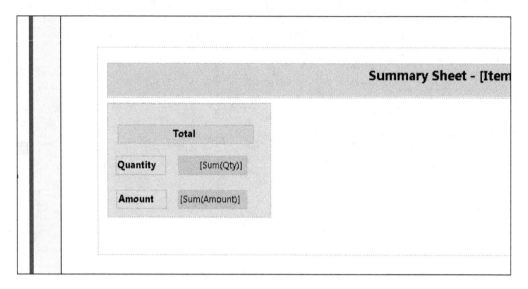

8. Stretch the list box to increase the height and below the total insert a radial gauge. On the pointer properties, set the field to `Avg(Price)`. Add a textbox that provides a title for the **Gauge** control as `Average Price`:

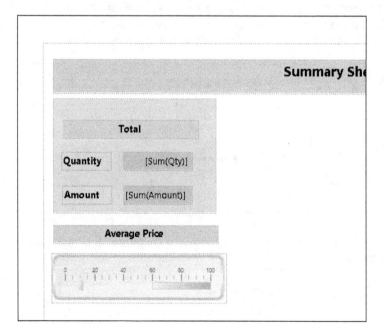

9. In the rest of the available area in the list we will create two charts. One is a bar chart that indicates the quantity sold across items and the other will be a line chart that indicates the price graph across the items.

10. To insert a chart, choose the **Barchart** option and then drop **ItemId** to the categories and **Quantity** to the Data. Delete the axis titles and legends to make space for the graph.

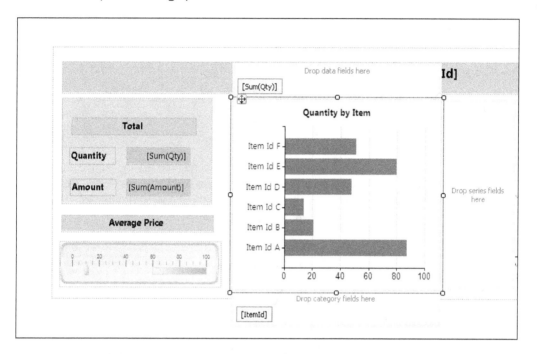

11. Similarly, insert a line chart and add `ItemId` to the categories and `Price` to the `Data`. Give it a title after removing the axis titles and the legend.

12. The final design of the report should be as shown here:

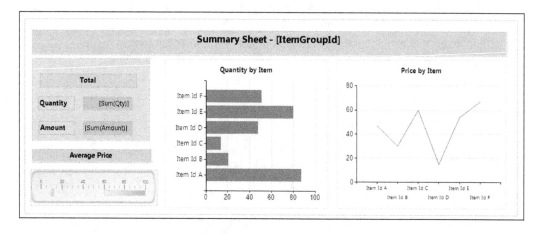

13. Since this is a summary, it is preferable to print each summary in a single sheet. To activate this go to **Group properties | Page Breaks (Tab)** and enable the **Between each instance of a group** flag. This will enable printing one summary per sheet. Preview the report to see the summary print per page:

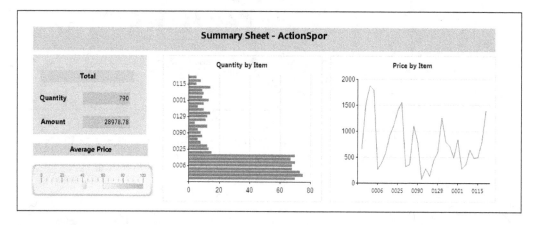

How it works...

Surprisingly, the list data region is also a Tablix control with altered configuration. It helps setting up a format that can be repeated for every record in the dataset. To experiment how a list data region works, do the following. Drag a list data region, connect it to a dataset, and then add a field from the dataset. When previewed, you will see that the list is repeated for each record in the dataset. In the example discussed here, since a grouping is added on the **ItemGroupId** it repeats only for the number of item groups in the system.

Adding reports to the role center

Reports that consolidate like financial statements or present analysis like Top 10 customers are used by the top level management. These reports might need to be integrated to their respective role center to make it visible. This recipe will discuss how any report can be added to the role center page.

How to do it...

1. Deploy a report and create a menu item for the report. In this case we will use `PktColumnChartReport` from **Create ColumnChartReport**. Give the menu item a label **Year To Year Sales order Report**.

2. Open the role center page that you wish to edit and click on the **personalize this page** option in the right corner. This opens a view that can be edited.

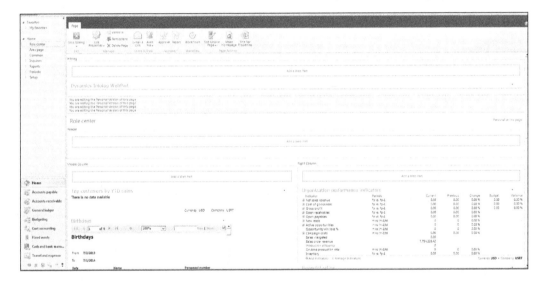

3. Click on **Add a web Part**.

4. A screen listing all the categories and web parts appears. Select **Microsoft Dynamics AX** from the category and **Report** from the Web Part. Click on **Add**:

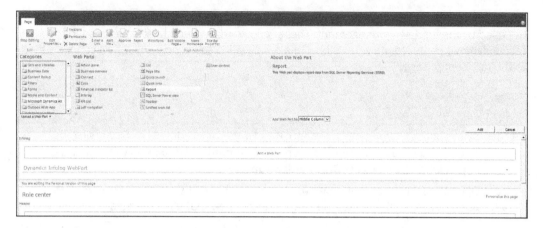

5. This adds the web part; this web part must be configured. Select the drop-down menu in the upper-right corner and then select **Edit Web Part**:

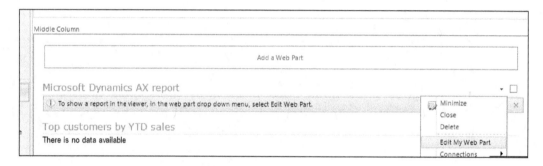

6. A report bar appears on one end of the web page. From this bar select the report, in this case the column chart. The list highlights the reports based on the report menu item label. Select the report and set the properties, such as parameter and layout. Click on **OK**:

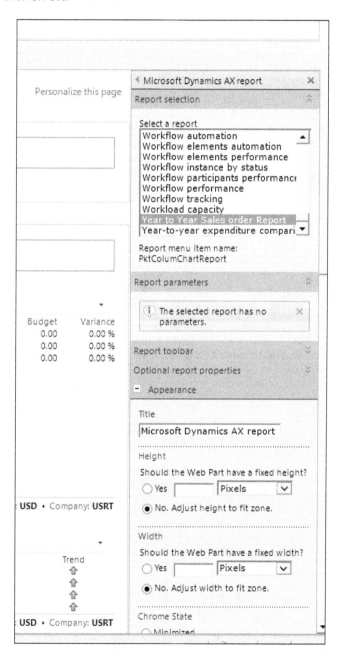

7. The report shows up in the role center. Click on **Stop Editing** on the toolbar to complete the setup. This recipe can be performed either in the Dynamics AX role center page or in the enterprise portal:

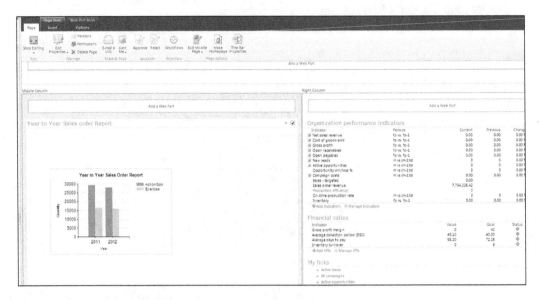

How it works...

The role center modifications can be done by an end user as well as administrators themselves. If a report is made visible at the role center, see that you don't have too many dynamic parameters.

7

Upgrading and Analyzing Reports

This chapter will cover the following recipes:

- ▶ Upgrading a report from the previous version
- ▶ Analyzing and modifying an existing report
- ▶ Implementing validation in reports
- ▶ Surrogate fields in reports
- ▶ Grouping and ordering controls in a report dialog
- ▶ RDP with multiple temporary tables
- ▶ Multi-value lookup
- ▶ Inventory dimensions in reports
- ▶ Financial dimensions in reports
- ▶ Financial dimensions in RDP reports

Introduction

This chapter will walk you through upgrading your reports from the previous versions to the new SSRS reporting framework; with this, you will also learn how to approach an existing report to identify the component parts of it. The next recipes will discuss about placing validations and structuring the report controls in a report dialog. You will also learn how to implement multi-value lookup reports, and how to return multiple tables from an RDP. The last sections of this chapter will discuss the frequently used patterns such as inventory and financial dimensions for reports.

Upgrading a report from the previous version

As learned earlier, reporting has gone through a major change with the new versions of AX. Though SSRS reports were introduced in AX 2009, there were only a handful by then, that too with limited framework support. AX 2012 uses SSRS as a mainstream report while still supporting the legacy framework. Moving reports from AX 2009 to AX 2012, though termed an upgrade, is in reality a redevelopment. This recipe will basically discuss how to map the different implementations in an AX 2009 report to the new framework, and it assumes that the report in AX 2009 is completely custom-developed and not found in AX.

How to do it...

Migrating reports from the older version is a multistep process, since it is a complete redesign. This process is broken down in to major headings and is described as follows:

Defining the datasource

Designing a report starts with making the choice of the report datasource. If the existing report uses only a report query, the ideal choice in AX 2012 would be using an AOT query.

Even if there are simple display methods or computations present in the `fetch` method, it is fine to use a report query. Choose to go with an RDP only when there is pure business logic placed in a report. The following are the decisional points that should help you choose the datasource:

- Source of the data contained in the report dataset
- Elements of the report that are from the report business logic
- Calculated columns based on Microsoft Dynamics AX data
- **Extended Data Types** (**EDTs**) that are used to format data

Mapping the parameters and fields

The next step is based on the datasource you choose to work with. Create the necessary parameters and decide the fields that are required in the report:

1. **For Query**: If there are parameters from the old report dataset, add them to the ranges node in the newly created AOT query. This will add them as dialog fields using dynamic filters.

2. **For RDP**:

   1. The next step is to identify the data that is needed for the report, and create one or more temporary table based on the business logic. For example, `SalesConfirm` and `ProjInvoice` are reports that use more than one temporary table.

   2. After the temporary table is created, create the RDP class and move the business logic placed inside the `fetch` method into the RDP. Also to be moved are any computed columns that are implemented as display methods in AX 2009. The display value is mapped to the field in the temporary table and is filled by the RDP.

   3. When creating the RDP, you will identify the parameters that are necessary, and create a contract class with the list of parameters.

Mapping the design

Once the datasource decision is complete, the next step is to work on the design part. As AX 2009 has auto design and generated design, AX 2012 has auto design and precision design. The generated design is what maps as precision design in AX 2012, but before simply moving all the generated design to precision design, consider rethinking the strategy. Sometimes, it is possible that what was achieved through generated design in AX 2009 could be achieved with the help of auto design and RDP in AX 2012. Take in to account the following points as you do your design mapping:

1. **Choice of control**: SSRS reports have a wider choice of presentation methods such as charts, matrix, and list. So, consider if you can use an alternate way to display your data.

2. **Segregate display methods**: Display methods must be carefully redesigned. In AX 2009, it was a common practice to write a display method for even fetching a value using a foreign key. Such methods can be eliminated in AX 2012. Here are a few suggestions for the commonly found display methods:

- **Find methods**: If a query is the report datasource, it allows you to add display methods present in the table as datasource fields. So, directly choose the display method when choosing the fields in the query selection window in the report designer.

- **Simple computations**: There can be conditional computations such as `If (PriceDiscTable.Value) then Total = Total + Value`. For such conditional computations, try to use expressions. If the expressions are proving difficult, use the business logic in the report design to create a method, which can be referenced from the expressions. Refer to the *Data methods in business logic* recipe in *Chapter 3, A Report Programming Model*.

Business logic in C# must be used only for simple mathematical computations. For anything that involves access to AX business logic, the recommended approach would be an RDP.

- **Formatting changes**: For simple formatting purposes such as background color, prefer to use expressions.
- **Business logic in computations**: If there are business logic inside computations, make it a part of the RDP and add a field in the temp table.

3. If the company logo must be displayed in the report, prefer to use the precision design over auto design.

Datasets in AX 2012 versus AX 2009 reports

Datasets demystified: As compared to the report dataset in AX 2009, the AX 2012 report dataset has stark differences:

1. Two datasets cannot be related or joined with each other.

2. The dataset is flattened and it is accessed by the dataset name, unlike in AX 2009, where when there are `SalesTable` and `SalesLine`, there is two cursors to identify them individually.

3. To achieve header and line pattern as in AX 2009 reports, use the **group by** property in AX 2012; the header row in the group represents the parent data while the details are placed in the table body.

Refer *Grouping in reports* in Chapter 1, *Understanding and Creating Simple SSRS Reports*.

4. There are no multiple header, footer, or prolog sections in AX 2012. There is only one header and footer for each report.

5. Programmable sections are not present in AX 2012. To display designs conditionally, use expressions for the visible property.

6. This completes the migration of a report.

Developing the controller

If your report also uses `RunbaseReport`, then proceed with the following steps:

1. **Multiple design/reports**: If the `RunbaseReport` class chooses the report or design at runtime, a controller must be created in AX 2012. The controller class can be used to choose the report at runtime.

2. If the ranges in the query are modified based on the caller in the `RunbaseReport` class or in the report, use the controller class in AX 2012.

Handling UI events

UI events can be handled as follows:

1. **Adding dialog fields**: Simple dialog will be constructed by the framework, using the contract parameters. If any dialog modifications are required, create a UI controller class.

2. **Reacting to the dialog field changes**: Any changes such as lookup modification or dependency fields must be implemented in the UI controller class.

3. **Validations**: Any validations must be placed in the contract class.

4. **Align the report dialog controls**: Use `SysOperationAttribute` to order the controls in a contract class. For more complex restructuring, use the Visual Studio parameter nodes to create groups.

See also

- The *Calling multiple reports from a controller* recipe in *Chapter 3, A Report Programming Models*

- The *Adding ranges from unbound parameters to the query* recipe in *Chapter 3, A Report Programming Models*

- The *Modifying the report query in the controller* recipe in *Chapter 3, A Report Programming Models*

- *Adding data methods in business logic* recipe in *Chapter 3, A Report Programming Models*

- The *Grouping and ordering controls in a report dialog*

Analyzing and modifying an existing report

This recipe is to guide you on how you can approach to identify the components involved in an existing report, either for the purpose of upgrading your report or to make your customizations. The easiest way would be updating a cross-reference but the chances of having a cross-reference updated system are low and hence this recipe will help you proceed with an approach that doesn't require the cross-reference to be updated.

How to do it...

An existing report can be analyzed and modified as follows:

1. The first step is to identify the report you need to work on. Here are several places where your starting point might be and the corresponding methods to find the report name:

   - **Moving from AX 2009**: If you are moving from AX 2009, use the following links to search for the report name in the current version, `http://technet.microsoft.com/EN-US/library/gg731909.aspx`, if it doesn't exist, check at `http://technet.microsoft.com/EN-US/library/gg731897.aspx`. This will help you identify the report name.

   - **End user tells the main menu navigation**: If the main menu navigation is known, navigate to **AOT | Menus**. Expand the corresponding module and identify the output menu item. If the menu item is connected to a controller class, and check the **Linked Permission Object** property for the name of the report, whether the **Linked Permission Type** is **SSRSReport**; otherwise, open the controller class and look for the `parmReportName` method to identify the reports that are being used for the controller.

- **Knowing the report name but not sure which report layout is used**: Say from the previous step you identify the controller but are still not sure which layout is used, since there are many layouts being referenced, then use this approach. Place the debugger at `\Forms\SrsReportViewer\Methods\init` and when the debugger hits this point, choose `Classes\SrsReportRunController` from the stack trace and look for the `reportname` variable under **this** in the watch window. This will clearly indicate the report name and design. This will also help you identify the controller.

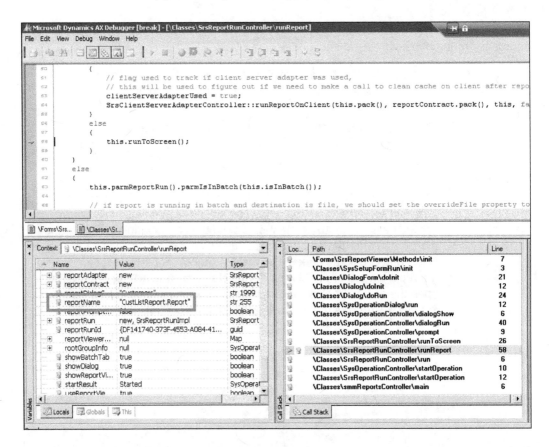

- **Searching for an example**: If you are looking for an example report to learn about a certain type of report, download the Excel sheet from `http://www.microsoft.com/download/en/details.aspx?id=27877`. This contains the complete list of reports with different details based on their usage, design, and so on. This can help you choose the report that might serve you as a good example.

2. After knowing your report name, the next step is to explore the kind of data sources used in it. To do this, navigate to your report, right-click and navigate to **Add-ins | Cross reference | Using (Instant View)**.

> This will work even if your cross reference is not updated.

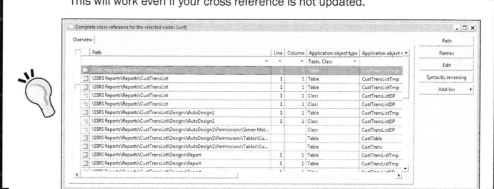

3. This will help you identify the query, temporary table, RDP contract, and any business logic project present as part of the report. What you don't find is the Visual Studio project to which the report belongs.

4. There are two ways to find the project; one is to go by the naming convention. The standard naming convention for a project is <ReportName>Report. For example, `CustTransListReport`. In case you don't find it, the alternate way is to visit `http://msdn.microsoft.com/EN-US/library/hh496433.aspx`, where all the reports are listed with the associated project name.

5. If you identify that the report uses RDP, the next step is to figure out if it has any contract and if the UI builder is being used. To identify the contract, navigate to the RDP class and on the class declaration look for the contract class passed to `SRSReportParameterAttribute`. The `SRSReportQueryAttribute` will help you identify the query that it uses.

6. Further, the contract class can be optionally associated with a UI builder. To identify the UI builder adopt the same approach that was used for identifying the contract.

7. The report can have an RDL contract and optionally a UI builder as well; finding an RDL contract without the cross reference updated is not a straightforward approach. The best approach here would be trying to go by the naming convention; if that is not successful, use the type hierarchy browser.

8. Navigate to the `SRSReportRDLDataContract`, right-click on **Add-ins** and select **Type Hierarchy Browser**. The **Type Hierarchy Browser** window shows all the extended classes from where you can shortlist the appropriate RDL contract class. Following these steps can help you identify all the artifacts related to your report.

9. **Modifying your report**: There are different approaches that can be adopted in modifying a report design and the choice depends on the level of requirements. Here are a few approaches that you can adopt:

    1. **Modify the design**: Use this approach when the number of changes are minimal and are not country/context specific. If too many changes are made, it becomes cumbersome to handle changes when the standard report is modified in later releases. This is the simplest of all that are discussed and similarly can be adopted only for minor changes.

    2. **Create a new design**: Here, the standard design is duplicated and the design is altered. Use this approach when the report is heavily modified or you are implementing it for a specific country but the RDP contract and UI builder can still be shared. The choice of the design at runtime can be made through the controller class.

    3. **Create a new report**: A completely new report is designed and used instead of the existing report. Adopt this approach when the RDP logic used by the standard report or the UI classes cannot be shared and the report also goes for deeper changes. The reports, however, can share the temp table and contract if possible.

10. **Merging changes**: Modifying a standard report throws up new challenges such as manageability in the longer run, since each cumulative update release from Microsoft can bring in more changes to the report design. As of now, there are no efficient tools inside AX for merging report changes. There are no references from Microsoft but there are a few blogs that discuss widely about the usage of external code-compare tools to do the merge. Though it is not a standard approach it can work. Please visit `http://www.k3technical.com/using-code-compare-to-merge-ssrs-reports-in-dynamics-ax-2012/` to understand how you could merge changes between different layers.

How it works...

The steps discussed in the recipe, help you in identifying all the components involved in a typical reporting project. Create a separate project and add the elements to it; this will make it easier to perform the required changes. Also apply the design guidelines to see how you can accommodate the changes.

Implementing validation in reports

Validations are important to ensure integrity of the process, here in this recipe, let us see how we can implement validations for reports.

Getting ready

The example discussed is extending the `InventBatch` report discussed in *Creating an advanced RDP report* in *Chapter 4, Report Programming Model – RDP*.

How to do it...

You can implement validation in the reports, as follows:

1. To make a parameter mandatory in the report model in Visual studio, expand and open the parameter that you wish to make mandatory. On the **Properties** node ensure the **AllowBlank** property is **False**. Modify it to **True** if the parameter needs to be optional. This property by default is **False**, so any property is mandatory by default. Also, you can use a default value if you want. This is particularly useful for Boolean type of parameters where the default value can be **True** in some cases.

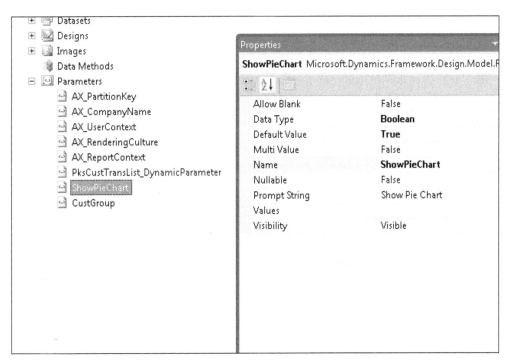

2. Sometimes, the validations go beyond verifying mandatory; in that case, the validate operation must be implemented in the contract. As we have learned from the previous chapters, there are two kinds of contracts and in the next steps, let us see how to implement the validations in each of the contracts.

3. To implement the validation in an RDP contract, the contract must implement the `SysOperationValidatable` interface. Once this interface is implemented, the `validate` method is automatically triggered by the framework.

4. After implementing the interface, write the `validate` method. This `validate` method can be used to place all your validations. Here is an example of how the validation might look like:

```
class PktInventBatchTransContract implements
  SysOperationValidatable
{
}
public boolean validate()
{
   boolean isValid;

   if (this.parmProdDate() > today())
   {
      error("Production date must be in the past.");
      isValidate = false;
   }
}
```

5. In case of an RDL contract, the approach differs. There is no need to extend the interface since the RDL base class `SSRReportRdlDatacontract` already implements it. Override the `validate` method from the base class and write your validation, as follows:

```
[
    SrsReportNameAttribute(ssrsReportStr(PktRdlCustTransList,
   CustTransList)),
    SysOperationContractProcessingAttribute(classstr(PktRdlCust
   TransListUIBuilder))
]

class PktRdlCustTransListRdlContract extends
  SrsReportRdlDataContract
{
   Date fromDate, ToDate;

   #define.FromDate('FromDate')
```

```
      #define.ToDate('ToDate')
   }

   public boolean validate()
   {

     boolean isValid = super();

     fromDate = this.getValue(#FromDate);
     toDate = this.getValue(#ToDate);

     if(fromDate && toDate)
     {
       if(fromDate > toDate)
       {
         isValid = checkFailed("@SYS120590");
       }
     }

      return isValid;
   }
```

How it works...

Implementing validations in a report is summarized as follows:

- **RDP contract validation:** The RDP contract validation is invoked by verifying if the contract class is implementing the interface. The framework triggers a validate call, automatically after the user input. This is because the RDP contract doesn't extend any class unlike the RDL contract.

- **RDL contract validation:** The RDL contract has a base class `SRSReportRDLDataContract` and it is used for all reports. The base class carries the framework-level validations for the reports. To implement a custom validation for a specific report, extend this class and decorate it with the attributes to indicate the report for which it should work. Since the RDL contract stores and retrieves values based on their names, the first lines in the `validate` method are to retrieve the values followed by the validation logic. Remember not to prevent the `super` method as it contains the validations.

Surrogate fields in reports

The surrogate key that was introduced with AX 2012 is a powerful feature but at times creates ambiguity on the usage. The goal of this recipe is to clarify and showcase examples that use surrogate keys in the possible patterns. This is divided into two sections; the first section will discuss the usage of surrogate keys in a query based report, followed by the second section that details the application in RDP-based reports.

How to do it...

The following steps show how to implement surrogate fields in reports:

1. To be able to implement this recipe, we will use the example of Student and Student Marks tables. Create these tables and relate the Student Marks table to the Student table, using the surrogate key. For the Student table add student id as replacement key in the table properties:

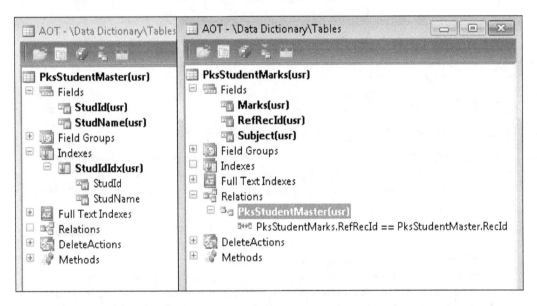

2. Create the surrogate key by creating a new relation in Student Marks and then using the options **New | Foreign Key | Primary Key Based**. On the relations property make sure **CreateNavigationPropertyMethods** is set to **Yes**.

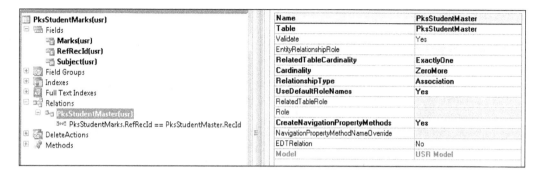

Name	PksStudentMaster
Table	PksStudentMaster
Validate	Yes
EntityRelationshipRole	
RelatedTableCardinality	ExactlyOne
Cardinality	ZeroMore
RelationshipType	Association
UseDefaultRoleNames	Yes
RelatedTableRole	
Role	
CreateNavigationPropertyMethods	Yes
NavigationPropertyMethodNameOverride	
EDTRelation	No
Model	USR Model

3. Add a method that returns the student ID in the `Students Marks` table, similar to the following code:

```
public display PktStudId studId()
{
    return this.PktStudentMaster().StudId;
}
```

Surrogate keys in query-based reports

Surrogate keys can be implemented in query-based reports, as follows:

1. Create a query for the `Student Marks` table and add the surrogate key to the range.

2. Open Visual Studio and create a new reporting project and add a new report. Add a new dataset to the report and click on the datasource property. In the query prompt window, select the query that was created, and in the fields selection window you will see the display method that was written for student ID. Check the display method and once you click on **OK**, you will see it gets added as a dataset field. This is one way to bring the information from related tables through a surrogate key.

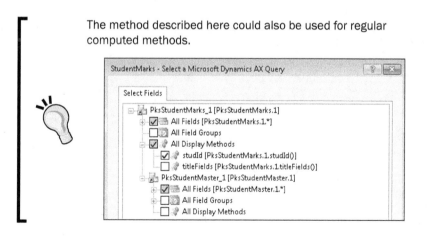

The method described here could also be used for regular computed methods.

3. Now deploy and run the report in AX. When the report opens up, the range is seen as `Recid`. This may not be a convenient way for the user to make the selection. This approach can be used when the report needs to show only the relation and no selection is needed.

4. For reports that use the `selection` field from the parent table, adopt the approach where the parent table is added as a child datasource. Drop all the fields, leaving only the relevant field that needs to appear in the selection dialog and in the report. In this case, the `student master` is added to the child datasource and the `student id` is added to the range. The rest of the report remains the same. So when a report dialog is shown, the user is able to see the students list instead of `recid`.

Surrogate keys in RDP

Surrogate keys can be implemented in RDP, as follows:

1. In an RDP report, the temporary table that is created can be used to directly store the replacement values. In this example report, the temporary table for student's marks will have the `student id` field instead of `ref RecId`.

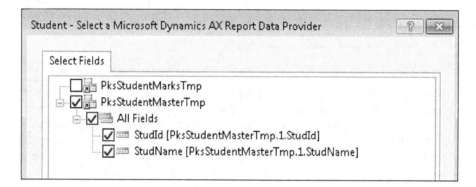

2. Create an RDP for this temporary table. The process report method must be a simple query that fills this temporary table as follows:

```
[SysEntryPointAttribute(false)]
public void processReport()
{
    Query                   query;
    QueryRun                queryRun;
    QueryBuildRange         studIdRange;
    QueryBuildDataSource    qbds;

    PktStudentMarks           studMarks;
    PktStudentMarksContract   studContract;
```

```
studContract = this.parmDataContract() as
PktStudentMarksContract;

query = new query();
qbds = query.addDataSource(tableNum(PktStudentMarks));

//set the range
studIdRange = SysQuery::findOrCreateRange(qbds,
   fieldNum(PktStudentMarks,     RefRecId));

   studIdRange.value(int642str(studContract.parmStudIdSFK()));

queryRun = new queryRun(query);

while (queryRun.next())
{
   studMarks = queryRun.get(tableNum(PktStudentMarks));
   this.insertTmpTable(studMarks);
}
}
```

3. The contract has the surrogate key as the parm method, since the `StudentMarks` don't have other values:

```
[
   DataMemberAttribute('StudentId'),
   SysOperationLabelAttribute(literalStr("Student")),
   SysOperationHelpTextAttribute(literalStr("Student
   Details")),
   SysOperationDisplayOrderAttribute('1')
]
public StudISurrogateKey parmStudIdSFK(StudISurrogateKey
   _idSFK = idSFK)
{
   idSFK = _idSFK;

   return idSFK;
}
```

4. Create a report in Visual Studio, and add the RDP created as a datasource. Preview and deploy the report to AX.

5. When you open the report, you can see that the lookup appears for the replacement key and not the surrogate key. When the user selects the student ID the appropriate `recid` is stored in the contract.

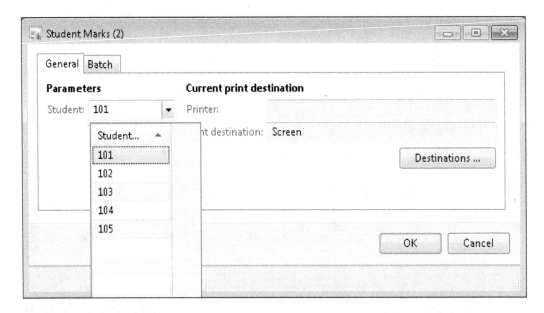

How it works...

Summarizing the approach of surrogate keys in reports:

1. **Surrogate keys in query-based reports**:

    1. If you want the replacement fields only to be displayed in the report, use display methods present in the table.

    2. If the replacement values are added as selection fields, use a multilevel query where the parent table is added as a child datasource, and the appropriate replacement keys are retained from the child data source.

2. **Surrogate keys in RDP reports**:

    1. Create new fields in the temporary table for the replacement fields and fill them in the RDP class.

    2. If the contract uses a surrogate key as the parm method, the lookup is shown appropriately, based on the replacement key set up in the table.

Spin-off idea

For the RDP report discussed here, try to increase the replacement key to more than one field and see how the report dialog behaves. In this case, the student name is also added along with the student ID. The resulting dialog is as seen in the following image:

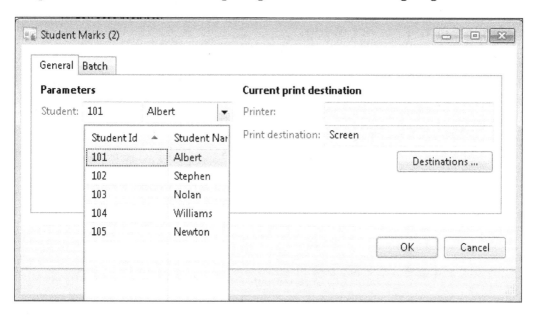

Grouping and ordering controls in a report dialog

A report dialog is constructed automatically by the UI builder in Sysoperationframework, but sometimes you want to influence how the controls are visualized in the dialog. In this recipe, let us see the different options available for grouping and ordering controls in the report. There are multiple options for this; we will start with a simple grouping mechanism and move on to the sophisticated changes.

Getting ready

This recipe will extend the PktRDLCustTransList report built in *Chapter 3, A Report Programming Model* and the PktInventBatchTrans report built in *Chapter 4, Report Programming Model – RDP*.

How to do it...

This section will discuss how to perform grouping control at the model level, that is, in the VS editor, followed by how to implement it in the UI builder and at contract level.

Grouping in the report model

This applies to the RDP and query-based reports:

1. In the Visual Studio report, expand the parameters node. Right-click and navigate to **Add | Parameter Group**. Specify the **Date Range** label in the caption property. Drag the **FromDate** and **ToDate** controls into the report.

2. Similarly add another group called **Options** and specify the label.

3. Create another parameter group, drag both the groups inside this new group and modify the layout direction to **Horizontal**. This will align all the components inside a group in the horizontal direction while the default mode is vertical:

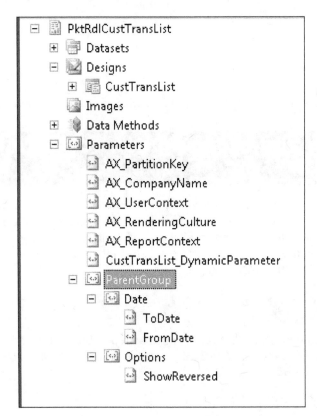

4. Save and deploy the report. The modified report dialog should appear as follows:

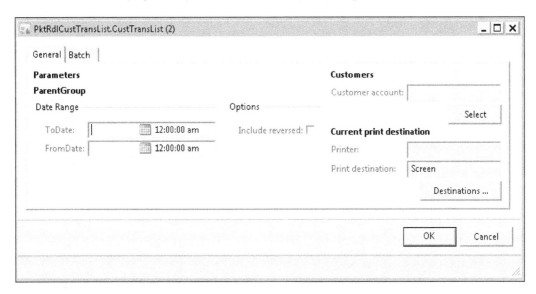

When creating report parameters that are hidden from the end user, follow the best practices for creating a separate hidden group. This will help easily identify the fields that are part of the report parameters but are not exposed to the user.

Grouping in the UI builder

This grouping mechanism can be applied to both RDP and query-based reports:

1. The modification here is done completely in the UI builder. Open the `PktRdlCustTransListUIBuilder` UI builder.

2. Declare a new field in the class declaration for a dialog group:

```
class PktRdlCustTransListUIBuilder extends
SrsReportDataContractUIBuilder
{
    DialogField dialogFromDate;
    DialogField dialogToDate;
    DialogField dialogReversed;

    DialogGroup dialogDateGroup;

    #define.ShowReversedParam('ShowReversed')
```

```
      #define.FromDate('FromDate')
      #define.ToDate('ToDate')
   }
```

3. Modify the `addDateFields` method to include a new group. Additionally, we will make this group into a checkbox-enabled group. This deactivates the entire group control, if the checkbox is deactivated.

 The other important change noticeable here is setting the number of columns to 2. If this is not set up, the groups will get added vertically.

```
private void addDateFields()
{
   dialog                           dialogLocal;
   PktRdlCustTransListRdlContract   transContract;
   SRSReportParameter               reportParameter;
   FormBuildGroupControl            buildGroupControl;

   dialogLocal     = this.dialog();
      buildGroupControl = dialogLocal.curFormGroup();
   buildGroupControl.columns(2);

   transContract   =
      this.getRdlContractInfo().dataContractObject()
         as PktRdlCustTransListRdlContract;

   dialogDateGroup = dialogLocal.addGroup("Date Range");
   dialogDateGroup.frameOptionButton
      (FormFrameOptionButton::Check);
   //enabled by default
   dialogDateGroup.optionValue(1);

   dialogFromDate  = dialogLocal.
      addFieldValue(extendedTypeStr(FromDate),
         DatetimeUtil::date
            (transContract.getValue(#FromDate)),"@SYS5209");
   dialogToDate   = dialogLocal.addFieldValue(
      extendedTypeStr(ToDate),DatetimeUtil::date
         (transContract.getValue(#ToDate)),"@SYS14656");
}
```

4. Now when the report is opened, the report dialog has a new group with a checkbox at the top. The checkbox can be used to enable and disable the controls under this group.

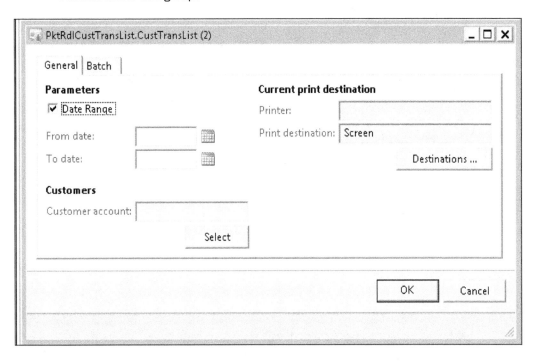

Grouping in the contract

The grouping mechanism described here applies only to RDP-based reports.

1. In the RDP contract for the `PktInventBatchTrans` report, modify the class declaration to add two new groups. This will add groups to the report dialog:

```
[
    DataContractAttribute,
    SysOperationContractProcessingAttribute
        (classStr(PktInventBatchTransUIBuilder),
            SysOperationDataContractProcessingMode::
                CreateUIBuilderForRootContractOnly),
                SysOperationGroupAttribute('BatchGroup',
                    "Batch",'1'),SysOperationGroupAttribute
                        ('DateGroup', "Date", '2')
]
class PktInventBatchTransContract implements
```

```
       SysOperationValidatable
       {
           InventDimViewContract          inventDimViewContract;
           InventBatchProdDate            prodDate;
           InventBatchId                  batchId;
           boolean                        dummyValue;
       }
```

2. Modify the `BatchId` and `ProdDate` parm methods to include the new attributes:

```
       [
           DataMemberAttribute('Batch'),
             SysOperationGroupMemberAttribute('BatchGroup'),
               SysOperationDisplayOrderAttribute('1')
       ]
       public InventBatchId parmBatchId(InventBatchId _batchId =
         batchId)
       {
         batchId = _batchId;

         return batchId;
       }


       [
           DataMemberAttribute('ProdDate'),
             SysOperationGroupMemberAttribute('DateGroup'),
               SysOperationDisplayOrderAttribute('1')
       ]
       public InventBatchProdDate parmProdDate(InventBatchProdDate
         _prodDate = prodDate)
       {
         prodDate = _prodDate;

         return prodDate;
       }
```

3. Include a new dummy parm attribute to verify the display order:

```
       [
           DataMemberAttribute('Verifydisporder'),
             SysOperationGroupMemberAttribute('DateGroup'),
               SysOperationDisplayOrderAttribute('2'),
                 SysOperationLabelAttribute("Dummy Value")
       ]
```

```
public boolean parmDummyValue(boolean _prodDate =
  dummyValue)
{
  dummyValue = _prodDate;

  return dummyValue;
}
```

4. Run the report to see that two new groups, **Date** and **Batch** are added. The dummy value appears second since its display order attribute was 2:

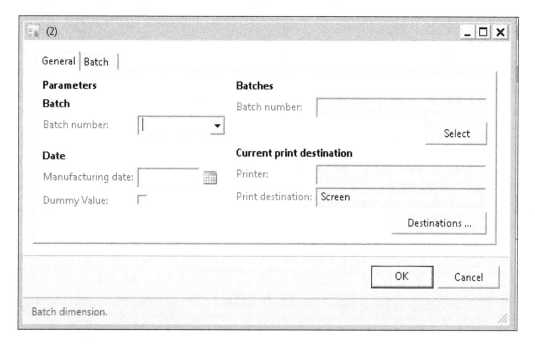

How it works...

In this section, we saw several short recipes that explain how you can control grouping in reports. The important point to keep in mind is what sort of grouping works for what kind of report. In case of query-based reports, only the first two models apply, while all three models can be used for RDP.

In the RDP contract, choose one of the grouping methods, either the RDP contract or the Visual Studio method. The Visual Studio grouping overrides the RDP grouping.

RDP with multiple temporary tables

This is another simple recipe that will show you the possibility of using RDP with multiple temporary tables. RDP is a data provider, and a single RDP can be used to create different datasets in the report. Walk through this recipe to understand how this can be done.

Getting ready

This recipe requires you to complete the report discussed in the *Surrogate fields in reports* recipe in this chapter.

How to do it...

An RDP can be used with multiple temporary tables, as follows:

1. In this recipe, we will use the `Student` table that we used for the *Surrogate fields in reports* recipe. Create two temporary tables `Student` and `Student Marks`.

2. Create an RDP class that will fill these two tables, using the process report method. Generally the RDP has a method with `SRSReportDataSetAttribute` that is used to return the temporary table. When you have more than one temporary table, create two methods, one for each temporary table as follows:

```
[
    SRSReportDataSetAttribute(tableStr(PksStudentMasterTmp))
]
public PksStudentMasterTmp getStudentTemp()
{
    select studentTmp;
    return studentTmp;
}


[
    SRSReportDataSetAttribute(tableStr(PksStudentMarksTmp))
]
public PksStudentMarksTmp getStudentmarksTemp()
{
    select studentMarksTmp;
    return studentMarksTmp;
}
```

3. Open Visual Studio, create a report and on the new dataset, select RDP. Click on the **Query** node and select the RDP just created. There will be two datasets that will be returned by the RDP, one for each temporary table; add the Student dataset to the report:

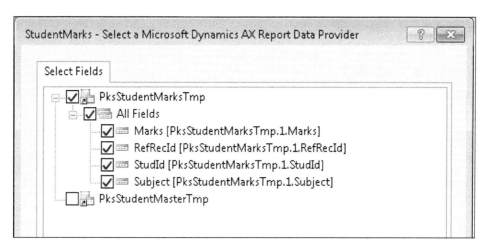

4. Similarly, add another dataset and use the RDP. Follow the similar process to choose the second temporary table, Student Marks.

5. The two datasets are not related in AX and are independent of each other. In this example, we create two multiple data regions where one lists Students and the other lists Student Marks.

6. Drag the datasets to create two different data regions and then run it to see the data being rendered.

How it works...

The standard reports such as SalesInvoice and SalesConfirm adopt the same approach. In these cases, there is a header table that stores all the header-related information such as company address, email, and VATnum that is common across all reports while the other stores the line-level information. RDP can return any number of temporary tables and not just two.

Multi-value lookup

All the report dialog controls that we have seen so far in this book only store a single value, but there can be cases where you want the users to be able to choose multiple values. This recipe is going to show you how to do it.

Getting ready

This recipe will extend `PKtInventBatchReport` built in *Chapter 4, Report Programming Model – RDP*.

How to do it...

A multi-value look lookup can be implemented in reports, as follows:

1. This recipe will add a multi-value lookup for the batch ID, so that the user can select multiple batches to be printed in the report. The first step is to create a parm method in the contract of list type. The parm method should appear as follows:

```
[
    DataMemberAttribute('MultipleBatch'),
    SysOperationLabelAttribute("Multiple Batch"),
    AifCollectionTypeAttribute('return', Types::String)
]
public List parmMultiBatch(List _multiBatch = multiBatch)
{
    multiBatch = _multiBatch;
    return multiBatch;
}
```

2. Once the parm method is added, the dialog already shows a report with a list control, but the lookup has no values in it. To enable the lookup, the UI builder class must be modified. The framework makes it very easy to add lookup for multi-select controls, even the override of the event is automatically done. Use the following code to enable multi-batch lookup:

```
class PktInventBatchTransUIBuilder extends
SysOperationAutomaticUIBuilder
{
    DialogField batchDialog, dateDialog;
    DialogField multiBatchDialog;
}
```

```
public void multiBatchLookup()
{
  Query          query;
  QueryBuildData qbds;
  TableId        multiSelectTableNum = tableNum(InventBatch);
  container      selectedFields      = [multiSelectTableNum,
    fieldName2id(multiSelectTableNum, fieldStr(InventBatch,
      InventBatchId))];


  query = new Query();
  qbds = query.addData(tableNum(InventBatch));
  qbds.addSelectionField(fieldNum(InventBatch,
    InventBatchId));
  qbds.addSelectionField(fieldNum(InventBatch, ItemId));


  SysLookupMultiSelectCtrl::constructWithQuery
    (this.dialog().dialogForm().formRun(),
      multiBatchDialog.control(), query, false,
        selectedFields);
}

public void postRun()
{
  //super();

  this.multiBatchLookup();
}
```

3. We have so far added the list control and enabled a multi-value lookup, the next step
    is to use it in the RDP class. To do this, modify the RDP class in the process report
    method, where the list values are enumerated and added to the query range:

```
[
  SysEntryPointAttribute(false)
]
public void processReport()
{
  Query                  query;
  QueryRun               queryRun;
  QueryBuildRange        batchRange, dateRange;
  QueryBuildDataSource   qbds;
```

```
InventBatch              inventBatch;
InventTrans              inventTrans;
InventDim                inventDim;
InventTransOrigin        transOrigin;

InventDimViewContract       viewContract;
PktInventBatchTransContract batchContract;

List                     batchList;
ListEnumerator           listEnumerator;

batchContract = this.parmDataContract() as
  PktInventBatchTransContract;
viewContract  =
  batchContract.parmInventDimViewContract();

query = this.parmQuery();
qbds = query.dataSourceTable(tableNum(InventBatch));

if (batchContract.parmProdDate())
{
  dateRange = SysQuery::findOrCreateRange(qbds,
    fieldNum(InventBatch, ProdDate));
  dateRange.value(SysQuery::value(
    batchContract.parmProdDate()));
}

batchList = batchContract.parmMultiBatch();
listEnumerator = batchList.getEnumerator();

//copy the range from the list to the
//to the query
while (listEnumerator.moveNext())
{
  dateRange = qbds.addRange(fieldNum(InventBatch,
    InventBatchId));
  dateRange.value(SysQuery::value(
    listEnumerator.current()));
}

info(query.dataSourceNo(1).toString());

queryRun = new queryRun(query);
```

```
while (queryRun.next())
{
  if (queryRun.changed(tablenum(InventBatch)))
  {
    inventBatch = queryRun.get(tableNum(InventBatch));
  }

  if (queryRun.changed(tablenum(InventTransOrigin)))
  {
    transOrigin =
      queryRun.get(tableNum(InventTransOrigin));
  }

  inventTrans = queryRun.get(tableNum(InventTrans));
  inventDim   = queryRun.get(tableNum(inventDim));

  this.insertTmpTable(inventBatch, transOrigin,
    inventTrans, inventDim);
}

}
```

4. Open the Visual Studio project for the report, expand the dataset and refresh the dataset by right-clicking and selecting **Refresh**. This will add the new contract parameter to the report. Optionally, set the values such as **AllowBlank** and **Nullable**.

5. Run the report and see that the report dialog shows multiple values:

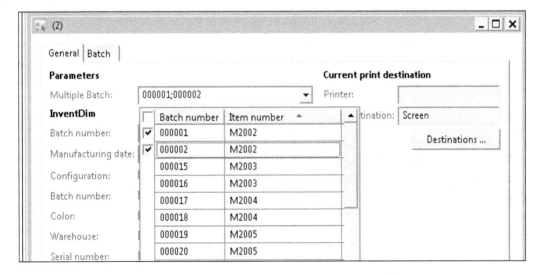

How it works...

Multi-value lookups are easy to build due to the framework support offered in building lookups and in maintaining list values. Care must be taken to appropriately use the list data returned from multi-select in RDPs.

Inventory dimensions in reports

The inventory dimensions is like a lifeline for trade and logistics and its presence in reports is indispensable. There is usually a good framework support for the inventory dimension in AX and that continues in the reporting framework. We will explore how to use the standard framework to easily handle inventory dimensions in this recipe. This recipe will also demonstrate nested contract through this example.

The recipe will add inventory dimensions to the report design and create control parameters that determine if an inventory dimension is displayed in the report.

Getting ready

This recipe will extend `PKtInventBatchReport` built in *Chapter 4, Report Programming Model – RDP*.

How to do it...

Inventory dimensions can be implemented in reports, as follows:

1. Modify the temporary table of the report to include the dimension field.
2. Open the contract and then add a parm method as in the following code. This will add a Boolean flag for each `inventdim` field:

```
[
  DataMemberAttribute('InventDimViewContract'),
  SysOperationControlVisibilityAttribute(false)
]
public InventDimViewContract
  parmInventDimViewContract(InventDimViewContract
    _inventDimViewContract = inventDimViewContract)
{
  inventDimViewContract = _inventDimViewContract;

  return inventDimViewContract;
}
```

3. Modify the process report method to fetch the inventory dimension, using **inventrans** and fill the temporary table. The code changes are that simple and completed with this step.

4. Open the corresponding Visual Studio report, expand the **Refresh** dataset. The new fields will be added to the dataset and the parameters will also show the Boolean dimensions flag for each dimension.

5. Open the precision design and modify the design to include the dimensions from the dataset. The next step is to enable these dimensions based on their corresponding parameter.

6. On the **Row Group** and **Column Group** window at the bottom-right corner, click on the dropdown and select the **Advanced Mode** option. This will make the static control visible in the column group:

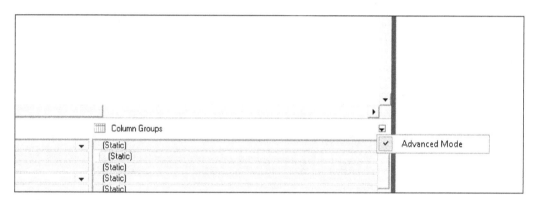

7. Each static control represents one column in the active row. Identify the column count where the inventory dimensions start, and traverse to the corresponding static control column. On the left, the **Properties** window will show the property for each control. Once the static control is selected, choose the hidden property from the **Properties** window. Open the expression editor and enter the following expression:

```
"=Not(Parameters!InventBatchTrans_ViewConfigId.Value)"
```

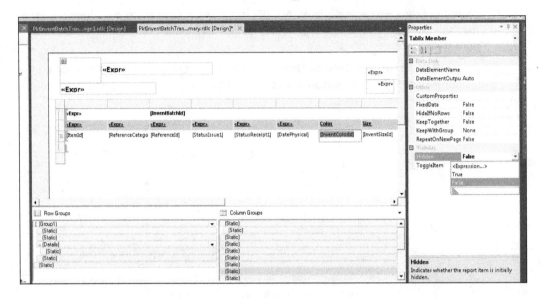

8. Build and deploy the report. The report dialog will show all the inventory dimension parameters and choosing the parameter should print it in the report:

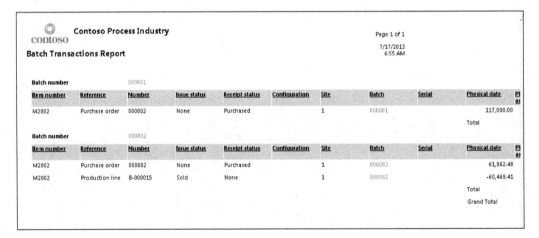

How it works...

Nested data contract: A nested data contract is a sort of an abstraction where commonly used parameters can be grouped and used in other contracts. The usage of an RDP contract is not much different from the other parm methods, except that it returns a class object. The framework automatically creates the parameters in the report design and the dialog by expanding it. The recipe uses `InventDimViewContract` as a nested contract, avoiding the hassle of rebuilding the entire list of parm methods.

Financial dimensions in reports

As inventory dimension influence trade and logistics reports, so does financial dimensions for finance reports. In this recipe, we will extensively see how financial dimensions can be used in the design of a report, in the report dialog, and so on. There are two recipes discussed, one is using financial dimension in a simple query report and the other is based on an RDP report.

Financial dimensions in query reports

This report will discuss how to use dimensions in a simple query-based report.

How to do it...

Financial dimensions can be used in reports, as follows:

1. Create a new query and add the `LedgerJournalTrans` table. Set the **Dynamic field** property to **Yes**.

2. In Visual Studio, create a new project. Create a new report and add a dataset.

3. In the query property, click on the **Browse** button to open the query list. Select the query that was created and check the **journalNum**, **Txt**, and **LedgerDimension_String** fields.

4. Expand the **AXDimensions** node. This shows all the applicable dimensions for this query. Select **CostCenter**, **Department** and click on **Ok**.

5. Drag the dataset to the auto design node to create the design. Previewing the report shows all the **ledgerjournaltrans** records with the **Costcenter** and **Department** dimensions.

6. To add a filter based on this dimension, implement the following steps:

   1. Create a new parameter under the parameters node of string type.
   2. Click on the ellipsis button on the **Values** property.
   3. This shows the value window. Here select the **From Dataset** radio button, followed by setting the following field values:

Property	Value
Dataset	LedgerDimension
Value Field	Department
Label Field	Department

7. Step 6 will help the user to choose the value that he wants to filter. This filter value must be passed on to the query so that the data is filtered. The easiest way to do this is to create a filter, in the table data region.

8. In the filters node in auto design, right-click on the **Filters** node and click on the **Add Filter** option. In the new filter set the following properties:

Property	Value
Expression	=Fields!Department.Value
Name	DepartmentFilter
Operator	Equals
Value	=Parameters!DepartmentParameter.Value

9. The filter region restricts the data that shown in the auto design. So when the report is previewed, the report shows only the dimension selected by the user:

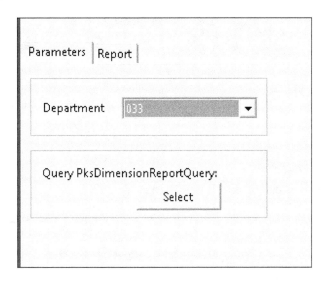

| Parameters | Report |
| Department | 033 ▼ |

Query PksDimensionReportQuery:

Select

LedgerDimension   Page 1 of 1
Contoso Retail USA   7/17/2013
LedgerDimension   5:54 PM

Journal batch number	Description	Account	CostCenter	Department
00001		112100--033-5637144576-ANNAPOL-1-000073		033
00007		112100--033-5637144576-ANNAPOL-1-000073		033
00007		112120--033-5637144576-ANNAPOL-1-000073		033
00001		112120--033-5637144576-ANNAPOL-1-000073		033

How it works...

The AX query framework is programmed to automatically bring up the dimensions related to a dimension record. These are the reason behind the query showing all the dimensions table while what was actually added was only `LedgerJournalTrans`.

The lookup setup works by executing the query and retrieving all the values from the database, using the query. This is then exposed in the lookup and when the user selects the value, it is applied to the auto design filter. It is important to understand that when using filters the whole query is executed, since filters restrict data only in the specific region.

Financial dimensions in RDP reports

This recipe will extend the simple steps that we learned in the previous recipe to build a more sophisticated report. In this report, the user will be given the option to choose a dimension and a range for it. The report will list all the general journal entries for the selected dimension in the specified range.

How to do it...

The financial dimensions can be added in RDP reports, as follows:

1. Since this is an RDP report, start with creating a temporary table as follows:

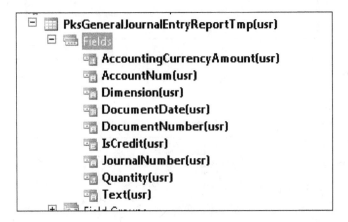

2. Create a new contract with the following code. The contract has four fields, one for the account, one for the dimension attribute, and the other two for the dimension ranges:

```
[
    DataContractAttribute,
        SysOperationContractProcessingAttribute
            (classStr(PktGeneralJournalReportUIBuilder),
                SysOperationDataContractProcessingMode::
                    CreateUIBuilderForRootContractOnly)
]
class PktGeneralJournalReportContract
{
    Name            dimensionAttribute;
    MainAccountNum  account;
    DimensionValue  fromDimensionValue;
```

```
  DimensionValue  toDimensionValue;
}


[
  DataMemberAttribute('Account'),
  SysOperationLabelAttribute(literalStr("@SYS182387")),
  SysOperationDisplayOrderAttribute('1')
]
public MainAccountNum parmAccount(
  MainAccountNum _account = account)
{
  account = _account;
  return account;
}
[
  DataMemberAttribute('DimensionAttribute'),
  SysOperationLabelAttribute(literalStr("@SYS24410")),
  SysOperationDisplayOrderAttribute('5')
]
public Name parmDimensionAttribute(
  Name _dimensionAttribute = dimensionAttribute)
{
  dimensionAttribute = _dimensionAttribute;
  return dimensionAttribute;
}
[
  DataMemberAttribute('FromDimensionValue'),
  SysOperationLabelAttribute(literalStr("@SYS105870")),
  SysOperationDisplayOrderAttribute('2')
]
public DimensionValue parmFromDimensionValue(
  DimensionValue _fromDimensionValue = fromDimensionValue)
{
  fromDimensionValue = _fromDimensionValue;
  return fromDimensionValue;
}
[
  DataMemberAttribute('ToDimensionValue'),
  SysOperationLabelAttribute(literalStr("@SYS103530")),
  SysOperationDisplayOrderAttribute('6')
]
public DimensionValue parmToDimensionValue(
  DimensionValue _toDimensionValue = toDimensionValue)
{
  toDimensionValue = _toDimensionValue;
  return toDimensionValue;
}
```

3. The UI builder for the financial dimension plays a crucial role, since that is where the dimension and dimension range must be set by the user. The standard comes to our rescue by offering a whole set of logic that can be reused. This ranges from the lookup method to the validate logic. To harness this, the UI builder class must extend the `LedgerAccountReportUIBuilder` class. The UI builder implementation logic can be as follows:

```
class PktGeneralJournalReportUIBuilder extends
    LedgerAccountReportUIBuilder
{
    DialogField dialogFieldAccountName;

    Name          dimensionAttribute;

    #define.Columns(2)
    #define.DialogFieldLength(30)
}

public void build()
{
    FormBuildGroupControl    formBuildGroupControl;

    super();

    formBuildGroupControl = this.dialog().curFormGroup();
    formBUildGroupControl.columns(#Columns);
}

public void dimensionAttributeLookup(FormStringControl
    _dimensionAttributeDialogControl)
{
    super(_dimensionAttributeDialogControl);
}

public boolean dimensionAttributeModify(FormStringControl
    _dimensionAttributeDialogControl)
{
    if (dimensionAttribute != dialogFieldAttribute.value())
    {
        /*If modified "Dimension Attribute" is different with
          previous,set the "From Dimension" and "To Dimension"
            as null*/
        dialogFieldFromDimension.value('');
        dialogFieldToDimension.value('');
```

```
        dimensionAttribute = dialogFieldAttribute.value();
    }

    return true;
}

public boolean dimensionAttributeValidate(FormStringControl
    _dimensionAttribute)
{
    boolean ret;

    ret = super(_dimensionAttribute);

    return ret;
}

public void dimensionValueLookup(FormStringControl
    _dimensionValueControl)
{
    super(_dimensionValueControl);
}
public boolean dimensionValueValidate(FormStringControl
    _dimensionValue)
{
    boolean ret;

    ret = super(_dimensionValue);

    return ret;
}

protected void modifyOverrideMethod()
{
    this.overrideDialogFieldLookup(dialogFieldAttribute,
        methodStr(PktGeneralJournalReportUIBuilder,
            dimensionAttributeLookup));
    this.overrideDialogFieldLookup(dialogFieldFromDimension,
        methodStr(PktGeneralJournalReportUIBuilder,
            dimensionValuelookup));
    this.overrideDialogFieldLookup(dialogFieldToDimension,
        methodStr(PktGeneralJournalReportUIBuilder,
            dimensionValuelookup));
```

```
      this.overrideDialogFieldMethod(dialogFieldAttribute,
        methodStr(FormStringControl, Modified),
          methodStr(PktGeneralJournalReportUIBuilder,
            dimensionAttributeModify));
      this.overrideDialogFieldMethod(dialogFieldAttribute,
        methodStr(FormStringControl, Validate),
          methodStr(PktGeneralJournalReportUIBuilder,
            dimensionAttributeValidate));
      this.overrideDialogFieldMethod(dialogFieldFromDimension,
        methodStr(FormStringControl, Validate),
          methodStr(PktGeneralJournalReportUIBuilder,
            dimensionValueValidate));
      this.overrideDialogFieldMethod(dialogFieldToDimension,
        methodStr(FormStringControl, Validate),
          methodStr(PktGeneralJournalReportUIBuilder,
            dimensionValueValidate));
    }

    public void postBuild()
    {
      SysOperationUIBindInfo binfo = this.bindInfo();
      Object                 contract =
        this.dataContractObject();

      dialogFieldAttribute        =
        binfo.getDialogField(contract,
          methodStr(PktGeneralJournalReportContract,
            parmDimensionAttribute));
      dialogFieldFromDimension    =
        binfo.getDialogField(contract,
          methodStr(PktGeneralJournalReportContract,
            parmFromDimensionValue));
      dialogFieldToDimension      =
        binfo.getDialogField(contract,
          methodStr(PktGeneralJournalReportContract,
            parmToDimensionValue));
      dialogFieldAccount          =
        binfo.getDialogField(contract,
          methodStr(PktGeneralJournalReportContract,
            parmAccount));

      super();

      dialogFieldAccount.displayLength(#DialogFieldLength);
    }
```

4. The next step is to get the RDP class. Create a new RDP class and add the following code:

```
[
  SRSReportParameterAttribute(
    classStr(PktGeneralJournalReportContract))
]
class PktGeneralJournalReportDP extends
  SRSReportDataProviderBase
{
  PksGeneralJournalEntryReportTmp reportTmp;
}
[
  SRSReportDataSetAttribute(
    tableStr(PksGeneralJournalEntryReportTmp))
]
public PksGeneralJournalEntryReportTmp getJournalTmp()
{
  select   reportTmp;
  return   reportTmp;
}

private void insertinTmp(
  GeneralJournalAccountEntry            accountEntry,
  GeneralJournalEntry                   journalEntry,
  DimensionAttributeLevelValueView      restrictView,
  DimensionAttributeLevelValueView      accountValue)
{
    ;

  reportTmp.initValue();
  reportTmp.AccountNum = accountValue.DisplayValue;
  reportTmp.Quantity   = accountEntry.Quantity;
  reportTmp.AccountingCurrencyAmount =
    accountEntry.AccountingCurrencyAmount;
  reportTmp.Text        = accountEntry.Text;
  reportTmp.IsCredit   = accountEntry.IsCredit;
  reportTmp.JournalNumber = journalEntry.JournalNumber;
  reportTmp.DocumentNumber = journalEntry.DocumentNumber;
  reportTmp.DocumentDate = journalEntry.DocumentDate;
  reportTmp.Dimension     = restrictView.DisplayValue;
  reportTmp.insert();
}
```

```
  [
    SysEntryPointAttribute(false)
  ]
  public void processReport()
  {
    GeneralJournalAccountEntry        accountEntry;
    GeneralJournalEntry               journalEntry;
    DimensionAttributeLevelValueView valueView, restrictView;
    DimensionAttributeLevelValueView accountValue;

    DimensionAttribute       dimensionAttributeTable;

    PktGeneralJournalReportContract contract;

    Name            dimensionAttribute;
    MainAccountNum  account;
    DimensionValue  fromDimensionValue;
    DimensionValue  toDimensionValue;

    contract = this.parmDataContract();

    dimensionAttribute = contract.parmDimensionAttribute();
    dimensionAttributeTable =
      DimensionAttribute::findByLocalizedName(
        dimensionAttribute, false,
          SystemParameters::find().SystemLanguageId);

    fromDimensionValue = contract.parmFromDimensionValue();
    toDimensionValue   = contract.parmToDimensionValue();

    account            = contract.parmAccount();

    delete_from reportTmp;

    ttsBegin;

    while select DisplayValue from accountValue
      where   accountValue.DisplayValue == account
      join AccountingCurrencyAmount, Text, quantity from
        accountEntry
      where accountEntry.LedgerDimension ==
        accountValue.ValueCombinationRecId
        join journalNumber, DocumentDate, DocumentNumber from
```

```
journalEntry
 where journalEntry.RecId ==
accountEntry.GeneralJournalEntry
 join restrictView
 where restrictView.ValueCombinationRecId ==
  accountEntry.LedgerDimension
 &&    restrictView.DimensionAttribute    ==
   dimensionAttributeTable.RecId
 &&    restrictView.DisplayValue          >=
   fromDimensionValue
 &&    restrictView.DisplayValue          <=
   toDimensionValue
{
   this.insertinTmp(accountEntry, journalEntry,
     restrictView, accountValue);
}

ttsCommit;

}
```

5. The process report method is designed to find all general journal entries for a specific account number in a specified range. A DML is used to retrieve this data.

6. Once the coding changes are complete, create a new report in Visual Studio and link the RDP report that was just created.

7. Create a precision design with a table control as shown in the following image. Choose the fields. For the dimension attribute field in the precision design, enter =Parameters!JournalData_DimensionAttribute.Value so that the label printed will be based on the dimension selected. The image indicates how the report design would look like:

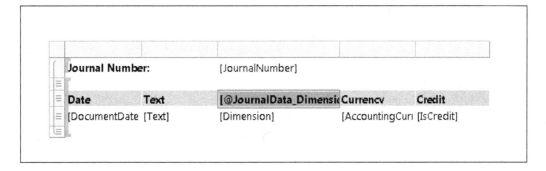

8. Compile and deploy the report. Create a menu item for the report and run the report to see whether the report prints only the specified range in the selected dimension:

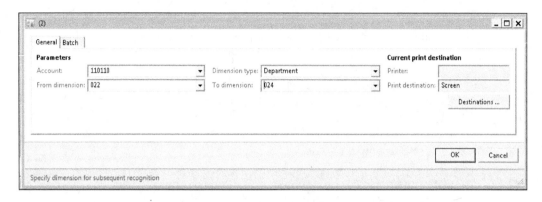

Journal Number:		000045		
Date	**Text**	**Department**	**Currency**	**Credit**
1/1/2012	Vendor invoice	023	25,325.00	No

Journal Number:		000049		
Date	**Text**	**Department**	**Currency**	**Credit**
1/1/2012	Vendor invoice	023	25,325.00	No

Journal Number:		000055		

How it works...

AX makes it really easy to add financial dimensions, using the standard support for frequently used dimension methods. In this report, the lookup for the dimension attribute and the ranges are derived from the base class.

8
Troubleshooting and Other Advanced Recipes

This chapter will cover the following recipes:

- ▸ Assessing report performance and usage
- ▸ Handling long running reports in AX
- ▸ Troubleshooting reports in AX
- ▸ Auto e-mail and Save as file tasks in reports
- ▸ Handling events post report completion
- ▸ Generating and displaying barcodes in reports
- ▸ Hiding controls by context
- ▸ Using AXEnumProvider as dataset for parameters in reports
- ▸ Adding a new report design to print management
- ▸ Deploying language-specific reports to speed up execution time
- ▸ Making your reports function better

Introduction

A good work-through with the previous chapters should have helped you gain a good command of SSRS reports by now. This chapter will help handle problems that you might face executing SSRS reports and a few handy recipes that are required over and over in report customizations, such as barcodes, hiding controls, and e-mailing. The last part has very useful inputs that can aid to get the right fundamentals for effective report development.

Assessing report performance and usage

The introduction of SSRS also brings up more interesting capabilities as we have been seeing in the last chapters. Here is another interesting aspect to add to the list; the SSRS report logs. The SSRS reports log key usage parameters into the system automatically. The free report log viewer tool can unravel a lot of useful production data that helps to understand what reports are being used, what is consuming a lot of time, and what reports fail. This recipe will throw some light on how to configure and use the log viewer for this purpose.

Getting ready

Download the SSRS report log viewer and install it from: `http://www.microsoft.com/en-us/download/details.aspx?id=24774`.

How to do it...

1. The report log viewer, by default, is installed in the following location, `Program Files (x86)\Microsoft\Reporting Services LogViewer\RSLogViewer.exe`. Open the log viewer, select the **Catalog** tab, and then click on the **Connect** button.

2. In the prompt dialog box enter the details of the report server:

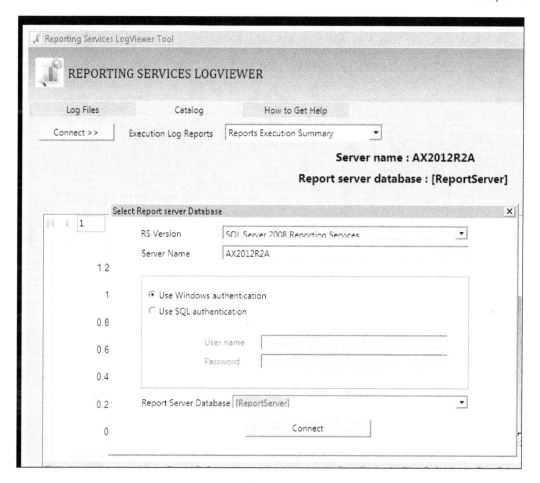

3. On the **Execution Log Reports** field choose **Reports Execution summary**. This gives a detailed insight into overall report performance. Click on **Show Filters** and apply a date range among the different kinds of ranges available.

4. These reports reveal the time for data retrieval, report processing, and report rendering for reports in the selected filter criteria:

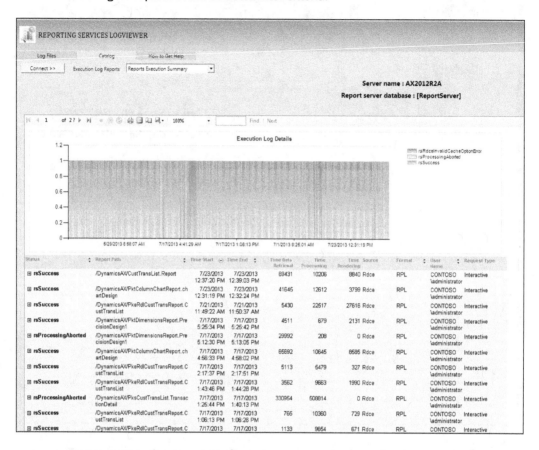

5. The **Catalog** view offers other reports, such as **Reports by User** and **Reports by Month** as seen here. These offer more beneficial parameters that help in fine-tuning the report performance and usage:

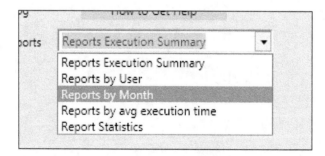

6. Here is another sample report that lists the report usage by month:

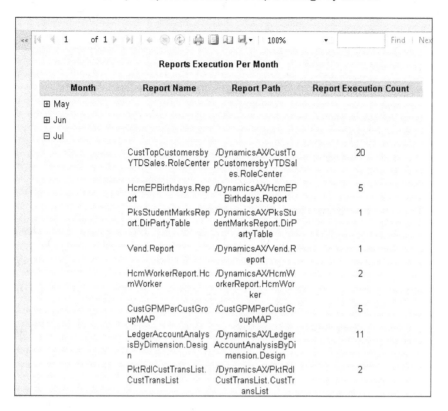

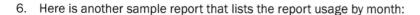

How it works...

The log viewer connects to the report server database and offers a presentable view of the data from the SQL tables. It also has the capability to analyze the logs generated; this is discussed in the section _Expression-related Issues_ under the recipe _Troubleshooting reports in AX_ in this chapter. This is a non-intrusive analysis, which means you could do this even when the production systems are up and running. There is no need to stop or restart them to have this analysis working.

Some sections in your report may not have data, but the custom header sections might print. In these cases to make it informative for the user a **No data available** message might be helpful, since the user is then assured that there is no data for that particular data section. Select the **Tablix/List/Matrix** control where you want the message to be available, and then open the properties window, Find the property **NoRowsMessage**. This property can be filled in with text or with dynamic text using expressions. Type in something, such as **No data available**.

Handling long running reports in AX

Reports are relatively used to render from a couple of pages to a larger volume of copies. There can be many cases when a report may not render the data in an acceptable performance which can be identified using tools such as the report log viewer. This recipe is to list out the various approaches that can be used to manage performance related issues in reports.

How to do it...

This section will discuss approaches to resolve long running reports through adopting best practices at design time and at runtime through configuration changes.

Design-based resolution

The following factors can be verified and modified to see if it improves the report performance. The modifications referred to here are changes to the components involved in a report and so must not be implemented in a production environment before taking it through a testing cycle:

- **Reindex**: If the report uses a query directly or uses one in RDP, see if the indexes have been properly used in the tables.

- **Restrict the data**: If no index-related issues are found, then see if the following design-level changes can be made:
  - Improve the performance by showing only a limited set of data; for example, the first 1000 records.
  - Improve the performance by limiting the data. To do this, add a range to the dialog box so that the user can narrow down the data.

- **Inefficient report parameters**: If the issue is caused by the user not utilizing the ranges and running the report for the broadest of parameters then consider implementing this change.

  On the controller method for the report, override the `prerunvalidate` method, and then write code that will warn the user based on the number of records the query might return. When the user executes this report and if it returns a large number of records, it will throw an error advising to use a better range.

```
protected container preRunValidate()
{
    /* More than 100,000 rows will take at least 12 minutes on a
warm box with low volume and not under load while 1,000 records
will take about 10 seconds, so these are used as the warning and
error limits.*/
    #Define.ErrorLimit(100000)
    #Define.WarningLimit(1000)
```

```
    /* Using the query from the contract, count up to the error
limit + 1 since anything over the error limit will return the same
error*/
    container    validateResult;
    Query        query = this.getFirstQuery();
    int          rowCount = queryRun::getQueryRowCount(query,
#ErrorLimit + 1);

    if (rowCount > #ErrorLimit)
    {
        validateResult = [SrsReportPreRunState::Error];
    }
    else if (rowCount > #WarningLimit)
    {
        validateResult = [SrsReportPreRunState::Warning];
    }
    else
    {
        validateResult = super();
    }

    return validateResult;
}
```

▶ **Implement preprocess**: If during design or at later point you identify that the delay in the report data is caused because of the data insertion into the temporary table in the `processReport` method, then enable preprocessing.

▶ SSRS uses WCF to connect to AOS for data access. This connection has a threshold limit and it might fail if a report takes a longer time to execute. The report server execution waits for RDP to process the data and return. In the event where the RDP takes a longer time to execute, the reporting service might fail. Preprocessing is a strategy to beat through this issue. To understand how to enable preprocessing for reports read the *Preprocessing reports* recipe from *Chapter 4, Report Programming Model – RDP*.

Configuration-based resolution

Report execution time must be always kept minimum by applying the design time principles and best practices discussed in the previous section. The configuration-based methods must be adopted to make sure the overall reporting experience is smooth.

▶ **Data extension-based timeout**: This timeout occurs when there is a delay for the reporting services to fetch the data from Dynamics AX. It is to be understood that the AX-specific data extension uses the WCF based query service to access the data. So any data-related timeout has to be configured by fine-tuning the WCF timeout. WCF has two ends, the client and the server, so the timeout has to be adjusted at both ends.

Server-side WCF timeout:

1. Locate the `AX32Serv.exe.config` file located at `\Program Files\ Microsoft Dynamics AX\ <version>\Server\Microsoft DynamicsAX\Bin`.

2. Open the file for editing (Notepad/Visual Studio) and identify the element `QueryServiceBinding`.

```
<system.serviceModel>
  <bindings>
    <netTcpBinding>
      <binding name="QueryServiceBinding" sendTimeout="00:10:00" transferMode="StreamedResponse" maxBufferSize="65536" maxReceivedMessageSize="1048576000" listenBacklog="200" maxConnections="200">
        <readerQuotas maxStringContentLength="1048576000" />
      </binding>
      <binding name="InteractionServiceBinding" maxReceivedMessageSize="524288" listenBacklog="200" maxConnections="200" />
      <binding name="MetadataServiceBinding" sendTimeout="00:05:00" receiveTimeout="00:10:00" maxBufferSize="1048576" maxBufferPoolSize="3145728" maxReceivedMessageSize="1048576" listenBacklog="200" maxConnections="200">
        <readerQuotas maxDepth="128" maxStringContentLength="1048576" maxArrayLength="524288" maxBytesPerRead="1048576" maxNameTableCharCount="1048576" />
      </binding>
    </netTcpBinding>
```

3. Increase the `sendTimeout` property. The default value is set to 10 and can be changed to a longer time as needed. The range must be decided based on your longest running report.

4. Save the changes.

Client-side WCF timeout:

1. Open the **Run** window and type `AXclicfg` to open the client configuration.

2. Create a new client configuration and give it a name.

3. In the **Connection** tab, click on the **Configure Services** button. A message is displayed as seen here. Click on **OK** to continue.

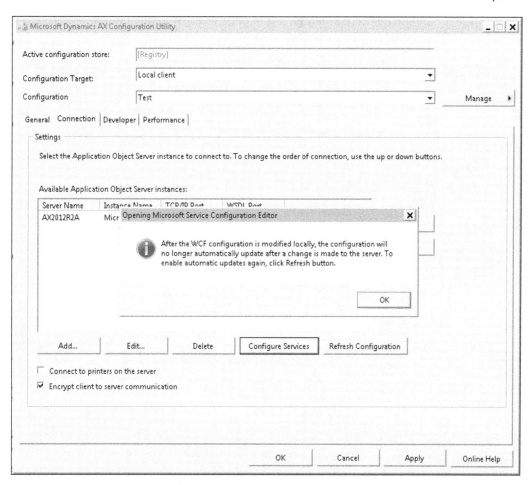

4. In the **Configuration** window that opens up, select the **Bindings** node from the tree node and identify the sibling **QueryServiceEndPoint**(**netTcpBinding**).

5. On the adjacent **Bindings** tab, find the property **SendTimeOut**, and then increase it from the default value of 10 to the desired amount:

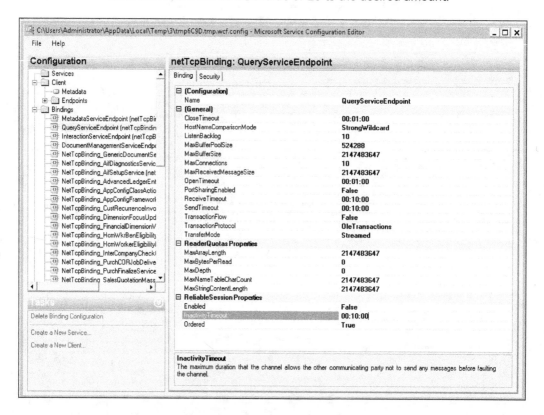

6. Similarly, on the **MaxReceivedMessageSize** property increase the message size from the default value to the desired value. The max value is the `int64` limit since this is an `int64` field.

7. Click on **Apply**, and then **OK**.

▶ **Report execution timeout**: This setting decides how long the report attempts to keep the execution going before it stops the execution through a timeout. The time specified here ideally must be the time taken by the longest report in the application. This can be defined for the all reports or a specific report.

Specify for all reports:

1. Open the Report Manager available at the URL; for example, `http://[SSSRSServerName]:80/Reports`.

2. Click on **Site Settings** to open the **Properties** page.

3. In the **Properties** page under **Report Timeout** specify the number of seconds.

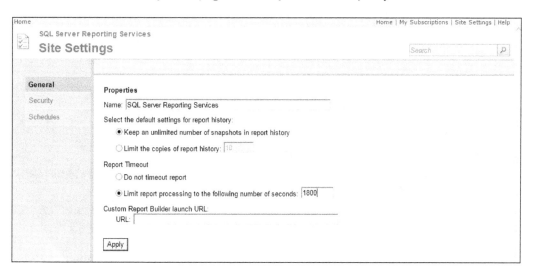

4. Click on **Apply** to save the changes.

Specify for a specific report:

1. To specify for a specific report, select the report, click on the drop-down arrow, and then click on **Manage**. On the **Properties** page, set the **Report Timeout** that will apply to that specific report.

▶ **User-session timeout**: Though this has nothing to do with performance, this governs the total time a user is allowed to have his or her session open untouched. This value must be greater than the Report Processing timeout.

1. Create a file **timeout.rss** with the script shown here and save it to the drive:

```
Public Sub Main()
    Dim props() as [Property]
    props = new [Property] () { new [Property] (), new
    [Property] () }

    props(0).Name = "SessionTimeout"
    props(0).Value = timeout

    props(1).Name = "SessionAccessTimeout"
    props(1).Value = timeout

    rs.SetSystemProperties(props)
End Sub
```

2. In the command prompt, run the `rs.exe` command in the format shown here. The `rs.exe` command can be generally found in `\Program Files\ Microsoft SQL Server\110\Tools\Bin`:

```
$>rs.exe -i C:\timeout.rss -s http://[SSSRSServerName]:80/
Reports -v timeout="72000" -l 0
```

3. This will set the timeout to 20 hours for both **SessionTimeout** and **SessionAccessTimeout**.

See also

▶ The *Preprocessing reports* recipe from *Chapter 4, Report Programming Model – RDP*

When working on precision designs a lot of time is spent on waiting for the preview to run. If your precision design is run by an RDP, here is a simple tip to speed up testing:

▶ Convert your temporary table to persistent by modifying the **TableType** property to `Regular`.

▶ Now, run the report once either from Visual Studio or from inside AX. This fills the data in the temporary table.

▶ Comment the code inside the `processreport` method or simply write a `return` statement on the first line of the method.

Remember to revert back once you are done and don't let it go to production.

Troubleshooting reports in AX

With the multitude of technologies involved in a report it is not devoid of issues. This recipe will discuss the possible issues that come during the development of a report, and the approaches that could be taken to identify the cause and resolution. The issues mostly seen in SSRS fall into three broad categories, such as the deployment, data-related, and rendering issues. While deployment and rendering are mostly on the SSRS end, the data-related issues concern X++ or the programming elements. This recipe will discuss issues by placing them in one of these broader categories.

How to do it...

This section is classified into three broad categories; deployment, data, and rendering-related issues.

Deployment-related issues

These are issues concerning deploying reports from AX or Visual Studio and getting them updated in AX.

Unable to deploy

1. **Verify SSRS configuration**: The first step to ensure when you face a deployment is configuration. Ensure the configuration specified in System **Administration | Setup | Business Intelligence | Reporting Services | Reporting servers** is accessible and valid. Try opening the SSRS reporting services manager through the browser.

2. **Rebuild versus project**: Open the Visual Studio project along with the reference assemblies, if any, and rebuild the project.

3. **File lock errors**: On receiving file lock errors restart the report server.

Unable to refresh

1. **Restore report**: Open the **SSRS report** node and navigate to your report. Right-click and select **Restore**.

2. **Refresh cache**: Since caching is enabled, there might be cache-related issues. Go to **Tools | Caches | Refresh Elements**.

3. **Redeploy**: Delete the report from the reporting service manager and redeploy the report:

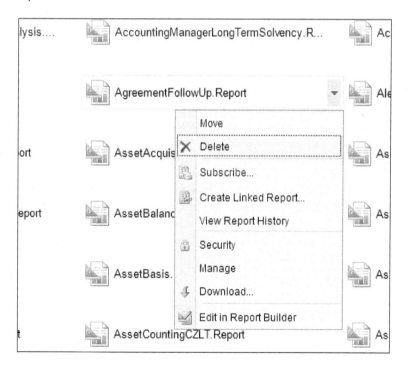

4. **Restart client/reporting server/AOS**: RDL is not parsed every time and is cached in AX. So restart the client/reporting server/AOS to clear the cache and reload the report.

5. **Default values**: For changes in default values update the parameter in Report Manager. The **Parameter** window can be opened from the drop-down menu under each report, and then choose **Manage**:

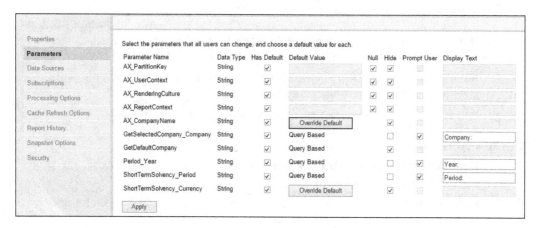

Rendering-related issues

This section will further discuss how issues that come at the time of report rendering can be handled:

1. **Parameter issues**: If you have issues with the parameters and not able to identify what parameters are passed to the report; try to render the parameters in the report design so that the parameters are visible. Navigate to the **Auto design** node and set the **Render** parameter property to true. This will display the parameters in the **Auto design** node window. In the case of precision design, parameters have to be added to the report area manually as there is no option as in auto design.

> Make sure the **Allow Blank** property is set to `true` for optional parameters as this can cause the issue of a missing report parameters error when running reports from AX.

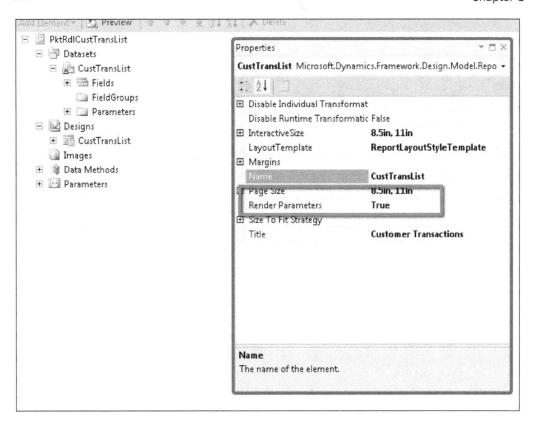

2. **Dynamic parameters**: In case of dynamic parameters, verify the range in the query node and if there is any initialization done in the controller. Ranges for dynamic parameters come from the range node in a query.

3. **Issues with label/grouping**: Grouping can be implemented at various levels in a report and it varies based on the report. Make sure to verify the places in the following list to identify and resolve issues related to grouping:

   ❏ For query-based reports, visit VS project/UI builder

   ❏ For RDP-based reports, visit Contract/VS project/UI builder

4. **Initialization and validation issues**: Check the contract/controller classes for issues related to initialization and validation.

5. **Formatting issues**: Use color coding to understand the spacing between controls. This will give the knowledge of the control that is taking up the space, based on which you can modify the parameters to fine-tune the spacing, and then later remove the color coding.

6. **Localization issues**:

1. Use Visual Studio preview to quickly switch between languages and verify the report rendering in different languages:

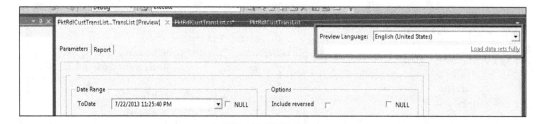

2. **Enum translation issues**: Each enum field in a query or contract when added to the dataset results in two different fields. One holds the label and the other holds the system name; always use the Enum.Label field in report rendering. In the screenshot seen here, you can see two fields being rendered for the field TransType. The name type can be used in programming references while the label can be used for rendering purposes:

7. **Control visibility issues**: Expressions are mostly used to handle the visibility of controls. Whenever an issue arises, verify the expression attached to the visible property of the control.

8. **Group headers**: Use the **Advanced** mode to fine-tune headers. Refer to the recipe *Inventory dimension in reports* in *Chapter 7*, *Upgrading and Analyzing Reports* to understand how to use **Advanced** mode.

9. **Expression-related issues**:

    1. Try to translate the expression into a data method and do a unit testing. Refer to unit testing business logic in the recipe *Debugging business logic* from *Chapter 3*, *A Report Programming Model* to identify how to test data methods.

    2. Break down the expression into simple pieces rather than one long expression to analyze the data method.

    3. **Enable verbose logging**: To enable the log, open the location `ReportingServices\ReportServer\bin` in the reporting server and identify the file `ReportingServicesService.exe.config`. Open the file and set the value to `4` for the properties **DefaultTraceSwitch** and **Components**. This enables the log to a verbose mode which creates more detailed logs of the actions in the report server. The log files can be found typically at `%ProgramFiles%\Microsoft SQL Server\MSSQL .x\Reporting Services\LogFiles`.

 Remember to switch the value to 3 post debugging, as the value 4 adds load to the report execution.

```
ReportingServicesService.exe.config  ×   PktRdlCustTransList...TransList [Preview]      PktRdlCu
⊟<configuration>
⊟  <configSections>
     <section name="RStrace" type="Microsoft.ReportingServices.Diagno
   </configSections>
⊟  <system.diagnostics>
⊟     <switches>
        <add name="DefaultTraceSwitch" value="4" />
      </switches>
   </system.diagnostics>
⊟  <RStrace>
     <add name="FileName" value="ReportServerService_" />
     <add name="FileSizeLimitMb" value="32" />
     <add name="KeepFilesForDays" value="14" />
     <add name="Prefix" value="appdomain, tid, time" />
     <add name="TraceListeners" value="file" />
     <add name="TraceFileMode" value="unique" />
     <add name="Components" value="all:4" />
   </RStrace>
⊟  <runtime>
     <alwaysFlowImpersonationPolicy enabled="true"/>
⊟     <assemblyBinding xmlns="urn:schemas-microsoft-com:asm.v1">
         <dependentAssembly>
```

10. **Use the log viewer to read the log**: The log file though can be opened and read using Notepad, it is cumbersome to read it in a raw format. Use the log file viewer discussed in the recipe *Assess report performance and usage* in this chapter. Open the report log viewer and on the **Log Files** tab, navigate to the folder where the log files are located; for example, `Microsoft SQL Server\MSRS11.MSSQLSERVER\ Reporting Services\LogFiles`. Choose `Today` in **Date Range**, and then `Raw` in **View details** textboxes. This will present the log in a way that is easier to analyze.

> Enable the **Show filters** option. This shows different filters that can be applied to narrow down the search results; for example, the **Filter by trace level** option allows you to view only errors, warnings, or info.

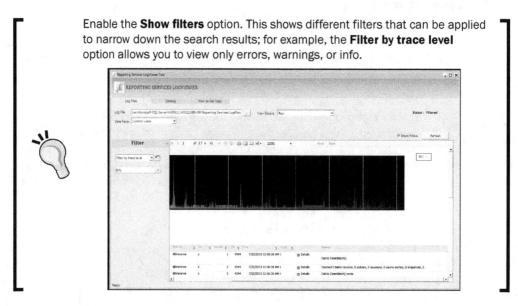

Data-related issues

The first step in a data-related issue is to identify the source of the data. Based on the report data source, handle the issue.

Query-based reports

To handle issues of data not showing in a query-based report, use the following approaches:

1. Verify if the user running the report has access to the data in the company.
2. Verify if the query returns data:
    1. Write a job to verify the query.
    2. Add the query to a form and see that the data is returned.
    3. Use the query service through services such as InfoPath to ensure it returns data.

3. **Queries are cached**: Delete data from the `SRSReportQuery` and `SRSReportParameters` tables to clear the cache.

4. If any changes are made to the query/contract, then open the Visual Studio project and refresh the dataset and redeploy.

5. Ensure the correct query is used by accessing the query in the controller. You can place the following code in the `preRunModifyContract` method to get the query displayed in the infolog:

```
info(this.getFirstQuery().toString());
```

RDB-based reports

To handle data issues for RDP adopt the following approaches:

1. Debug by adding the keyword `breakpoint` in the `processreport` method and ensure the flow is smooth.

2. If the RDP uses a query or DML, ensure that it returns the data by running it in a job.

3. Try to invoke the RDP through a job by converting the `Temptable` instance to a persistent table. Refer to the recipe *Testing the RDP* in *Chapter 4, Report Programming Model – RDP*

Controller issues

For runtime design selection issues look into the controller. Use the `prePromptModifyContract` and `preRunModifyContract` methods in the `controller` class for debugging. This is a good entry point.

See also

▸ The *Testing the RDP* recipe in *Chapter 4, Report Programming Model – RDP*

▸ The *Inventory dimensions in reports* recipe in *Chapter 7, Upgrading and Analyzing Reports*

▸ The *Debugging business logic* recipe in *Chapter 3, A Report Programming Model*

When you use configuration files to start your AX client (saved as `.axc` files) and also work on Visual Studio; make sure your default client configuration is pointing to the same layer as in the configuration file.

This is because Visual Studio opens in the layer that is specified in the default settings in the **AX Client Configuration** window. Though your AX client is on the VAR layer, if your default client configuration setting is pointing to the USR layer then the Visual Studio reporting project gets saved to the USR layer. You end up deleting and reimporting the entire project. So make sure to verify the layer setup before you start working on reporting projects.

To set up the default layer configuration, open the **Run** window and type `axclicfg`. In the window that opens, create a new configuration or on the existing configuration go to the **Developer** tab and verify the layer information including the license.

Auto e-mail and Save as file tasks in reports

There are some reports that demand no user interaction and are expected to be directly saved in a file or e-mailed. This simple recipe will share how the printer settings contract can be used to achieve this in a simple manner.

How to do it...

This recipe is in two sections, the first section details how to save the report to a file followed by sending it through an e-mail.

Saving the report to a file

To save the file to the printer, carry out the following steps:

1. Create a new static method in the `controller` class or in the class from where the report is invoked.

2. On the method, place the following code to save the report. Here the file location is hard coded but you may want to turn it into a parameter or refer to a table location:

```
public static void saveReporttoFile(Args _args)
{
/*if the controller is not overriden for your report then use
appropriate controller*/
    SrsReportRunController controller = new
PktRdlCustTransListController();
    SRSPrintDestinationSettings printSettings;

    controller.parmReportName(ssrsReportStr(PktRdlCustTransList,
CustTransList));

    // get print settings from contract
    printSettings = controller.parmReportContract().
parmPrintSettings();

    // set print medium
    printSettings.printMediumType(SRSPrintMediumType::File);
    printSettings.fileFormat(SRSReportFileFormat::PDF);
    printSettings.overwriteFile(true);
    printSettings.fileName(@"C:\Temp\CusttransReport.pdf");

    // suppress the parameter dialog
    controller.parmShowDialog(false);

    controller.startOperation();
}
```

Sending the report through an e-mail

To send the file through an e-mail the procedure is not much different except the need to pass an e-mail contract:

```
public static void mailReport(Args _args)
{
    SrsReportRunController controller = new
PktRdlCustTransListController();
    SRSPrintDestinationSettings printSettings;
    SrsReportEMailDataContract emailContract;

    // set report name
    controller.parmReportName(ssrsReportStr(PktRdlCustTransList,
CustTransList));

    // create email contract
    emailContract = new SrsReportEMailDataContract();

    // fill in the email contract details
    emailContract.parmAttachmentFileFormat(SRSReportFileFormat::PDF);
    emailContract.parmSubject("Customer Transactions");
    emailContract.parmTo("admin@contoso.com");

    printSettings = controller.parmReportContract().
parmPrintSettings();

    printSettings.printMediumType(SRSPrintMediumType::Email);
    printSettings.parmEMailContract(emailContract);
    printSettings.fileFormat(SRSReportFileFormat::PDF);

    // suppress the parameter dialog
    controller.parmShowDialog(false);


    controller.startOperation();
}
```

How it works...

The printer setting is a contract similar to the RDL and RDP contracts. The printer setting can be modified inside the controller if it requires manipulation. This must be performed in the preRunModifyContract method in the controller. If the report is required to be opened through a code, then all that is needed is to invoke the code that is given in this recipe and keeping the printer setting-related changes is optional.

When reports that are meant for printing on a specific paper size or export format, the page size must be setup accordingly for a proper rendering. Using just the page setup in the printer dialog box without modifying the page size in design might make the report look odd; say when you print a report configured for portrait as landscape.

Open the **Properties** window in the designer window (*F4*), and on the drop-down menu in the **Properties** window type `Report`. Find the property **Page Size**, expand it, and enter the **Width** and **Height**. So, to change the page from A4 portrait to A4 landscape, you set the width to 11in and height to 8.5in. Once set up here, the **Print** option on the report, by default prints, it to A4, A3, Portrait, or Landscape.

Handling events post report completion

To handle events post reporting completion, the reporting framework in AX gives the ability to hook custom events that will be called after a report is complete. This event can be used to find when a report execution is complete and take the corresponding actions. The recipe here discusses a sample implementation.

How to do it...

1. In this example, let us say that we update the `Printed` field in the table with status `Yes` after the report is printed. The reporting framework has the delegate `renderingCompleted` that is invoked once a report is complete. Create a method that can be linked to this delegate.

2. The method's signature must match the delegate while the rest such as the name, instance method, or a static method doesn't matter:

```
public static void renderingComplete(SrsReportRunController _
sender, SrsRenderingCompletedEventArgs _eventArgs)
{
    Query              query;
    QueryRun           queryRun;

    InventBatchId      batchNum;
    PktBatchPrintStatus batchStatus;

    SRSReportExecutionInfo executionInfo;

    executionInfo = _eventArgs.parmReportExecutionInfo();

    if(executionInfo && executionInfo.parmIsSuccessful())
```

```
        {
            // Get the report's query
            query = _sender.getFirstQuery();

            // Mark all the records as printed
            queryRun = new QueryRun(query);

            ttsbegin;
            while(queryRun.next())
            {
                batchNum = queryRun.get(tableNum(InventBatch)).
(fieldNum(InventBatch, inventBatchId));
                update_recordset batchStatus
                    setting Printed      = NoYes::Yes,
                            PrintDateTime = executionInfo.
parmExecutionDateTime();
                    where batchStatus.inventBatchId == batchNum;
            }
            ttscommit;
        }
    }
```

3. The next step is to hook the event to the delegate. This can be done anywhere before the `preRunModifyContract` event but the standard recommendation is to write it inside the `preRunModifyContract` method.

```
protected void preRunModifyContract()
{
    this.renderingCompleted += eventhandler(PktInventBatchTransCon
troller::renderingComplete);
}
```

4. When the report execution is completed, the method will be invoked and the records fetched through the query will be updated.

How it works...

Since SSRS report execution is asynchronous as it connects to the AOS via the WCF service, the rendering complete will be the best approach to hook events post the report complete. Though the method attached to the delegate here is a static method instance, methods can also be used. The arguments controller gives complete access to the report that was executed. The `SRSRenderingCompletedEventArgs` class has access to the object `SRSReportExecutionInfo`. The execution info carries several information pertaining to the report that was just executed, such as number of pages, if print was successful, layout, execution time, and many more.

Make sure the event is hooked in `preRunModifyContract` to ensure it gets called both during batch and interactive modes.

 There can be cases where you want a contract in the attribute but do not want the UI builder to expose it to the user. The reporting framework in AX provides a very easy way to incorporate this. Open the parm method in the contract that you don't want to expose. Add the attribute shown here along with other attributes. This attribute when found in the parm method will automatically prevent the UI builder from adding this to the dialog.

`SysOperationControlVisibilityAttribute(False)`

Generating and displaying barcodes in reports

Shop-floor and warehouse reports require barcodes to be printed for handling goods, and many other reports also demand barcode strings to be printed on the report. This recipe is focused on guiding you to build barcodes in SSRS. Here we will attempt to print the barcode of the inventory batch table.

How to do it...

1. Create a simple query, and then add the `InventBatch` table as a datasource. Keep the fields selective only with `InventBatch` and `ItemId`.

2. This will be an RDP-based report so create a temporary table with the fields shown here. The fields `Barcode` and `BarcodeHR` will store encoded values and so must extend the EDT `BarcodeString`:

3. Create a `Contract` class as shown here. The **barcode setup** field in the `Contract` class is used to choose the format of barcode, such as Code39/EAN:

```
[
    DataContractAttribute,
    SysOperationGroupAttribute('BatchGroup', "Batch", '1')
]
class PktInventBatchBarCodeContract
{
    InventBatchId           batchId;
    BarcodeSetupId          barcodeSetupId;
    FontSize                batchFontSize;
    FontName                barcodeFontName;
}


[DataMemberAttribute('Batch'),
SysOperationGroupMemberAttribute('BatchGroup'),
SysOperationDisplayOrderAttribute('1')]
public InventBatchId parmBatchId(InventBatchId _batchId = batchId)
{
    batchId = _batchId;
    return batchId;
}
[

    DataMemberAttribute('BarcodeSetupId'),
    SysOperationGroupMemberAttribute('BatchGroup'),
    SysOperationHelpTextAttribute(literalStr("@SYS102646")),
    SysOperationDisplayOrderAttribute('2')
]
public BarcodeSetupId parmBarcodeSetupId(BarcodeSetupId _
barcodeSetupId = barcodeSetupId)
{
    barcodeSetupId  =   _barcodeSetupId;

    return barcodeSetupId;
}


[

    DataMemberAttribute('BarcodeFontName'),
    SysOperationGroupMemberAttribute('BatchGroup'),
    SysOperationDisplayOrderAttribute('3')
]
```

```
public FontName parmBarcodeFontName(FontName _barcodeFontName =
barcodeFontName)
{
    barcodeFontName     =   _barcodeFontName;

    return barcodeFontName;
}
```

4. Create an RDP class using the code here. The RDP class will apply the selected barcode setup chosen by the user in the **report** dialog box to encode the batch number to the barcode;

```
[
    //bind query - shows in the report dialog
    SRSReportQueryAttribute(queryStr(PktinventBatchBarCode)),
    //bind the contract
    SRSReportParameterAttribute(classStr(PktInventBatchBarCodeCont
ract))
]
class PktInventBatchBarCodeDp Extends SRSReportDataProviderBase
{
    BarcodeSetupId   barcodeSetupId;
    FontName         barcodeFontName;
    FontSize         barcodeFontSize;

    PktInventBarCodeTmp   barCodeTmp;
}


[SysEntryPointAttribute(false)]
public void processReport()
{
    QueryRun                        queryRun;
    PktInventBatchBarCodeContract   contract;
    BarcodeSetup                    barcodeSetup;
    Barcode                         barcode;
    QueryBuildRange                 batchRange;

    breakpoint;

    contract = this.parmDataContract() as
PktInventBatchBarCodeContract;

    barcodeSetup    = BarcodeSetup::find(contract.
parmBarcodeSetupId());
```

```
    barcode          = barcodeSetup.barcode();

    contract.parmBarcodeFontName(barcodeSetup.fontName);

    batchRange   =   this.parmQuery().dataSourceTable(tableNum(Inve
ntBatch)).addRange(fieldNum(InventBatch,InventBatchId));
    batchRange.value(contract.parmBatchId());

    queryRun = new QueryRun(this.parmQuery());

    while (queryRun.next())
    {
        this.insertBarCodeTmpTable(queryRun.
get(tableNum(InventBatch)) as InventBatch, barcodeSetup, barcode);
    }
}

protected void insertBarCodeTmpTable(
        InventBatch       _inventBatch
      , BarcodeSetup      _barcodeSetup,
        Barcode           _barcode)
{
    int                      currentInfologLine;
    SysInfologEnumerator     infoEnumerator;

    // encode barcodes
    barCodeTmp.clear();

    if(_barcodeSetup)
    {
        currentInfologLine = infologLine();

        if (_barcodeSetup.validateBarcode(_inventBatch.
inventBatchId))
        {
            _barcode.string(true, _inventBatch.inventBatchId);

            if (_barcodeSetup.FontName)
            {
                barCodeTmp.Barcode = _barcode.barcodeStr();
            }

            barCodeTmp.BarcodeHR        = _barcode.barcodeStrHR();
```

```
            barCodeTmp.InventBatchId      = _inventBatch.
inventBatchId;
            barCodeTmp.insert();
        }
        else
        {
            infoEnumerator = SysInfologEnumerator::newData(infol
og.copy(currentInfologLine + 1, infologLine()));
            return;
        }
    }
}

[SRSReportDataSetAttribute(tableStr(PktInventBarCodeTmp))]
public PktInventBarCodeTmp getBarCodeTmp()
{
    select  barCodeTmp;
    return  barCodeTmp;
}
```

5. Create a **Controller** class as shown here. The **Controller** class will find the barcode setup and set the **FontName** and **Fontsize** accordingly. This makes it possible to dynamically change the barcode type at runtime:

```
public class PktInventBatchBarCodeController extends
SrsReportRunController
{
}

public static void main(Args _args)
{
    PktInventBatchBarCodeController controller = new
PktInventBatchBarCodeController();

    controller.parmReportName(ssrsReportStr(PktInventBatchBarCode,
InventBatchBarCode));
    controller.parmArgs(_args);
    controller.startOperation();
}

public void preRunModifyContract()
{
    BarcodeSetup                        barcodeSetup;
    PktInventBatchBarCodeContract    contract =
this.parmReportContract().parmRdpContract() as
PktInventBatchBarCodeContract;
```

```
    barcodeSetup = BarcodeSetup::find(contract.
parmBarcodeSetupId());

    if (barcodeSetup)
    {
        contract.parmBarcodeFontName(barcodeSetup.FontName);
        contract.parmBatchFontSize(barcodeSetup.FontSize);
    }
    else
    {
        contract.parmBarcodeFontName('');
        contract.parmBatchFontSize(0);
    }
}

public void prePromptModifyContract()
{
    BarcodeSetup                    barcodeSetup;
    PktInventBatchBarCodeContract    contract;
    Query                           query;
    InventBatch                     inventBatch;
    QueryBuildDataSource            queryBuildDataSource;
    QueryBuildRange                 qbrInventBatchId;

    contract = this.parmReportContract().parmRdpContract() as
PktInventBatchBarCodeContract;

    if (!contract.parmBarcodeSetupId())
    {
        select firstonly barcodeSetup
            where barcodeSetup.BarcodeType == BarcodeType::Code39;

        if (barcodeSetup)
        {
            contract.parmBarcodeSetupId(barcodeSetup.
BarcodeSetupId);
        }
    }

    query                  = this.getFirstQuery();
    queryBuildDataSource    = SysQuery::findOrCreateDataSource(que
ry, tableNum(inventBatch));
```

```
    if (this.parmArgs()
     && this.parmArgs().record() is InventBatch
     && this.parmArgs().record().isFormDataSource())
    {
        inventBatch = this.parmArgs().record() as InventBatch;
        qbrInventBatchId    = SysQuery::findOrCreateRange(queryBu
ildDataSource, fieldNum(InventBatch, InventBatchId));
        qbrInventBatchId.value(queryValue(inventBatch.
inventBatchId));
    }
}
```

6. Create a report and attach the RDP class as datasource.

7. Create a new precision design and add a table control.

8. In the table control, delete all the columns except the first column and select the InventBatchId field in the first column.

9. Insert three columns at the bottom and select the field barcode, BarcodeHR, and barcode sequentially.

10. Select the text boxes for the field barcode. On the font toolbar modify the font to **BC C39 3 to 1 HD Wide**, set the size to **48pt**, and set the alignment to center. This is a static way of specifying the barcode setup:

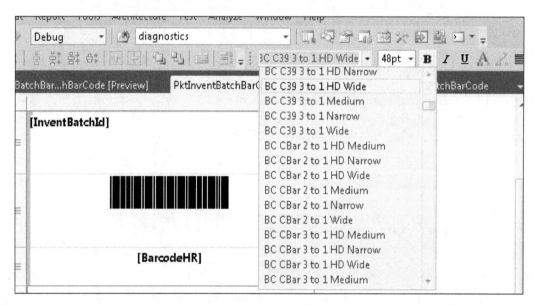

11. Select the last barcode box at the bottom, and on the **Properties** window set the **WritingMode** property to vertical. This will print the barcode in the vertical direction.

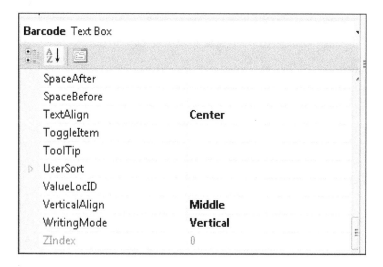

12. Select the barcode and on the **Properties** window for font family set the following expression; this will make the font dynamic so that it can be chosen at runtime:

```
=iif(IsNothing(Parameters!BarcodeFontName.Value),"Tahoma",
Parameters!BarcodeFontName.Value)
```

13. Resize the barcode textbox to fit the barcode when printed.

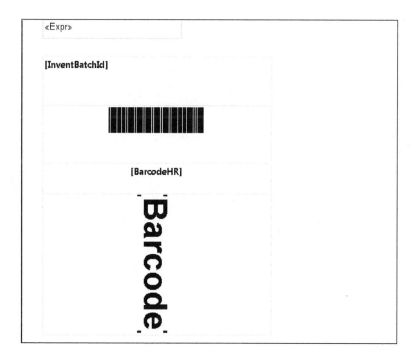

14. Run the report and choose the barcode setup in the report dialog.

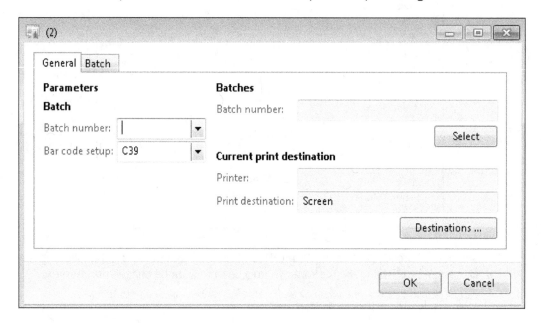

15. The report output shows the barcode that is horizontally and vertically aligned.

How it works...

Dynamics AX has inbuilt classes that support encoding for most types of barcodes and more can be added easily by extending the `Barcode` class.

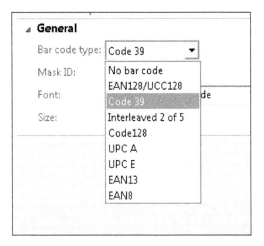

The report here flexibly allows the user to choose the encoding mechanism at runtime. The report picks up the available barcode from **Organization administration | Setup | Barcode**.

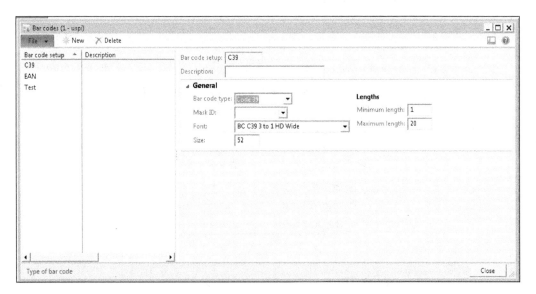

RDP receives this setup parameter through the contract and instantiates the appropriate barcode class. This helps in building more dynamic and generic solutions since the barcode report can run for any kind of barcode without changing the font for each format. Also, to be noticed is the easy way to print barcodes vertically compared with AX 2009 where the only feasible solution is to save it as a vertical image and print it on the report.

Sometimes you may want to create an interactive text in the reports but still use the standard labels as part of the message; for example, Page 1 of 10 where the strings **Page** and **of** are plain strings. In the case of pages, the value comes from the global variable but you may also want to use labels to construct such texts. In that case use the **String format** option. Open the report control properties and on the property `Value`, select the **expression** option and place your text in the format seen here:

```
=System.String.Format (This is a label ID converted
at runtime {0}, Lables!@SYS1560)
```

Hiding controls by context

Among the customization that is done on a report, one of the most frequented is to disable certain report controls by context. This recipe will showcase the pattern on how to hide a report control in the report design using the context.

How to do it...

1. Create a new report in Visual Studio with the `CustTable` query as datasource.

2. Add an auto design and drag the datasource to the design.

3. On the **Parameter** node, add a new parameter of type `Boolean` and call it **showDlvMode**, and then set the following properties:

Property	Value
Nullable	True
AllowBlank	True
Default value	False

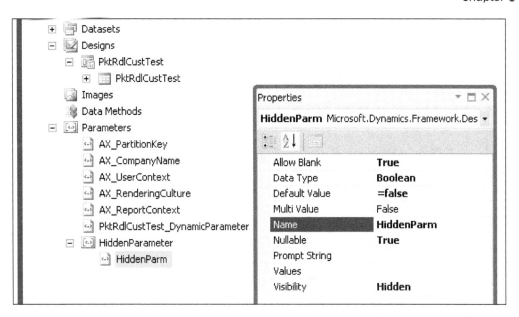

4. On the **Design** node, navigate to the control that must be toggled based on the flag. In the **Property** window set the visible property through an expression to point to the newly added parameter:

```
=Not(!Parameter.HiddenParm.Value)
```

5. The next step is to set this flag from the controller based on the context. To do this, navigate to the `Controller` class and on the `preRunModifyContract` method access contract and set the value as shown here:

```
class PktRdlCustTransListController extends SrsReportRunController
{
}
protected void preRunModifyContract()
{
    #ISOCountryRegionCodes
    SrsReportRdlDataContract    contract    =
                                 this.parmReportContract().
parmRdlContract();

    if(SysCountryRegionCode::isLegalEntityInCountryRegion([#iso
IN]))
    {
        contract.setValue("HiddenParm", true);
    }
```

```
      }

      public static void main(Args args)
      {
          PktRdlCustTransListController controller;

          controller = new PktRdlCustTransListController();
          controller.parmReportName(ssrsReportStr(PktRdlCustTransList,
      CustTransList));
          controller.parmArgs(args);
          controller.startOperation();
      }
```

6. Redeploy the report and run the report to see the field getting disabled or enabled based on the context.

How it works...

This recipe, in spite of its simplicity, will be immensely applicable as an idea in report development to toggle report controls. A best practice to keep in mind is to add the hidden parameter by creating a separate group under the **Parameter** node. This will help in understanding and extending at a later point.

Using AXEnumProvider as the dataset for parameters in reports

When you use `Enum` as a parameter in reports it works well within the AX client, but to deploy it to the EP, the parameter lookup must be built through the AX Enum provider. This recipe will discuss how an `Enum` provider can be added to a report and used in parameters.

Getting ready

To verify the recipe output you may require the enterprise portal configured for your Dynamics AX installation.

How to do it...

1. On the report identify the `Enum` field that must be added to the parameters. Drag it to the **Parameter** node to create a new parameter.

2. Create a new dataset and set the **Data Source Type** to `AXEnumProvider`. Click on the ellipsis button (**...**) on the **Query** property.

3. In the **Application** explorer, navigate to **DataDictionary** | **Tables** | (Select the table that has the enumerator) | **Fields** | (Select the Enum field) and identify the Enum that it uses. Type the value in the **Query** property in the dataset:

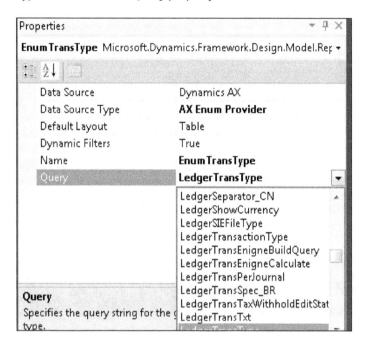

4. This will add a dataset with fields **Name**, **Value**, and **Label**:

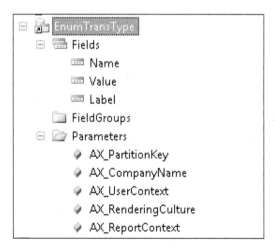

5. Go to the **Enum** parameter that was added in the **Parameters** node, click on the ellipsis button (**...**), and then on the **Select values** set these properties:

Field	Value
Dataset	Enum provider dataset that was added
Value	Value
Label	Label

6. This completes the process. Once this is done you are good to deploy the report. The system will automatically take care of filling the enum values at runtime and display them in the lookup both in EP and the rich client.

The header and body sections in an SSRS report are completely alienated, meaning you cannot reference global values, such as page number in the body section and dataset elements in the header section. This is because of the way SSRS reports are executed. The body is executed even before the header and footer are executed.

Adding a new report design to print management

Print management allows the end users to specify the print format and type (print/e-mail) of reports based on hierarchical relations, such as modules, accounts (customer/vendor), and transactions (picking/packing). The goal of this recipe is to set out how you can make a new report design for one of the existing document type as an option for users to choose in the print management setup.

How to do it...

1. This recipe assumes that a new design ready for one of the document types supported by print management say, **SalesInvoice**, is available.

2. Open the `PrintMgmtReportFormat` table and add a new record as shown here. If a report must be applied for a specific country, then fill the country additionally:

3. If it is required to make this the default report in print management, then in the class `PrintMgmtDocType` modify the `getDefaultReportFormat` method to replace the report name for the document type. If the report layout is country specific then apply the appropriate condition:

```
if (SysCountryRegionCode::isLegalEntityInCountryRegion([#isoIN]))
        {
                return ssrsReportStr(SalesInvoice, Report_Custom);
        }
```

4. Navigate to **Accounts Receivable** | **Setup** | **Forms** | **Forms Setup**. Click on the **Print Management** button.

5. In **Print Management** navigate to the **Customer Invoice** record and click on the drop-down list to see the **Report Format** field that was added:

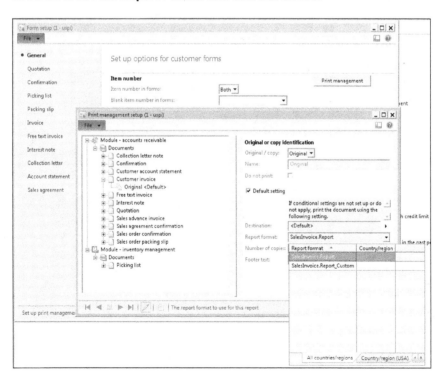

AX SSRS though is an extension of SSRS, it still does stop a few SSRS features from being directly used such as the reset of page numbers after a group change, use of maps in the reports and a few chart types, such as spark line.

Deploying language-specific reports to speed up execution time

Generally, when a report is deployed to a report server it is deployed once and is rendered per language, but for large-scale transactional reports, such as Sales Invoice that run in batch operations, can harness this option to speed up processing. Walk through this recipe to see how it can be done.

How to do it...

1. Navigate to **SystemAdministration** | **Setup** | **Business Intelligence** | **Reporting services** | **Report Deployment settings**.
2. In the **Report Deployment** settings, create a new record for the report and activate **Use static Report Design**.

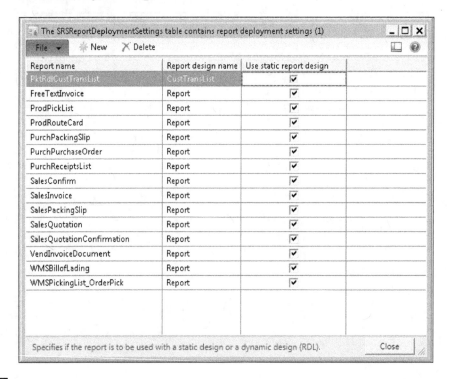

3. Redeploy the report to the report server.

How it works...

Enabling the static report design speeds up the report as it uses what is called a static RDL. A static RDL is different from a dynamic RDL because the labels are pre-rendered. This works by creating a language-specific version in the report server for each language making the processing of the report faster. However, keep in mind that changing a label means the report must be deployed again and when redesigning any report on this list make sure to uncheck **Use report static design**.

Making your reports function better

Designing a report and making it function better relies on getting it fundamentally right. This recipe will speak about some simple steps that when implemented can help design a better, faster, and reliable report.

How to do it...

1. **Use query**: Prefer to use a query-based report over an RDP-based report wherever possible and use an RDP only if there is a compulsion to use the business logic for the query.

2. **Use SSRS for totals**: Use the `totals` functions in SSRS for running totals and don't calculate them in the RDP logic.

3. **Use relations in RDP**: Create relations in the RDP table to get automatic drill-through on reports.

4. **Make parameters optional**: Remember to set **Allow blank** to **true** and **Nullable** to **true** for optional report parameters.

5. **Use Run on property for menu items**: On the menu item that invokes a report make sure the property is called from; otherwise, it may not be invoked from a batch process.

6. **Use SSRSReportStr**: When specifying the design in reports avoid strings and use the inbuilt function `SSRSReportStr(ReportName, DesignName)`. This validates the design at compile time.

7. **Concentrate computation in the RDP**: Complete all computations in the RDP and don't spread logical computations to the report through data methods.

8. **Limit C# data methods**: Use C#-based data methods to do formatting-related changes and avoid using it to invoke AX services for querying and so on.

9. **Limit display methods from the query node**: Though you are allowed to choose display methods using the query datasource, always limit the number of methods and consider each is really needed in the report. When there are a lot of display methods or a performance delay is noticed, create a view. This can bring a significant difference to the performance of the report.

10. **Use query ranges**: Strive to place select conditions as much possible as ranges on the query rather than using the **Filter** option in the report design or by adding `if` conditions in the RDP.

11. **Use set-based processing RDP**: Evaluate if the RDP requires a query to collect the user inputs. If not, try to use set-based operations, such as `insert_recordset` and `update_recordset` operations to bulk-process records to the temporary table used in the RDP as these operations are exponentially faster.

12. **Resize images**: The AOS service has a limit of 1 GB for streaming data to the reporting service. When using reports that contain images and bulk number of transactions, this can cause choking or slowing down. Avoid using the `.bmp` file format and use compressed image formats, such as JPG or PNG instead.

Introduction to SSRS

Introduction

This section will discuss the reasons that led to the transformation to SSRS from the legacy reporting system. It is followed by an introduction to the SSRS reporting architecture. A comparison between AX2012 and AX 2009 is discussed and the artifacts involved in the new reporting model are described in detail. The last part of this appendix will list the configurations that must be ensured before starting to work SSRS.

Why SSRS?

This appendix section will give you a brief introduction to the AX 2012 reporting system and the reason that is driving this major shift.

To justify the shift to SSRS, let's understand the drawbacks of the legacy reporting system:

- The legacy reporting system was a client side solution that means the framework needs to be installed in the client system.
- It uses the capabilities of the client to print a report.
- The system works only with tables in AX. It cannot be connected to an external database or a web service.
- The reports cannot be exposed outside the AX client that means the report can only be viewed through the AX client.
- The rendering reporting framework is very weak when it comes to graphical, tabular, and interactive reports.

> ▶ Solving these problems to enrich the legacy reporting system may not be a wise approach when we have a robust technology that can enable SSRS. So, the obvious choice would be to have a road map to get SSRS working with Dynamics AX. The preliminary works started with AX 2009 resulting in an early framework with certain limitations, which has been re-engineered in the current version (AX 2012) to be seamless and more powerful.

Reporting architecture

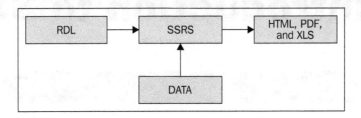

The major components in the architecture include the database, report server, and the Report Manager.

The report database

It is an SQL server database that stores reporting services data, such as report definitions, report metadata, cached reports, snapshots, and resources.

The report server

It is a server component that includes several subcomponents that work together to process the data and render it as a report. The subcomponents include designer, ad-hoc report builder, and more.

The Report Manager

Though a subcomponent of report server, it is used as the major interface to access, manage and view the contents of a report.

A report design is stored as a **Report Definition Language** (**RDL**) and whenever a report is requested through the report manager the report server uses the RDL to identify the data sources and fetch the data. The data is then transformed into a report using the design stored in the RDL.

Report Definition Language (RDL)

This is a format in which the report models are stored. RDL is an XML that contains all the information that is required to generate the report, such as the data sources, extensions and the design of the report.

Dynamics AX reporting extensions

SSRS has been designed ground-up to support multiple data sources and flexible rendering mechanisms. SSRS adopts an extension-based design through which you can have your own custom extension to control different processes in the generation of a report, such as:

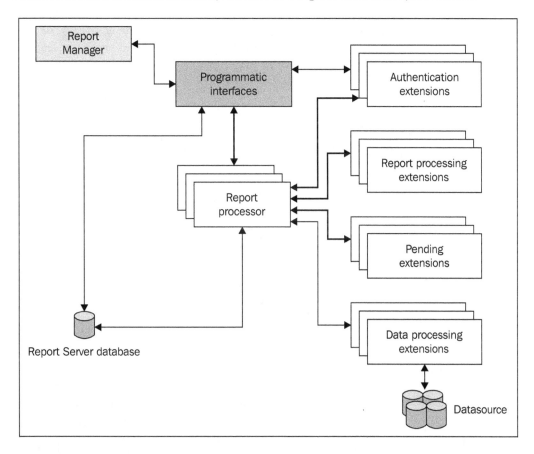

The key part to enable the integration to work is to get the ability to access data from AX and apply the context-based modifications, such as labels, authentications, and data restrictions. To achieve this AX-specific reporting extensions have been developed. There are two major extensions that are built for AX.

Data Processing Extensions (DPE)

SSRS uses different DPEs based on the type of data source to be used. These DPEs are data source specific, such as for XML and SQL. To enable SSRS to support AX data sources, AX-DPE is developed as part of the AX reporting extension.

The purpose of this DPE is to query the AX data source and return the data in a flattened row set to the report processor.

Report Definition Extensions (RDE)

RDE processes the RDL file dynamically based on the context to apply the right view. RDE processes the RDL file dynamically based on the context to apply the right view. The context is determined by the user, the company in which he is logged to and the security and privileges setup for the user. The context is used by the RDE to define what data and fields are viewed by the user. RDE is responsible for the following transformations:

- ▸ Reference and translation of labels from Dynamics AX
- ▸ Display data for which the user has permissions
- ▸ React to changes such as EDT width, field group additions, configuration keys, roles, and security

The simplified architecture of SSRS is redrawn to include the extensions:

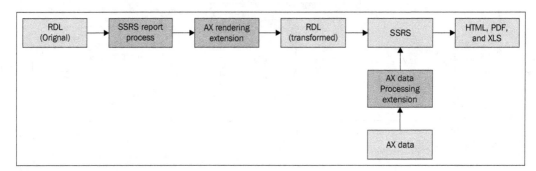

DPE and RDE come as a part of Dynamics installation and must be installed to enable AX-specific reports.

AX 2009 versus AX 2012

SSRS has evolved as a mature framework for Dynamics AX. Here is a listing of the major changes that came through the latest version in comparison to the previous version.

Development

AX 2009	AX 2012
Used `.Net` business connector to communicate to Dynamics AX	Uses the Dynamics AX services framework (system services/ metadata services/document services)
Control formats had to be defined explicitly	Control formats are derived from the corresponding types EDT/fields
Large data sets are first stored in a data table and then rendered causing a delay in loading of the reports	Data streaming is possible that enables data to be read in pages or streams of data
Limited interactivity and no charting capabilities	Rich charting and interactive capabilities
Labels for each locale had to be created separately as a `.resx` file	Standard AX labels can be referenced and the framework translates them according to the locale
One report for each locale (English, Arabic, and so on) was created	Only one report is created and is rendered in different languages
Record-level security didn't apply to report data	The entire security model (duties, privileges, and XDS) is honored by the reports
Deployed through the project deployment form.	Uses PowerShell to deploy reports
No cross reference for reports	Reports are cross referenced

Apart from this, the AX 2012 SSRS framework has also implemented popular features of the MorphX reporting framework, such as auto report, filtering and sorting report data, printing reports in batches, and print management.

Understanding AX reports

This section will detail the different artifacts that are involved in creating and running a report. Individual components inside the report model are also briefly discussed.

Artifacts

AX SSRS reports are managed through multiple AOT components.

Reports (AOT\SSRS reports)

The SSRS report node in AOT stores the metadata for the report in XML format that includes the RDL and cross reference entries. There is no code written in this part of the report. A report can be part of any number of reporting projects.

Reporting projects (AOT\Visual Studio Projects\ Dynamics AX Model Projects)

A reporting project holds references to multiple reports and provides the provision to create business logic associated with the reports. The business logic created here can be shared across the reports included in the project. Business logic can be written either in Visual C# or Visual Basic.

To customize a report it is important to identify the report and associated report project. Though mostly, they may have similar names, sometimes they may not. It is recommended to use the following list to identify the associated project and report: `http://msdn. microsoft.com/EN-US/library/hh496433.aspx`.

Report model

A report consists of datasets, designs, parameters, data methods, and images.

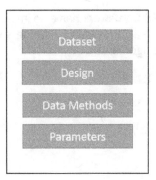

Datasets

A dataset contains the details of the data source and the means to retrieve the data through it. The dataset is shared across multiple designs in the report. A dataset represents flattened data, and hierarchical relations are not represented. Here is a list of data sources and fetch options currently supported:

Data Source	Option
Dynamics AX	▸ AOT queries
	▸ Report data provider AX classes
	▸ Data methods in reporting project
SQL	▸ TSQL query
	▸ Stored procedure
	▸ Dynamics AX OLAP
OLAP	▸ MDX query

The data fetched from Dynamics AX honors the security-related to roles for both metadata and data; for example, a field that is hidden and a setup to show only the records created by the user running the report. The other cases of SQL and OLAP security must be employed at the database level.

Design

There are two different designs that are supported.

Auto design

A design is automatically generated based on the report data. The placement and the layout of controls are decided by the system with limited options for the user. It is simple and easy to create.

Precision design

A design is to be done by the developer through the SQL report designer. It helps in designing a to-the-scale design but is time consuming.

Apart from this, a report model contains several elements; here is a quick overview of different components in a model with a brief description.

Element	Icon	Description
Data method		This contains code to retrieve and process data for a report. The code for a data method is written in C# or Visual Basic, depending on which project template is used.
Data region	List Matrix Pie or Doughnut Chart Table XY Chart	This is an area in a report that displays data. Data can be displayed in table, list, matrix, or chart formats.
Parameter		This lets you parameterize data for a report.
Filter		This is used to filter or restrict the data that is displayed in a report.
Grouping		This lets you organize data that displays in a report by grouping fields.
Sorting		This lets you control the order in which data is displayed in a report.
Image		Any image that is utilized by the report is defined here.
Layout template		This specifies the styles that are applied to the header, footer, and body of a report. One layout template can be applied to many reports.
Style template	List Matrix Pie or Doughnut Chart Table XY Chart	This defines the template for a data region and can be applied to more than one data region. Templates are data region dependent, that is, a certain template is applicable only to a certain data region.

Installation and configuration checklist

The following section will cover what you need to ensure as a developer before you start developing your reports and the general anatomy of the report.

Components to be installed

- ▸ Run the prerequisite validation checklist to identify any missing components or updates
- ▸ Install reporting extensions from standard Dynamics AX installation
- ▸ Deploy the out-of-the-box reports using PowerShell

Configurations in Dynamics AX

The following form must be configured to ensure that SSRS reports can be accessed and deployed through Dynamics AX:

System Administration | Setup | Business Intelligence | Report Servers.

Reporting services configuration manager

The report services configuration must be started and run without any issues to be able to use SSRS reports. The configuration manager has diagnostic capabilities to indicate the missing setup. This can be accessed from the SQL server configuration tools.

Native mode versus SharePoint integrated mode

Native mode is where the reports can be accessed through the report manager web services. In that case, the report server can be accessed through the URL, `http://[SSRSServerName]:80/Reports`.

Starting with Dynamics AX2012R2, SharePoint integrated mode is supported for reporting services. If installed in SharePoint integrated mode, your reports are available as a part of a document library in the SharePoint site.

Index

report query, modifying 52
controller class 260
controller issues 259
controls
hiding, by context 274-276
control visibility issue 257
customer summary OLAP report
about 125
creating 125-129

D

data extension based timeout 248
data method
versus expressions 68
data methods, business logic 66-68
Data Processing Extensions (DPE) 286
data regions
about 24
adding, to report 27
chart data regions 29
creating, steps 25, 26
filters, adding 42, 43, 44
list data regions 29
matrix data regions 29
table data regions 29
data related issues
handling 258
dataset
auto design, creating 11-14
dataset, report model 289
datasource
adding, through business logic 108-111
spin-off recipes 114
XML feed, using as 112-114
deployment related issues
about 253
reports, unable to deploy 253
reports, unable to refresh 253, 254
design-based resolution 246, 247
designs, report model
about 289
auto design 289
precision design 289
DLL (dynamic-link library) 70
DML (Data Manipulation Language) 86

document map navigation
adding, to report 44, 45
drill down navigation
adding, to report 45, 46
drill up navigation
adding, to report 45, 46
Dynamic Filter property 17
dynamic filters 42
dynamic parameter issue 255
Dynamics AX
reporting extensions 285
Dynamics AX 2012
reporting overview 6

E

e-mail
reports, sending through 261
enum translation issue 256
events post reporting completion
handling 262, 263
existing report
analyzing 201-204
modifying 201-204
expressions
about 32
implementing, in reports 33, 34
URL, for info 34
versus data method 68
expressions related issue 257
Extended Data Types (EDTs) 196
external datasource
report, building through 120-123
external datasource query
parameter, adding 124
External Data Sources 41

F

file
reports, saving to 260
filters
adding, to data regions 42-44
financial dimension
in RDP reports 232-240
in query reports 229-231
formatting issue 255

P

parameter issue 254
parameter lookup
  adding, for OLAP 129-135
  building, business logic used 115-119
parameters
  adding, for external datasource query 124
  system parameters 40
  user-defined parameters 40
parm method 264
precision designs
  about 81
  creating 81-84
  subreport, creating 157-160
prePromptModifyContract method 53
preRunModifyContract method 261
print management
  new report design, adding to 278-280
ProcessReport method 76

Q

query
  about 41
  using as data source in report 6-11
query-based report
  data, handling 258
query parameters 41
Query property 110
query reports
  financial dimension 229-231

R

ranges
  adding, from unbound parameters
      to query 53-59
  adding in reports 15, 16
RDB-based report
  data, handling 259
RDL 59, 284, 285
RDL contract validation 207
RDL data contract
  versus RDP data 59, 60
RDP
  about 41, 73, 78

debugging 99
existing temp table, using 100-103
multiple temporary table 220, 221
selecting, for report 79
testing 80
RDP class 78
RDP contract validation 207
RDP data
  versus RDL data contract 59, 60
RDP data contract 78
RDP report
  creating 74-77
  financial dimension 232-240
rectangle control
  about 186
  in reports 186-190
rendering related issues
  handling 254-258
report
  about 5, 24
  adding, to role center 191-194
  aggregating 35, 36
  auto e-mails, saving 260
  AXEnumProvider, using in 276-278
  barcodes, displaying 264-274
  barcodes, generating 264-274
  building, with company images 98, 99
  building, with headers 98, 99
  charts, adding 27
  data region, adding 27
  deploying 17, 18
  designing 281, 282
  document map navigation, adding 44, 45
  drill down navigation, adding 45, 46
  drill up navigation, adding 45, 46
  expressions, implementing 33, 34
  financial dimension 229
  formatting 38
  grouping 14, 15
  improving 281, 282
  inventory dimension 226-228
  menu item, creating 19-22
  opening, through controller 48, 49
  preprocessing 104, 105
  query, using as data source 6
  ranges, adding 15-17
  RDP, selecting for 79

Thank you for buying
Microsoft Dynamics AX 2012 Reporting Cookbook

About Packt Publishing

Packt, pronounced 'packed', published its first book "*Mastering phpMyAdmin for Effective MySQL Management*" in April 2004 and subsequently continued to specialize in publishing highly focused books on specific technologies and solutions.

Our books and publications share the experiences of your fellow IT professionals in adapting and customizing today's systems, applications, and frameworks. Our solution-based books give you the knowledge and power to customize the software and technologies you're using to get the job done. Packt books are more specific and less general than the IT books you have seen in the past. Our unique business model allows us to bring you more focused information, giving you more of what you need to know, and less of what you don't.

Packt is a modern, yet unique publishing company, which focuses on producing quality, cutting-edge books for communities of developers, administrators, and newbies alike. For more information, please visit our website: www.PacktPub.com.

About Packt Enterprise

In 2010, Packt launched two new brands, Packt Enterprise and Packt Open Source, in order to continue its focus on specialization. This book is part of the Packt Enterprise brand, home to books published on enterprise software – software created by major vendors, including (but not limited to) IBM, Microsoft and Oracle, often for use in other corporations. Its titles will offer information relevant to a range of users of this software, including administrators, developers, architects, and end users.

Writing for Packt

We welcome all inquiries from people who are interested in authoring. Book proposals should be sent to author@packtpub.com. If your book idea is still at an early stage and you would like to discuss it first before writing a formal book proposal, contact us; one of our commissioning editors will get in touch with you.

We're not just looking for published authors; if you have strong technical skills but no writing experience, our experienced editors can help you develop a writing career, or simply get some additional reward for your expertise.

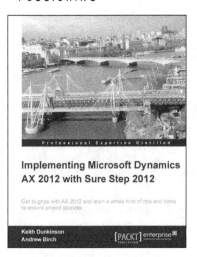

Implementing Microsoft Dynamics AX 2012 with Sure Step 2012

ISBN: 978-1-849687-04-1   Paperback: 234 pages

Get to grips with AX 2012 and learn a whole host of tips and tricks to ensure project success

1. Get the confidence to implement AX 2012 projects effectively using the Sure Step 2012 Methodology

2. Packed with practical real-world examples as well as helpful diagrams and images that make learning easier for you

3. Dive deep into AX 2012 to learn key technical concepts to implement and manage a project

---

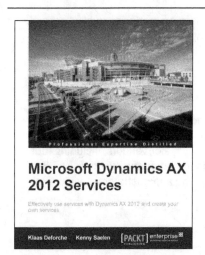

Microsoft Dynamics AX 2012 Services

ISBN: 978-1-849687-54-6   Paperback: 196 pages

Effectively use services with Dynamics AX 2012 and create your own services

1. Learn about the Dynamics AX 2012 service architecture

2. Create your own services using wizards or X++ code

3. Consume existing web services and services you've created yourself

Please check **www.PacktPub.com** for information on our titles

**Developing SSRS Reports
for Dynamics AX**

**Developing SSRS Reports
for Dynamics AX**

A step-by-step guide to Microsoft Dynamics AX 2012 report
development using real-world scenarios

Mukesh Hirwani

ISBN: 978-1-782177-74-6   Paperback: 128 pages

A step-by-step guide to Microsoft Dynamics AX 2012
report development using real-world scenarios

1. Build reports using AOT queries, report data
   provider classes, or an external data source

2. Learn how to deploy reports and manage
   SSRS reports in AOT, as well as customize
   standard reports

3. Discover best practices for Dynamics AX 2012
   reporting and learn common SSRS expressions,
   classes, and methods

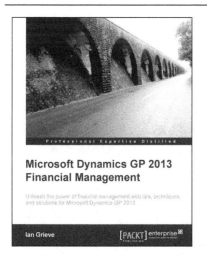

**Microsoft Dynamics GP 2013
Financial Management**

Unleash the power of financial management with tips, techniques
and solutions for Microsoft Dynamics GP 2013

Ian Grieve

**Microsoft Dynamics GP 2013
Financial Management**

ISBN: 978-1-782171-30-0   Paperback: 110 pages

Unleash the power of financial management
with tips, techniques, and solutions for Microsoft
Dynamics GP 2013

1. Discover how to improve financial management
   in Microsoft Dynamics GP 2013

2. Learn the key financial management modules
   in Microsoft Dynamics GP 2013

3. Improve your abilities with Microsoft Dynamics
   GP 2013 to gain a better understanding and
   control of your business

Please check **www.PacktPub.com** for information on our titles